Coals of Fire

The *Alton Telegraph* Libel Case

Thomas B. Littlewood

With a Foreword by
Rodney A. Smolla

Southern Illinois University Press
Carbondale

Copyright © 1988 by the Board of Trustees, Southern Illinois University
All rights reserved
Printed in the United States of America
Designed by Heidi Gunter
Production supervised by Natalia Nadraga
91 90 89 88   4 3 2 1

Library of Congress Cataloging-in-Publication Data
Littlewood, Thomas B.
  Coals of fire.
  Bibliography: p.
  Includes index.
  1. Green, James C.—Trials, litigation, etc.
2. Alton telegraph—Trials, litigation, etc.
3. Trials (Libel)—Illinois—Chicago. 4. Freedom
of the press—United States. I. Title.
KF228.G74L58   1988   345.73′0256   87-9844
ISBN 0-8093-1401-0   347.305256

The paper used in this publication meets the minimum requirements of American National Standard for Information Sciences – Permanence of Paper for Printed Library Materials, ANSI Z39.48-1984. ∞™

For Andrew, Kara, Kyle, and Timothy

It is a newspaper's duty to print the news and raise hell.
—Wilbur Storey, editor
of the *Chicago Times*,
1861

Every newspaper sees its defeats and its victories, and the wise newspaperman has learned not to gloat over his fallen adversary, for the fallen may rise to wreak vengeance, either with coals of fire or vindictive measures.
—From the seventy-fifth
anniversary issue of
the *Alton Evening
Telegraph*

Contents

	Foreword by Rodney A. Smolla	ix
	Preface	xv
1.	In a Plaintiff's Paradise	1
2.	Enter Jim Green the Builder	11
3.	Roll-overs and Straw Parties	23
4.	Blue Pencils at the *Telegraph*	29
5.	A True Newspaper in Alton	39
6.	The Memorandum	48
7.	The Fall of Piasa	62
8.	Jury Selection in Metro East	78
9.	The Law of Libel	93
10.	An Odyssean Journey	102
11.	Give Him the Money	114
12.	The Struggle to Appeal	153

13.	The Settlement	177
14.	The Chilling Effect	186
15.	The Price We Pay	195
	Summary of Key Cases	203
	References	207
	Notes	211
	Index	219

Foreword

Rodney A. Smolla

In 1987 America celebrated the Bicentennial of the American Constitution. The events described in Madison County, Illinois, in *Coals of Fire* resonate with messages from the past from the county's namesake, James Madison. Madison, the principal intellectual architect of the Constitution and the Bill of Rights, would have found in the strange and twisted tale surrounding the *Alton Telegraph*'s libel suit ample evidence to support his theories about politics and human nature. To put it bluntly, there is an eerie, haunting atmosphere to the Madison County described so vividly and artfully by Tom Littlewood, a sense that in Madison County all might not be as it appears.

James Madison would not be terribly surprised, for he assumed the inherent dangers of concentrated power. His genius was to set America off on a political adventure in which government would be established, quite deliberately, with the ever-present possibility of corruption in mind. To counteract that tendency two critical Madisonian themes permeate the Constitution and Bill of Rights. First, power is to be divided, not concentrated, with each locus of power checked and balanced by countervailing forces. Second, information about power is to be unrestricted; Americans are to have freedom of conscience in matters of religion, culture, and politics, and the test of truth is to be the power of an idea to get itself accepted in the open market.

When power is allowed to consolidate itself without open scrutiny and accountability, Madison taught that it will become corrupt. And so the First Amendment to the Constitution establishes the freedom of the press and of the people to cross-examine constantly government and all other influential actors in public life. *Coals of Fire* reveals what may happen when the system of checks and balances is short-circuited. Many of the cadre of lawyers and judges involved seem to be off in a self-serving world of their own, applying Byzantine legal rules in a murky fog reminiscent of Charles Dickens' *Bleak House,* a fog in which the real merits of a dispute never quite seem to be dictating the results. And the peculiar operation of that legal system in this case visited an extraordinarily punishing result on a classic small-town American newspaper, the *Alton Telegraph*.

The story is a parable of sorts for much that has gone wrong with James Madison's scheme, and an invitation for us to return to some of his guiding wisdom. At a time when we ought to be celebrating the First Amendment, America is in the midst of an explosion of libel suits against the media. And whatever the capability of *Time* magazine or CBS News may be to absorb the often gigantic legal costs these suits impose, their impact on small media outlets, such as the *Alton Telegraph,* can be devastating.

The press is now sued with regularity for its investigative efforts. American juries are increasingly willing to return multimillion-dollar libel judgments against the press, judgments that seem to have lost all proportion to the real reputational injury suffered by plaintiffs. This grass-roots antipathy for the press may well reflect the public perception that the media has grown too powerful, arrogant, and oracular, that the modern press does not merely report the public agenda, but purports to set it.

Recent national events do indeed provide compelling evidence of the awesome power of the modern press. Ronald Reagan's Teflon presidency was stripped of its protective coating by aggressive media coverage of the Iran-Contra affair. His presidency was forever altered by the scandal, and the adversarial postures of the White House and its press corps will always be indelibly stamped on our consciousness of the period. We will always remember Sam Donaldson of ABC defiantly asking Reagan, "Sir, how can you defend this duplicity," or the sight of Helen Thomas of UPI descending on the President as a press conference ended.

In the midst of the Iran scandal, America witnessed two other episodes revealing the power of the press to visit ruin on the powerful. Revelations of the Reverend Jim Bakker's sexual impropriety and dubious financial management of his PTL ministry, following on the heals of evangelist Oral Roberts' desperate fund-raising threats of impending forced ascension into heaven, triggered a virtual media orgy of critical reporting about television evangelists. And as if somehow to emphasize a sort of evenhanded karma to the universive of press aggression, the *Miami Herald* descended on Democratic presidential front-runner Gary Hart with a surveillance effort that revealed what was at least the appearance of an extramarital relationship with a Miami model. This story ultimately destroyed the candidate's quest for the presidency. In each of these cases we witnessed a striking phenomenon: for many Americans, the fact that the press had actually done its job of ferreting out the truth was counterbalanced by a backlash of resentment against the press for stirring up trouble. Wise journalists do not worry too much about this backlash as long as it is simply vocal opposition—for it is not the good journalist's destiny to be loved. When victims of adverse press reportage fight back verbally, they are doing precisely what the First Amendment calls for: fighting speech with counterspeech, and letting the market draw conclusions. When victims go to court, however, and when the legal system permits crippling judgments to be imposed without an adequate opportunity for a dispassionate appellate review, then all society eventually suffers, for that is precisely the course that leads to the erosion of Madison's elegant system.

"I'm all for the First Amendment," the old saying goes, "it's the newspapers I don't like." Americans are always happy to applaud freedom of speech as an abstraction; we will dutifully trot out the First Amendment with Mom and apple pie during Fourth of July declamations and toasts to the constitutional bicentennial. Freedom of speech, after all, is what makes us different from the Russians. But as an abstraction freedom of speech is meaningless—that freedom is listed as a paper guarantee in the constitutions of many nations in the modern world, including some of the most repressive and totalitarian regimes in the international community. The single most critical element distinguishing an open from a closed society is that in an open society freedom of speech is no mere slogan. And to be more than a slogan, freedom of speech must embrace speech that has the capability to hurt, speech that may topple the existing regime, ruin reputations, outrage prevailing sensibilities. Cautious and decorous speech needs no special protection. The First Amendment is not for the timorous, but for the bold. To the real journalist, the First Amendment is not merely a protective shield, it is an invitation to engage in gutsy, honest investigation—an invitation to dig.

Freedom of speech gathers meaning when a society accepts sacrifices to preserve it. The sacrifices are not the stuff of the glorious conquests of the Marines on Iowa Jima, but the smaller, day-by-day acceptance of many of the frictions and irritations of social life in a society that permits wide-open and robust discourse. In concrete terms, for speech to be free in America we must accept the freedom of Nazis and the Ku Klux Klan as much as the freedoms of the Anti-Defamation League and Martin Luther King. For speech to be free in America we must accept the freedom of the *National Enquirer* and *Penthouse* magazine as much as the freedom of *Newsweek* and the "MacNeil/Lehrer News Hour." For speech to be free in America we must accept the freedom of Larry Flynt as much as of Jerry Falwell. And perhaps most important of all, for speech to be free in America there must be freedom in our immediate surroundings.

There are national marketplaces of ideas and local marketplaces of ideas, and if they thought about it most Americans would realize that the local markets are where the ideal of free speech is truly most important. We too often act as if the First Amendment belongs primarily to Ted Koppel or Dan Rather. Yet, while few Americans ever find themselves injected into arenas of national attention, many Americans are active in events and controversies in their neighborhoods, their children's schools, their churches, and their workplaces. The institutions and persons of power immediately around us shape our lives as much as national institutions and leaders. The conduct of the local school superintendent, police chief, circuit court judge, real estate developer, and bank president may penetrate the fabric of our lives in immediately palpable ways. The local market of speech about the conduct of those local actors must be uninhibited and vigorous if life at the local level is to be truly open and free.

In Madison County, Illinois, this should mean that reporters for a newspaper ought to have the freedom to investigate a story on an issue of public interest, and having found suspicion of possible financial wrongdoing, to report their suspicions to law-enforcement authorities. Surely that modest exercise of the checking function of the press (modest because the *Telegraph* never even published the story) ought to be immune from civil liability. Across the nation, however, this sort of elemental wisdom is too often swept aside by legal machinery too far out of touch with Madison's ideals. I know of no more revealing example than the case of the hapless *Alton Telegraph*.

Preface

This is the story of a libel suit brought against a newspaper and two of its reporters. The newspaper is the *Alton Telegraph*, published in the city of Alton, Illinois, across the Mississippi River from St. Louis. It was a most peculiar case, this award of $9.2 million in damages—the biggest libel verdict in United States newspaper history. The case grew out of a decision not to publish some information the reporters had received, but rather to seek the cooperation of a federal law enforcement agency to check whether the information was true. And, after the jury had returned its verdict, the amount of damages was so large that the newspaper could not afford to post the necessary bond for an appeal to a higher court and had to file for protection under the bankruptcy laws.

In 1981, when this happened, the *Telegraph* was a modestly profitable, family-owned and operated newspaper that had been in the community for almost a century and a half. It is not to be found on any lists of great American newspapers. There are no Pulitzer Prizes hanging on the office walls. But the *Telegraph* reported the news of the community and the region with a vigor—at times a hell-raising vigor—uncommon for a paper of its size. By retracing the years of litigation against (and around) the newspaper in Alton, it is possible for us to examine one of the crucial questions of our time: Are the American people so disenchanted with the custodians of their First Amendment rights that they no longer want them pursuing unsettling truths?

As the scene of one of the important early incidents that led some years later to the Civil War, an incident involving a violent confrontation between a mob and an editor, Alton is an especially intriguing place in which to consider that question. Back in 1837, it was the biggest city in Illinois. It had dreams of overtaking St. Louis and becoming the dominant commercial center of the Mississippi River valley. Those aspirations were destroyed by the mob that killed antislavery editor Elijah Lovejoy and hurled his press into the river. The news of that terrible night of bloodshed "jolted the Yankee conscience like the shock of an earthquake," said John Quincy Adams. Alton never fully recovered from the stain on its national reputation.

The social and political tensions of Lovejoy's time continued to evolve in ways that will help us understand what happened to the *Telegraph*. Contrary to what newspaper publishers would sometimes have us believe, libel suits are seldom as clear-cut as they might seem. One of the aims of this book is to place the events in Alton in their proper context, so that we might also better understand the ambivalence with which the American people have always regarded their newspapers.

Newspapers, said Henry Ward Beecher a long time ago in his *Proverbs from Plymouth Pulpit*, "are schoolmasters of the common people." "That endless book, the newspaper, is our national glory," he said. Later, in this century, the editor of the *Cleveland Press*, Louis B. Seltzer, proudly described his newspaper as a community institution "striving to be with the people, always at their side, always beating with their hearts." Even then, when newspapers were acclaimed the fearless champions of the common man, there was a constant tugging between the constitutionally sheltered status of the privately owned press and the desire of prominent citizens in the public eye to protect what they liked to consider their most cherished possession: their "good name." Unlike many other countries where prosecution for seditious libel—libel against the state—is a potent political weapon for the suppression of dissent, libel actions in the United States have usually been restricted by the power of public opinion to personal "tort" claims in the civil courts. That means a person whose reputation has been injured by a written statement "published to a third party" may sue for the recovery of specific proven financial damages. Except for a brief period at the beginning of the Republic, using the courts to silence an irritating critic was never part of the American tradition.

But freedom of the press is much easier for most Americans to endorse than to understand. Toward the end of the 1970s, libel complaints against newspapers, magazines, and broadcasters that had been squelched by judges in the past without the expense of going to trial were being given to confused juries to decide. In an alarmingly frequent number of cases—alarming to journalists, at least, and to those who treasure the uninhibited flow of news and ideas—the jurors were bringing back large, punishing judgments against the press, often far in excess of any actual financial injury.

Coming so soon after the aggressive reporting of the Watergate scandal, civil turmoil over the war in southeast Asia, and the struggle against racial discrimination by some (but certainly not all) news media, this trend was interpreted as a sign of public displeasure with the power and performance of the constitutionally privileged profit-making media. In a dramatic turnaround, it would seem that many Americans now consider the media (a class which now significantly includes television news) too big, irresponsible, negative, and arrogant. To a majority of Americans, the carriers of the news are no longer anything resembling a national glory.

There is something else, too: the conglomeratization of the commercial enterprises to which we have entrusted the exercise of our First Amendment rights. Wilbur Storey's prescription of a newspaper's duty to raise hell is an anachronism in most communities. In all but the largest cities today, the typical chain-owned newspaper is an inoffensive, ever-cautious organ of commerce, responsible first and foremost to a battery of corporate ledger-keepers in some far-off headquarters city. It is, more often than not, a monopolistic institution that beats with the hearts of the powerful to please the shareholding investors.

The implications of this are profound indeed. Our system of representative government based on the consent of the governed cannot function without the unrestrained flow of information and opinions, and a free, courageous, independent—yes, a hell-raising—press. A press that is emasculated by either the lure of profits or the fear of the ruinous costs of hiring lawyers to defend itself in court is no more free than if the government had closed it down.

What follows is a work of nonfiction; there should be no misunderstanding about that. Nothing is imagined, fabricated, or simulated. As in all lawsuits, there are different versions of the facts and even more different interpretations of those facts. I have done my utmost conscientiously to sort out the truth as fairly and completely as possible. There is no malice, "actual" (to cite the currently operative word in the law of libel) or otherwise, in the telling of this narrative.

The fact-finding phase of this work began in the spring of 1982 and ended in the autumn of 1986. It could not have been done without the extraordinary cooperation of the former editor and publisher of the *Alton Telegraph,* Stephen Cousley. I am deeply indebted to him, not only because of the time and attention he gave to my inquiries during an extremely traumatic period in the life of the newspaper, but also because he made available the unexpurgated libel case files of the company.

The documentary foundation for this book is in the voluminous court records. The case files, motions, depositions, briefs, and other pleadings, the orders and opinions of the several judges, and of course the transcripts of the two trials involving James Green provided rich primary source material.

The human details that made it a book and not a legal treatise came from the dozens of interviews with knowledgeable involved people. I am especially grateful to John Hackmann, the late Paul S. Cousley, Mary Lou Cousley, Hope Cousley Apple, D. G. Schumacher, Jerome Pragacz, Helen Toncoff, Luke DeGrand, William Cox, Philip Tone, Susan Tone, Robert Patterson, Dr. Mather Pfeiffenberger, Albion Fenderson, Rex Carr, Edward Eckert, Gene Callahan, Dennis McMurray, Joseph Melosi, William Lhotka, Walter Sharp, the Rev. Cortley Burroughs, John Focht, John Taylor, Peter Simpson, Karl Monroe, and Henry McAdams.

For help with the manuscript, thanks are due Michael Lennon, Steven Helle, and Barbara Wasserman. The ever-patient typists were Marsha Poff, Nena Richards, Kathryn Brown, and Barbara Littlewood, the last of whom served invaluably as consultant and adviser.

Coals of Fire

1

In a Plaintiff's Paradise

The Mergenthaler linotype that stood dappled with rust like a weather-beaten cigar store Indian out in front of the *Alton Telegraph* was more than a curiosity, more than an artifact of the fabled days of hot-type newspapering. Out there in the open, exposed to the full fury of the elements, the ungainly contraption gave the community a symbol for all to see of the durability of the newspaper in whose service it faithfully clinked and clanked for so many years. The *Telegraph* had been in Alton a long time and had every reason to believe in the momentous newsmaking years of the 1960s and 70s that it would continue printing the news and raising hell, should that become necessary, on into the indefinite future.

Down the street a block, ingloriously paved over now with parking spaces, is the site of the last of the Lincoln-Douglas debates in 1858. A couple of blocks farther on Broadway, at the foot of State, is the flour mill. And then, just beyond the railroad spur, swiftly flows the Mississippi River. Approaching St. Louis from the north, the river swerves in an easterly direction, bending back on itself before resuming the journey south to the Gulf of Mexico. It is here at this superbly promising bend of the mighty waterway that Alton was settled beginning in 1818. Another great river—the Missouri—empties into the Mississippi just below Alton. The churning turbulence at that junction makes it necessary to divert barge traffic into a more sedate parallel ship canal. From the mouth of the Missouri, the city of Alton can be seen built into the tree-shaded bluff that extends along the bank of the Mississippi on the Illinois side.

Altonians young and old are uncommonly conscious of their history. Alton is showing its age. It is a worn city, a worked-out city that could be entering its dotage, a city that has always suffered more than its share of woe. Yet the past is called back in ways that connect it to the present, and to the river passing by at the bottom of the hill.

Sometimes this preoccupation with the past can be jarring. The downtown area around the *Telegraph* building, for example, is a melange of charming little dusty antique shops and the seediest of waterfront saloons. Mississippi River Lock and Dam 26 is at Alton. Barge crews kill time in the saloons while their cargoes are triple-parked on the water nearby, waiting their turns to ease their way through the narrow lock. Built in 1939, the facility is one of twenty-nine making a stairway of water between St. Louis and the higher elevations all the way to Minneapolis. The hour and a half "elevator ride" through the lock at Alton may come after several days of waiting in line. So downtown is a handy rest and recreation center. The downtown dives are staffed with husky barmaids who double as ladies of the night working around the clock entertaining the idle barge hands.

A new and much larger lock and dam is under construction two miles away, one of the few encouraging economic developments in a region hit hard by industrial obsolescence and unemployment. The water backs up behind the dam, creating a broad slack-water pool and a rare refuge for birds, fish, and wildlife. The traffic jam is a consequence of Alton's location between the confluences of the Mississippi to the south and the Illinois River, which branches off toward Chicago fifteen miles upriver. Congress finally authorized the $800 million plus public works project, but only after imposing fees for the first time on users of the inland waterway navigation system.[1]

Even if it were not such a convenient R & R billet for the men who work the tow fleets, Alton could not avoid being a river town. The flavor of Mark Twain's Mississippi is in the west wind; steamboat whistles echo from long ago. In the middle of the last century, a visitor from the East observed:

No part of the United States, not even the highlands of the Hudson, can vie in wild and romantic scenery with the bluffs of Illinois. On one side of the river, often at the water's edge, a perpendicular wall of rock rises to the height of some hundred feet. Generally on the opposite shore is a level bottom or prairie of several miles in width, extending to a similar bluff that runs parallel with the river. One of these ranges commences at Alton and extends, with a few intervals, for many miles along the left bank of the Illinois [River].[2]

Looking westward today, from the cliffs above the city, the setting sun turns the river a murky, bubbling orange clotted with streaks of blood red. Across the way the cottonwoods, willows, and wild grape on the flat Missouri wetlands are sprayed with a soft mist at dusk. When the river pilots switch on their rotating searchlights, the beams jerk across the darkening sky.

Next to the newspaper downtown is a building also owned by the *Telegraph* that houses a museum and the local historical society. At the rear of the museum, the second floor has been remodeled into a replica of an old steamboat pilothouse. The window of the pilothouse looks out from the stationary hilltop over the rolling river a few hundred yards away. Diesel towboats equipped with radar scanners now artfully nudge fleets of as many as forty barges lashed together, some of them containing a million gallons of petroleum. The Huck Finns and Becky Thatchers in the Alton schools can stand at the wheel and imagine themselves guiding a boat through the sandbars, timber snags, eddies, and shoals in the treacherous river.

Below Alton is the industrial floodplain known by archeologists as the American Bottoms. Residents of the rest of Madison County tend to be more pragmatic and less enchanted with the lore of the river. They sometimes poke fun at all the monuments and historical plaques in Alton. The heavy industry upon which the economy of the entire Illinois Metro East region was based is in severe decline these days, so there is good reason perhaps to look ahead creatively and not linger over the occasional glories and many vicissitudes of the past. But the people of Alton are conditioned by their cultural upbringing, more so than most, to be conscious of the long reach and the many snags of human history. In such a community, therefore, it is fitting that the local newspaper—the *Telegraph*—should put an unsightly old machine out in front of the building as a symbol for the world to see of its own sense of continuity.

One Saturday morning early in 1980, a candidate for the Democratic party's nomination in the Third Judicial Circuit primary election parked his car at the curb across from the outdoor linotype machine and walked on up to the third floor offices of the Cousleys. The *Telegraph* lobby is itself a miniature museum. One of the items on display in the lobby is a piece of memorabilia more important in the history of Alton than any other. It is a part of a reconstructed hand press that belonged briefly to Elijah Lovejoy in 1837. Until he was shot to death by a mob protesting Lovejoy's expressions of opposition to slavery, he was the editor of another newspaper in Alton. The mob smashed his press and threw the pieces into the river. Some of the parts were retrieved later and reassembled in the lobby of the *Telegraph*.

The *Telegraph* had come into being a year before Lovejoy's death. John A. Cousley, who was hired as a printer's devil on the paper in 1861, acquired a controlling interest in the company in 1889. Succeeding generations of Cousleys have been running the newspaper ever since. In 1980, Paul Sparks Cousley, or "Paulie," as he had been known since childhood, was the publisher. He was, at seventy-two years of age, still responsible for the editorial page. Stephen A. Cousley, forty-one, the fourth generation of *Telegraph* Cousleys, occupied the position of editor. Paulie's father and Steve's grandfather were brothers—sons of John Cousley.

In 1905, John D. McAdams merged the *Alton Daily Republican* with the *Telegraph*. Thereafter the McAdams family assumed responsibility for the business side of the operation. Twenty-six members of various Cousley and McAdams families owned shares of the newspaper company. Fifty-one percent of the 1,000 shares belonged to the Cousleys, the other 490 to the McAdamses. Four members of the board were Cousleys, three were McAdamses.

Though working every day in the same building—the McAdamses in the counting house on the second floor, the Cousleys in the newsroom on the third floor—the two families had a falling out over the overriding issue in small-city newspapers all over the United States: whether the local owners should sell out to one of the communications conglomerates at highly inflated prices. In Alton, the McAdamses wanted to sell, the Cousleys wanted to hold on.

Their visitor that morning in 1980 was not interested in buying the newspaper. He had been a judge for a couple of months, liked the job, and wanted to keep it. His name was Charles W. Chapman. A studious looking, full-faced young man wearing heavy-framed glasses, he was meticulously dressed but styled his dark hair in the mod fashion of the day. Chapman had been named to a vacancy on the Circuit Court of Madison County. Now he was standing for election to a full six-year term.[3]

The Circuit Court is the trial court in the Illinois judicial system. Many other states have adopted various forms of merit selection of judges in an attempt to separate the judiciary from partisan political pressures. The voters of Illinois were given an opportunity in 1970 to decide how they wanted their judges chosen, and a bare majority (50.2 percent) preferred the continuation of party elections. Judicial selection is one of the significant remaining vestiges of party patronage in the state. A lawyer who wants to become a judge usually must first be endorsed for nomination by whichever is the dominant party organization in the county. A judgeship is one of the tangible rewards for party service. One of the effects of this has been to stimulate the involvement (and consequently the influence) of lawyers in county party organizations (and throughout the political system). When the Judicial Article of the Illinois 1870 Constitution was overhauled in 1964, that reform provided for the retention of previously elected sitting judges who run for reelection "on their record" without party label or opposition. If they receive the favorable vote of 50 percent or more, they remain on the bench. The percentage was raised to 60 percent, but the rest of the 1964 Judicial Article to the Illinois Constitution remained basically the same in the "new" 1970 Illinois Constitution.

Attempts to dispense with the initial partisan elections met a hard core of opposition from the two urban Democratic machine strongholds in Illinois—Chicago and the two counties of Metro

East across from St Louis. It is naïve, of course, to suppose that the administration of justice, including the selection of judges, can ever be anything other than political. But what kind of "politics"? Who is to say, argue the local Democratic leaders, that the wisdom of some elitist bar association or the governor of the state (who is, more often than not, a Republican) is preferable to the democratic voice of The People?

In Madison County, the selection of judges is effectively controlled by a few very wealthy and politically powerful personal injury lawyers. *The American Lawyer* reported at about this time that a "peculiar and complex system of justice . . . prevails in Madison County—a system in which plaintiffs almost always win, both in court and at the settlement table. It is perpetuated by a few local plaintiffs' lawyers who have amassed fortunes in the process."[4] Often in recent years the number of damage awards of $1 million or more is higher in Madison County than in any other county in the nation.

Madison has acquired a national reputation as a plaintiffs' paradise. An article in the St. Louis *Post-Dispatch* described damage suit law in the county as "a multi-million dollar hidden industry . . . maybe one of the 10 biggest industries in the Metro East area . . . handled on what seems to be an assembly line, often by millionaire lawyers in front of sympathetic judges and juries".[5] One lawyer was quoted in the *Post-Dispatch* story as having pointed out that the legal fees trickle down through the local economy ("We rent a lot of buildings, pay a lot of taxes. We put out money from these judgements into the local banks. . . . We support a lot of services.")

Lawyers for the plaintiffs customarily pocket one-third of the money award as their fee. The balance represents a sizable transfer of wealth from insurance companies, generally, to blue-collar workers. The juries usually consist almost entirely of working-class residents. It is not out of the ordinary for jurors to award an injured worker a million dollars or more in a personal injury trial against a railroad or barge line and then line up after the verdict is announced to take turns embracing him.

In such litigious surroundings, the leading personal injury law firms have become the power brokers in the county Democratic party organization. A Republican who was unexpectedly elected state's attorney said: "It's the lawyers with the money who matter in politics here." The lawyers he was talking about do this by putting up the money to elect the judges of their choice and, when necessary, putting up the money for campaigns to deny the 60 percent vote of confidence to sitting judges who have displeased them, thereby unseating them.

One of the most influential is Morris B. Chapman, of the Granite City firm of Chapman and Carlson, which specializes in injury claims by railroad workers. Granite City is one of the "Tri-Cities" of Madison County, tucked away in the southwest corner alongside Venice and the municipality of Madison. This is the tough, heavily industrialized riverside section that has usually managed to dominate the Democratic party machinery. Alton, the county seat of Edwardsville and the semirural localities in the eastern end of the county are left on the outside looking in as far as party affairs are concerned.

Though unrelated to Morris Chapman, Charles Chapman joined the firm of Chapman and Carlson after receiving his law degree from St. Louis University in 1967 and clerking for a federal trial judge for a year. Young Chapman, from a blue-collar family background in Granite City, worked at a Veterans Administration hospital while attending law school in the evening. After demonstrating his ability to try and win personal injury cases, he became a partner in the firm. Ten years later, when one of the circuit judges was appointed to a lifetime job on the local United States District Court, the member of the Illinois Supreme Court who had been elected from Metro East—Joseph P. Goldenhersh—asked his colleagues to fill the temporary vacancy with Charles Chapman. Reaching the state bench by appointment of the State Supreme Court is a short cut to the beginning of a judicial career. A short time before, Chapman had given up his law practice and begun doing graduate work in economics at Southern Illinois University at Edwardsville, because he said he wanted to spend more time with his family.

He took his place on the court, sitting at the branch court in the city hall in Granite City. Before long, he carried $10,000 to the party leaders and sought their blessing for his election to a full term in 1980.[6] The $10,000 was the customary party contribution, in effect to purchase the endorsement of the organization and rent the campaigning services of the precinct foot soldiers. The practice is extinct in most cities, but in Madison County it was still a regular feature of campaign finance. The delivery of cash and the laying on of party hands traditionally occurred at Besserman's tavern in Madison, the unofficial clubhouse of the Democratic party.

This time, though, there was a complication. Chapman received the party endorsement, but another judge, Andreas Matoesian, decided to run, too. Matoesian, forty-two years old, was also from Granite City. He had worked his way through law school as a barber. The Illinois system provides for the appointment by the elected judges of a number of associate judges who also hear cases and are yet another kind of political patronage. Matoesian had been named to an associate judgeship with Goldenhersh's backing in 1965, and now he decided to oppose Chapman in the March primary for the slot occupied by Chapman, even though Matoesian had not been "slated" by the party, and without coughing up his $10,000.

So there would be a primary contest: Chapman against Matoesian. Ordinarily, the endorsed candidate would have an enormous advantage. There was, however, an ominous development in the race—Morris Chapman's neutrality. His decision not to weigh in on the side of his former partner—reportedly because of his many years of supporting Matoesian previously—would cancel out some of the value of the organization endorsement.

The purpose of Judge Chapman's visit to Paulie and Steve Cousley on that Saturday morning was to solicit the *Telegraph*'s editorial endorsement of his candidacy against Matoesian. Wherever candidates run for public office in Illinois, this is a familiar and honorable ritual: The candidate coming hat in hand to see the newspaper editors and inviting them to size him up. Lincoln did it. Stephen A. Douglas did it. Countless others have done it. Politicians are always looking for ways to flatter journalists. Here is a harmless way for the editors to feel important grilling the candidates about their opinions and their qualifications while the candidates try to sound as knowledgeable and self-assured as they can. Sometimes, if an editor is uncertain of an endorsement for a minor office, decisions may even be made in such auditions. Less so than before television, the newspaper endorsement interview is still a reminder of the power of the press to mold public opinion.

In a cramped office at the far corner of the newsroom, Cousley ancestors and other long-gone leaders of the *Telegraph* looked down from a gallery of portraits on the walls. In a special place of honor above the publisher's desk hung an original gilt-framed painting of Lincoln made during the 1858 senatorial campaign. Next to Paulie's office, fronting on the newsroom, was the editor's office, which is where the meeting with the judge took place that morning.[7]

The atmosphere in Steve's office was amiable but awkward. Paulie seemed preoccupied. Steve asked the usual questions about the judge's background and took a few notes. As a judge, Chapman said he was not kept as busy as he had been as a trial lawyer. He said he liked not having to work nights, allowing more time to be with his family. The meeting lasted thirty to forty minutes. Steve remembers that two of the judge's children were waiting in the car parked outside and that he volunteered to conduct them on a tour of the newspaper pressroom afterward, but their father declined.

Years before, while working his apprenticeship as a reporter in the *Telegraph*'s Edwardsville bureau, Steve Cousley had gotten to know and like Andy Matoesian. Were the *Telegraph* to make an endorsement in this contest, it would most likely belong to Matoesian.

But both the Cousleys realized this was one election they would be well advised to pass. The less said right now on the editorial pages of the *Telegraph* that might affect the future of Judge Charles W. Chapman, favorably or unfavorably, the better.

For lodged at that very moment on Judge Chapman's jury trial docket in the Circuit Court of Madison County was a case numbered 77-L-66—*James C. Green v. Alton Telegraph Printing Co., Joseph Melosi, and William Lhotka*—a libel suit seeking the recovery of $7,045,000 in actual damages plus $3,500,000 in punitive damages, or $10,545,000 in all. The case was about to be set for trial. Eight other libel suits against the *Telegraph* stemming from the same alleged act of defamation were also awaiting trial in Madison County. Altogether the nine complaints claimed something over $20 million in actual damages and $53 million in punitive damages, a sum many times greater than the worth of the *Alton Telegraph,* more than enough to silence the presses and drive the newspaper out of business.

To help the reader understand the complicated circumstances surrounding the lawsuits against the *Telegraph,* here is a brief preliminary synopsis of what they were all about: The two principal accusers were James C. Green and Robert L. DeGrand. Green was a real estate developer and builder in Madison County. His projects were financed by a savings and loan association in Alton—Piasa First Federal Savings and Loan Association. DeGrand was the chief operating officer of that association. Eventually, the federal agency that regulates S & Ls (the Federal Savings and Loan Insurance Corporation) determined that Piasa had made far more loans than Green could ever hope to pay back. Before that discovery was made, however, something happened, which is the fulcrum of this story. Two reporters for the *Telegraph* received unsubstantiated tips from a past and a present local law enforcement officer that the Green transactions were involved in the "laundering" of Mafia funds through Piasa. Being unable to verify that information, the reporters were invited by representatives of the United States Department of Justice to send them a memo describing the allegations. The reporters did so with the expectation that if the federal investigators found the information to be true, the *Telegraph* could have first crack at what would be a good news story. Though nothing came of the criminal investigation, the FSLIC did look more closely at the Piasa-Green relationship, bringing about Piasa's demise and the temporary retirement of Jim Green the builder. The central issue in the libel case was whether the reporters were negligent for putting on paper information they intended to be confidential and which proved to be unfounded. Green's lawyer contended (and the FSLIC denied) that the action against the savings and loan association would not have occurred had it not been for the sending of the memo to Washington.

2

Enter Jim Green the Builder

The connections between real estate development, political influence, banking, and the law are as old as Madison County. The founders of Alton were speculators, builders, bankers, lawyers, politicans. Rufus Easton, who had been a federal judge and postmaster in St. Louis, acquired the site of what was then called Lower Alton in 1814. Its natural harbor so near three navigable rivers made Alton look like a promotor's dream—an ideal turnaround port between the upper and lower Mississippi waterways.

Unfortunately for Mr. Easton, shifting river channels interfered with the harbor's accessibility at the same time that he was being victimized by his own reckless investment schemes. By then a delegate to Congress from the Missouri Territory, he unwisely pledged his real estate interests in Alton as security for the notes of the Bank of St. Louis, of which he was a director. The bank collapsed in the Panic of 1819 and Easton was ruined. A legal struggle ensued over title to Easton's land claim. In the best American tradition, when the matter was settled by the Court of Chancery in the county seat of Edwardsville in 1829, several prominent politicians grabbed some of the disputed lands. Among them were the then-governor of Illinois, Ninian Edwards (after whom Edwardsville was named), and Nathaniel Pope, a former judge of the United States District Court.[1]

Until the levee was built much later to keep out the river, the floodplain bottomlands along the Mississippi to the south of Alton were of little value to anyone. Later in the century, the draining and then the industrialization of the spongy bottoms made rich men of the landowners, many of whom were Altonians. A reporter who grew up in Alton compared the grimy industrial plain to the New Jersey flats across the Hudson River from New York—"odorous with steel mills, stockyards, brass mills, tanneries, and oil refineries that belch smoke by day and flames by night."[2]

Built on a rock ridge rising from the riverbank to the high bluffs above, the city of Alton attracted the wealthy industrialists and merchant businessmen. Their workers lived in other parts of town back away from the river, or in East Alton, Wood River, Roxana, Hartford, or farther south in Granite City. A regional historian pointed out in 1912 that "Granite City, a flourishing manufacturing city, has had a marvelous growth in the last decade, but its capitalists have necessarily been non-residents."[3] Which is a polite way of saying that a steel company executive might live in the pleasant tree-shaded neighborhoods of Alton but never in the sooty mill town of Granite City. With the passing of time, "the bluff" became a convenient social boundary in the Metro East region. Those who lived "below the bluff" on the old bottomlands were inferior to those who dwelled above the limestone bluff. Throughout its history, this bluff mentality has been an important divisive element in the politics and the social life of the region.

Jim Green grew up in the heart of the blast furnace and smokestack belt, in the lowland "Tri-Cities" of Madison, Venice, and Granite City. His parents moved there from the hills and hollows of the Ozark country in southern Missouri. He played basketball at Madison High School, but dropped out of school and a short time later did as his father had done before him: He went to work in the steel mills in Granite City. Briefly after marrying, Jim lived in a house trailer on his parents' lot in Venice.

As a teen-ager, Jim Green was already a good ol' boy—a quick learner, fast on the upbeat, gabby, streetsmart, full of it. He was good at small talk and made friends easily. He also worked well with his hands. Before reaching the age of 21, Jim built a house on Second Street in the city of Madison. After completing his shift as a pipefitter's helper in the mills, he would work on the house with his father in the evenings. He lived in the house for a while, then sold it at a profit and began building another on Sunset Drive in Granite City.

It was late one afternoon while the self-taught carpenter was hammering away on the new house that, according to the story both men would repeat many times thereafter in lawyers' offices and courtrooms, Robert Lee DeGrand stopped to ask directions. Bob DeGrand was executive vice president of Piasa First Federal Savings and Loan Association. He and Henry Wuellner, the president of Piasa, lost their way trying to find the address of a house they were going to appraise for a loan. DeGrand recalled that he had admired the workmanship on Green's house and invited him to come by the S & L in Alton for financing.

Piasa had been founded in 1887 by a man who epitomizes, better than any other perhaps, the convergence of building, banking, and politics in the area. Just before the Civil War, Lucas Pfeiffenberger left his German immigrant parents' home in Ohio to find gold in California.[4] Pausing in Alton, he received a message from his mother imploring him to wait out the winter there instead of risking the perilous journey over the mountains. Heeding his mother's advice, Pfeiffenberger stayed for the winter—and for the rest of his days. A carpenter by trade, he branched out into architecture and construction. He designed and built churches, schools, courthouses, stores, firehouses, libraries, factories, and many of the substantial brick and stone homes high above the bluff in Alton. Most of the people of Alton lived in primitive log shanties, but one historian noted that "Alton probably possessed a larger percentage of high class men, men of education, men of refinement, men of means than any city old or new in the country."[5]

Pfeiffenberger also became the leader of the local Democratic party. It was said that during his lifetime no Democrat was ever elected to party or public office in Alton without his endorsement. He began his own career in public office as chief of the local volunteer fire department, a position he used as a ladder to five terms as the elected mayor of Alton.

The Pfeiffenbergers were among a small group of local families who dominated Alton's economic and civic affairs throughout the late nineteenth century, led by men with conveniently mingled interests in real estate, moneylending, business and industry, the law, and, of course, politics. He and his wife had five sons, the youngest of whom—James Mather Pfeiffenberger—became a distinguished surgeon. Dr. Pfeiffenberger also carried on his family's leadership of the savings and loan association of which his father had been the founding president.

(The name "Piasa," incidentally, has unpleasant connotations for the Alton area. In the language of the Illini Indians who once inhabited the upper Mississippi, the Piasa [pronounced Pie-a-saw] was a monster bird that devoured men. When the Jesuit priest Father Marquette first explored the great river in 1673, he told of seeing the image of the devil bird carved on the face of a cliff near Alton that no human artist could have reached.)

Known originally as Piasa Building and Loan Association, the institution was federally chartered and renamed Piasa First Federal in 1958. The "Federal" in the title is reassuring to depositors, who are comforted by the knowledge that their savings are insured by the Federal Savings and Loan Insurance Corporation. FSLIC ("Fizzlick" to the industry) is part of the Federal Home Loan Bank Board system. The FHLBB is a source of reserve credit for S & L's that need it. In exchange for this service, chartered institutions are assessed fees to pay the cost of regulatory examinations by federal auditors. Although the system is financed entirely by the associations, without any support from the federal treasury, the supervisory powers of the federal agencies are extensive under federal law. The FHLBB can salvage an ailing S & L with an emergency infusion of funds—or it can elect to put the association out of its misery by ordering its absorption by a healthy S & L. Among twelve regional Federal Home Loan Banks, the one with jurisdiction over Madison County, Illinois, is in Chicago.

Piasa had come a long way since its founding in the last century. Many of Alton's most prominent citizens had sat on its board. Until his death, the second of the Cousleys to run the *Alton Telegraph*, Paul B. Cousley, was a member of Piasa's board for fifty-nine years. Wuellner, the owner of a clothing store in Alton, succeeded Dr. Pfeiffenberger as board president upon the surgeon's death in 1953. Three years after that, DeGrand was hired. The day-to-day operations were managed by the two members of the loan committee, namely DeGrand and Wuellner. They decided who would receive loans from Piasa.

Savings and loans are the main element of what is euphemistically called the "thrift industry"—lending institutions that compete for savings. People who put their money in S & L's generally do so because the interest earned on their shares (a mutual association such as Piasa is owned by its depositors) is higher than in a bank. And some S & L's advertise more aggressively for deposits and pay a higher return than others.

DeGrand was chiefly responsible for Piasa's vigorous growth policy. An institution that pursues increased savings by offering slightly higher interest earnings is under pressure to make enough loans at even higher interest to keep growing profitably.

S & L's were once confined by federal law to home mortgages. But most home loans were at fixed rates for long terms, which can cause severe problems if interest rates rise. As a consequence, "thrifts" were allowed to make construction loans in competition with commercial banks. During this period, Piasa was the first S & L in Metro East to begin making riskier construction loans to certain real estate developers. In 1962, when DeGrand and Green met, the going rate for passbook savings in Metro East S & L's was 4.5 percent. Piasa was paying 4.6 percent. Piasa was thereby able to grow from a meager $5.2 million in mortgages and other assets in 1962 to more than $100 million by the end of the 1960s, making it the biggest Illinois S & L south of Springfield.

With so much money coming in at the deposit windows, DeGrand had to scramble to make enough home loans to maintain the necessary reserves and meet the promised quarterly dividends received by depositors. Which could explain why he and Wuellner might pause on an errant appraising expedition to offer a construction loan to someone they knew nothing about.

Regardless of whether the Green-DeGrand acquaintance began the way they said it did or some other way, Jim Green did in fact go to see Bob DeGrand about a loan. What happened next almost surely involved the intercession of some politically attuned real estate business people who were either known to Green, or were already doing business at Piasa, or both.

In short order, high school dropout Green took a correspondence course in real estate, quit his job at Granite City Steel, formed his own construction company, and went into the real estate development business. From the outset, Piasa was his single source of loans. He applied for loans from other sources from time to time, but none were approved; they were too chancy. Although Green had no capital of his own with which to launch his venture, DeGrand encouraged the enterprise on behalf of Piasa the moneylender. There were new subdivisions to be built in the empty spaces above and below the bluff. Once he found out how easy it was to get the money to pay for the development, Jim Green asked: Why not by me?

The housing boom that had been going on in metropolitan areas all over America since the end of World War II was slow coming to Madison County. Some of the reasons for that go back a long time. Alton's dreams of competing with St. Louis for commercial dominance in the Mississippi valley were doomed to failure by something that happened in 1837: the martyrdom of Elijah Lovejoy.

After his ordination as an evangelist in the Presbyterian church, Elijah Parish Lovejoy settled in St. Louis in 1833 to start a religious newspaper. Lovejoy arrived under a halo of moral superiority. A streak of stubborn intolerance did not endear him to all of the fairminded faithful. He condemned outright anyone associated in any way with the Roman Catholic church, nor was he very fond of Baptists as a class.[6]

His editorials, published in the slave state of the Missouri Compromise, cried out against the sins of slavery. He wrote often about the sexual abuse of slave women by their white slavemasters, a tender subject many of his readers did not care to have brought to their attention. So, in 1836, a mob sacked the newspaper office in St. Louis, whereupon Lovejoy loaded the press and some machinery aboard the steamship *Palmyra* for the short journey upriver to what he presumed would be the more congenial climate in the free state of Illinois.

The press, left standing on the dock overnight, was shoved in the river by a band of ruffians. Prominent citizens in Alton, saddened by the vandalism, raised money to buy a replacement. The town fathers let the Rev. Mr. Lovejoy understand though that no good purpose would be served by inflaming the passions of the rabble-rousers, many of whom were without jobs and in a sour mood. The community leaders told him in so many words to cool it.

Lovejoy could not do that. His transplanted newspaper—now the *Alton Observer*—became a prominent platform for the abolition of slavery. Many folks in Madison County did not take kindly to being preached at in print about that or about their sinful lifestyle—particularly their boozing. The attorney general of Illinois, Usher F. Linder, happened to be from Alton. He had a reputation in Springfield as a heavy drinker and took pleasure in attacking with equal vigor Lovejoy and the temperance societies.

As the tensions increased, the new general circulation newspaper that had come into existence the year before, the *Alton Telegraph,* commented editorially that it did not intend to "interfere or meddle in any way," a spineless abdication of leadership done to avoid alienating advertisers of either persuasion.

On the night of Nov. 7, 1837, a mob marched on a stone warehouse near the river. Lovejoy, his new press, and an armed militia company of fourteen men were inside. The roof was set ablaze with lighted torches and tar balls. Scurrying to help put out the fire, Lovejoy was felled fatally wounded by five shots from somewhere in the crowd.

The *Telegraph* crammed a bulletin, or a "postscript" as it was labeled, into the front page:

Lamentable Occurrence

It is with the deepest regret that we stop the presses in order to state that, at a late hour last night, an attack was made by a large number of persons, on the Warehouse of Messrs. Godfrey, Gilman & Co., for the purpose of destroying a press, intended for the revival of the *Alton Observer;* which, shocking to relate, resulted in the death of two individuals—the Rev. E. P. Lovejoy, late editor of the *Observer,* and a man named Bishop. Seven others were wounded; two severely and the others slightly. We can add no more at this time, other than that the assailants succeeded in effecting their object.

By effecting their object the perpetrators gave the rest of the nation a picture of Alton as a city of terror and lawlessness. "Who but a savage or cold-hearted murderer would go to Alton?" said the

Lynn (Massachusetts) Record. "Meanness, infamy, and guilt are attached to the very name. Hereafter, when a criminal is considered too bad for known punishment, it will be said of him: 'He ought to be banished to Alton.'"

When the news spread to the East, "the country overflowed with passion," Edward Beecher recounted later. "Funeral sermons poured from the pulpits, public memorials and resolutions flooded the papers." Many of Alton's prominent citizens who were opposed to slavery moved away. "The streets were deserted, business had fled, all who could were leaving," said the Rev. A. T. Norton, pastor of the First Presbyterian Church.

Even at that early date, Madison County's bizarre judicial system would be depended on to behave in strange ways so as to compound the horror. Attorney General Linder persuaded a grand jury to indict, not the rioters, but Winthrop Gilman, the owner of the warehouse, and eleven others who had been in the warehouse that night, for inciting a riot! The jury needed but fifteen minutes to reject Linder's preposterous contention that the defenders of the press were responsible for the death of Lovejoy, by acquitting Gilman and the other defendants.

What does all this tell us about Alton? Twenty-some years later, the states of the Union would go to war over the issue of slavery. The Southern states had laws on the books making it a crime to publish anything that might incite slaves to insurrection (in Georgia it was a crime punishable by death). Perhaps the murder of Lovejoy could have happened anywhere near the North-South border. But it happened in Alton. A crusading editor who was not considered to be *of* Alton printed news and views that many did not want to read or hear—either because they took violent umbrage or because they knew that the debate would drive the two sides farther apart and be, in a sense, bad for business. Moreover, Alton's lower classes resented being harangued about their boozing and other bad habits. Why deny them what few pleasures working people could manage in their unhappy lives? Another of the lessons of the Lovejoy story was the willingness of respected individuals in the community to engage in rash unthinking recriminations when the editor's journal was seen as contrary to the best interests of Alton.

Winthrop Gilman was so sickened by the whole sordid affair that he sold his interest in the wholesale firm and left Alton for New York City and a successful career in Wall Street finance. His departure precipitated the city's withdrawal from the river trade because his company, the remnants of which soon went out of business, had owned large packets making the month-long journey to New Orleans. Gilman belonged to the inner circle of men who dominated commerce, finance, and politics in Alton. These men who were so scarred by the trauma of Lovejoy's murder gave way to a new generation of leaders, of whom Lucas Pfeiffenberger was so significantly a part.

Alton managed nonetheless to bounce back from repeated economic panics in the years ahead. At the end of the century, nearly half the city's working population was employed by one thriving firm—Illinois Glass Co. Other industries made flour, steel, boxboard, materials for shoes, and black powder for explosives. Skilled craftsmen came over from Europe to help build the magnificent limestone homes occupied by the industrialists and merchant princes on the Alton hill, many of the finest structures having been designed and constructed by Lucas Pfeiffenberger and his sons.

It would be wrong, however, to think of Alton as an upper-class suburb of St. Louis. Many poor people lived in Alton. A consultant who examined the city's problems in 1912 commented on the "stark contrast" between "slum residential areas inhabited by laborers . . . and the park atmosphere of the residential neighborhoods of the minority [in the professional-managerial class]." In his report, the consultant, Charles Mulford Robinson, cited the recent birth of a child in a hen house in Alton, in a room, he said, "just as the chickens left it." He was also struck by the excessive parochialism of the people of Alton. "The residents of the community were divided by neighborhood loyalties based on tradition and on common prejudices related to wealth, religion, and ethnic heritage," Robinson said.[7]

After the turn of the century, streams of eastern European immigrants poured into the industrial section along the river plain and on into neighboring St. Clair County. They were attracted by the unskilled jobs in the steel mills, oil refineries, railroad car shops, and in the coal mines on the eastern and northern flanks of the factory towns. Bulgarians, Croats, Slovaks, and Hungarians settled in Granite City, for example.[8] The two counties of Madison and St. Clair are a single regional entity—politically, economically, culturally. They are bound together politically by the East Side Levee and Sanitary District, an early venture in intergovernmental cooperation famous in Illinois for its patronage abuses. The most distinctive of the cities of St. Clair County is East St. Louis, a city with as outrageously corrupt a political history as any in the nation.

Among the various communities of Metro East, and within the city of Alton itself, the parochial attitudes that so impressed Robinson earlier in the century are still there. The most prominent of the four large Presbyterian churches in Alton is the First Presbyterian, a handsome edifice which rises like a European cathedral on a high point of Alby Street overlooking the downtown section. The First Presbyterian ministers to many of the area's social and economic elite. Dr. Mather Pfeiffenberger, grandson of Lucas Pfeiffenberger, is a member. So are the newspaper Cousleys, and a number of the leading lawyers and business executives. When Alton's version of white flight resulted in the growth of its own suburbs—Godfrey, Cottage Hills, Forest Homes, and the like—some of the members wanted to relocate the First Presbyterian in Godfrey. "But," says Steve Cousley, "the old money said 'we like it fine where it is,' and that was that."

The pastor of the First Presbyterian at that time was the Rev. Cortley Burroughs. The Rev. Mr. Burroughs is from the hills of east Tennessee, a part of the country from whence many of his 1,800 parishioners (or, more likely, their forebearers) hailed. Tennessee is far behind him now. He is an urbane, polished man with a manner that is courtly indeed. A seven-handicap golfer at Lockhaven Country Club, the minister was good enough to be runner-up in the 1982 club golf tournament.

When I asked him about the city's social structure today, he said: "We have a number of leading families who have been here several generations. So they are respected; they have a certain status within the community, both in a sense of leadership activities and social activities. Not so much though as in previous years when ownership and management were more of a local affair. Now they're part of a big business complex. Status and leadership in most communities are like a pyramid with a few people at the top. I have not seen that here. Here it's more like parallel lines. We have lots of doctors and lawyers. Not many of the doctors have been very active in community leadership. They have their own little pyramid. Then you have large industry, and the newspaper, and the bankers, and the local business community. But there is not that cross-current of intermingling you see in many communities. Each has its own power structure. If you have a problem of race and the poor and so forth, there isn't the intense effort to deal with that by the community. It's because of these parallel lines. Each group says, 'well, this is our interest here, this is our small world.' It's interesting that we don't have a public outdoor swimming pool here. There are club pools, but no public outdoor pool. You could not get the cohesion of the groups to bring about a public swimming pool."

Under the gaze of the riverboat pilot house in the museum, close by the old lock and dam on the bank of the river, is a city park. It is called Riverfront Park. Riverfront Park is a sorry excuse for a park. It is poorly kept up. The grass grows in uneven clumps. Smoke and fumes from the towboats waft over the greensward. The picnic grounds are infested with deckhands sleeping off their shore leave.

Back away from the path is a scruffy flower garden the size of a swimming pool. The reason why it is the size of a swimming pool is that it almost *was* a swimming pool. The space was planned and the pool was almost built when some important people in Alton suddenly realized that it would necessarily be patronized by all the children of Alton—black and white—swimming in the same water. The hole in the ground was hastily filled in with a flower garden—a perennial symbol of the condition of race relations in Alton.

For reasons more historic than willful, Alton is viewed with hostility by many of the people who live in the blue collar towns below the bluff because it is a place where *both* wealthy capitalists *and* low-income blacks hang their hats.

In this age of fair housing laws, the citizens of Metro East still categorize communities according to whether housing is available to blacks. One of the favorite underground railroads for fleeing slaves led to Alton, and the oldest black church in town dates back in 1836, the year the *Telegraph* was founded. After that church was firebombed in 1974, the newspaper organized a campaign to rebuild it. Alton has always had a sizable black population—in the 1980 census just under 20 percent of the total. According to that census, more than one-third of the black families in Alton were living on incomes below the poverty level.

Half of all the blacks in Madison County live in Alton—a city which accounts for less than 14 percent of the county's total population. Next door in Wood River, which has a large Italian-American population, there were exactly 12 blacks counted among the 12,449 residents. In Granite City, there were 96 black residents in the 1980 population of 36,815.

3

Roll-overs and Straw Parties

In the outer reaches of most metropolitan areas, real estate developers insinuated themselves into the local political structure after World War II, all the better to deal with zoning and other technical complications. In an article written in 1966 (entitled "The War on Gangsterism"), newspaperman Barney Wander suggested two reasons why builders and realtors had until then been insignificant political forces in Madison County, Illinois.[1] One was the severely fragmented nature of the county political system. And the other was that political leaders were making so much money out of illegal gambling and the mass marketing of other forms of vice that they didn't need to piddle around with chintzy land deals. As streams of immigrants poured into Metro East from eastern Europe and later from the hill country of the upper South to do the hard work in the factories, foundries, mills, refineries, and railroad yards, they were followed by organized crime, machine politics, and corrupt government. The strong exploiting the weak.

In due course, however, the flight from the older cities, and the greater mobility and spreading out of the population, created a need for new suburban housing in Metro East. The spaces to the north and west were open for development. Alton acquired its own suburbs, mostly all-white settlements with names like Cottage Hills and Meadowbrook and Rosewood Heights. Granite City had its Pontoon Beach and Cedar Brook.

This was also a period of much congressional and press attention devoted to labor union "racketeering." Metro East had a long tradition of very aggressive union organizing. Not many unions were ever led in a way that would confuse them with a bridge club or the PTA, and it is true, as many labor leaders have pointed out over the years, that one man's economic pressure may be another man's racketeering. But some of the building trade locals in Metro East were yet another example of the strong exploiting the weak. Some of the business agents for the carpenters' union (with which a contractor would necessarily come in contact) were accused of using their union jobs as covers for criminal activity. Some of them had criminal records and were believed by police to be involved in organized crime.

All of which is to observe that in the normal course of a building contractor's life he would know politicians, real estate brokers, moneylenders—and union representatives who perchance could be tied in some way to organized crime.

A few of the politically most important real estate brokers were or became friends of Jim Green's. He had, for example, known John Sobol in high school. Sobol, who was in the real estate business in Granite City, was associated with Raymond Kozielek, another real estate broker, who had been mayor of the city of Madison and was prominent in the county-wide Democratic organization.

Green began slowly with single-family houses. Piasa financed the construction of the thirty houses that Green's company built in 1964. The next year he branched out into clusters of four-apartment fourplexes, most of them in subdivisions that included an adjacent shopping strip. Green's projects were aimed at the low-rent market. He intended to satisfy a need for housing moderate-income blue-collar workers and their families. Though enticingly adorned with exotic names like Chateau des Fleurs, or Gaslight Walk, or this or that "Gardens," there was nothing idyllic about most of his housing. He sometimes apparently cut corners on costs and had occasional problems with building inspectors. On one occasion he was fined $600 for going ahead with construction before the proper county building permits had been obtained.[2]

Some of his units attracted a clientele of tenants characterized later by the FHLBB's appraisers as "motorcycle gangs" and their promiscuous women's auxiliaries.³ Despite the unquestioned social desirability of building housing for moderate-income tenants in a market needing that housing, ventures of this sort required a high degree of management skill. The potential maintenance and other problems were enormous. The projects were fraught with risk—for the builder and for the lender. At the very least, without much capital of his own to fall back on, the builder had to earn at least enough rental income, or sell the properties, to pay off the loans.

About this time, apparently, Green made the acquaintance of the first Madison County real estate developer to be bankrolled by Piasa—one Donald Hazel. Don Hazel, thirty years old in 1965, borrowed heavily from Piasa beginning in 1962 to build apartment housing in and around Bethalto, a growing, blue-collar suburb on the eastern fringe of Alton. Hazel was suspected by law enforcement officials in the county of being involved in organized crime. The *Telegraph* referred to him in its news columns as a "police character" and "an associate of hoodlums."

When Bob DeGrand was asked later in court whether he had inquired into Hazel's criminal record, DeGrand said he had only checked the contractor's credit rating and was unaware of Hazel's having been charged with anything more serious than a traffic ticket or two. In fact, between 1951 and 1959 Hazel was arrested for car theft, tampering with a motor vehicle, burglary, larceny, breaking and entering, issuing fraudulent checks, and contempt of court. He served two stretches in the state penitentiary at Pontiac for the car tampering and burglary and larceny convictions.⁴

Before Green began developing his own subdivisions, his company did some of the carpentry work under subcontract on Hazel's projects. On his own Green built more than 1,800 apartment units and 200 houses by the end of the decade. Starting in Madison County, he was soon also building in St. Clair and two other counties—Clinton to the east and Sangamon, where Springfield is located.

The FHLBB estimated later that Green directly or indirectly borrowed a total of $24.8 million from Piasa during this period.⁵ Under federal regulations, any one borrower is limited at any one time to an indebtedness of no more than the net worth of the S & L—then a little over $4 million in Piasa's case. So it was necessary for Green and Piasa to take several steps to avoid exceeding the limit when federal auditors came around every year to look at the records.

For one thing, Green "rolled over" between $10 and $12 million in loans. A common practice in real estate, the rolling over of a construction loan means that a buyer of the property assumes the loan as part of the purchase price, thereby reducing the builder's debt by that amount. What was different here, the FHLBB contended later when all the records had been unraveled, was that some of Green's rollovers were paper transactions with the builder's associates, arranged to allow Green to continue to borrow from Piasa while he retained control over the "sold" properties.

Kozielek, for example, testified at one of the many court proceedings that he had been deeded some of Green's rental properties as a "straw party" for this purpose. He said Sobol, who managed many of Green's rental properties after they had been built, arranged the transaction because Green had been at his borrowing limit.[6] Other loans were made by Piasa in Sobol's name and in the names of others for Green construction projects, according to the FHLBB, again permitting Green's various enterprises to keep on borrowing more.

The federal authorities also accused Piasa of inflated appraisals of Green's projects, and of an unusual use of "pledged savings accounts" that they said they had never seen before.[7] Green was launching new projects with little or no down payment of his own, financed entirely by Piasa. Piasa made this possible—again according to the FHLBB—by raising the amount of the loan beyond what Green needed and putting the excess in a "pledged" account in Green's name as security. By the middle of 1969, almost $1 million had been deposited in Green's pledged accounts. The ostensible purpose of a pledged account is to protect the lender against the failure of the project, although in this case the FHLBB said Piasa actually put up the money—deposits that were paying dividends to Green.

In this case, however, the arrangement appeared to make little sense to the borrower (Green). He was paying a higher interest cost (about 6.50 percent) on the extra loan then he was receiving (about 4.75 percent) on the money in his savings account. For its part, Piasa presumably could have loaned the same money out to some other borrower at less risk and greater profit.

Some of his projects encountered unusual delays and were only partially completed. Others were poorly maintained, and the vacancy rate much higher than normal. The cash flow from rents was not enough to meet the interest payments on the loans, so Green needed new loans to make the payments on the old ones. It is difficult to understand how even an experienced managerial genius—which Jim Green was not—could continue to forge ahead under the circumstances.

In the late 1960s, however, the former steelworker was flying high. In addition to his own projects, he owned 60 percent of a mobile home park, 50 percent of a steak house, 20 percent of two skating rinks, 20 percent of a project called Fairway Estates (in which Madison County Democratic leader Mike Sasyk owned another 20 percent).

Ever the cocky optimist, Green enjoyed quoting the wisdom of Norman Vincent Peale and W. Clement Stone. One of his favorites from supersalesman Clement Stone promised: "Whatever the mind of man can conceive and believe, it can also achieve." He traveled abroad. He drove expensive cars. He was a frequent guest in Piasa's box at Busch Stadium in downtown St. Louis. The money kept coming from Piasa. Green had big plans for shopping centers, theaters, mobile home parks, and more housing projects.

Just then, at the beginning of 1969, an important event occurred in the life of Bob DeGrand, a cause for elation for him and his family. Robert Lee DeGrand's ancestors were French Canadians. His grandparents came to Alton not long after Lucas Pfeiffenberger and the first of the Cousleys. They lived in a different social stratum: the Roman Catholic middle class. DeGrand's father, Alfred, owned a small foundry in Alton, but died at the age of thirty-five. The boy's mother married again, but Bob and his stepfather did not get along, so he went to live with an aunt and uncle.

After serving as a cryptographer in the Army Air Corps, DeGrand married Nancy Hellrung, the daughter of a successful construction company owner in Alton. The DeGrands were a devout Catholic family. For sixteen years, the nine children and their parents said the rosary every night as a family unit in the living room of their home. The first of their sons, Robert Lee, Jr., became a priest.

Their small house in the Christian Hill section was inadequate for such a large family. An unexpected opportunity presented itself, however, when the Hellrung children inherited a magnificent big solid house that had been built originally for their mother on East 11th Street. Eleventh Street is in the "Middletown" neighborhood, near Henry Street, where some of the grandest mansions are located, and close to the older, more traditional, and most prestigious of the Catholic churches—St. Mary's.

Containing five bedrooms and five baths, the house was worth well over $100,000. The DeGrands borrowed money to purchase the interests of Nancy DeGrand's brothers and sisters. They moved into the remodeled residence in February. For reasons symbolic as well as practical, the move represented Bob DeGrand's arrival above the bluff.

4

Blue Pencils at the *Telegraph*

> *It's a Republican newspaper, the* Telegraph. *They're good people in their own way, I guess, but they're different . . . Presbyterian or something. And then Alton has always been cliquish. If you're not born into money, it's hard to be accepted there.*
>
> —A former Madison County judge who lived in Alton

Not long after the death of Lovejoy, the struggling young *Alton Telegraph* reported the news of a mild incident of local rowdyism with this explanatory aside: "We would publish the names were we not advised that liquor was the cause. They were Democrats. If a Republican should be guilty of such conduct, he would be instantly turned out of the party."[1]

In that one pronouncement is incorporated the two principles of faith that would guide the newspaper into this century. The Republican party, like the *Telegraph,* was still in its infancy. But from the publication of the first issue of the *Telegraph* on January 15, 1836, the editors were devoted with every drop of ink at their disposal to the causes of temperance and emerging Republicanism. Down through the decades the editorial policy would reflect the values of Alton's managerial-professional class and the Presbyterian New England background of many of its leading citizens. As European immigration made the region more strongly Democratic, Catholic, and blue-collar working class, the editorial judgments of the newspaper clashed often with the cultural and political traditions of a large segment of the Madison County populace.

One of the founders of the *Telegraph,* twenty-two-year-old Lawson A. Parks, had been pastor of a church in Troy, in eastern Madison County, and associated with Lovejoy in the publication of the *St. Louis Observer* before Lovejoy moved his operation across the river. Many years later, the *Telegraph* noted in an anniversary issue that Parks had "carried his religion into the paper as long as he lived."

His partner, Richard M. Treadway, died the very next year, in 1837, at the age of thirty-two, but Parks lived until 1875. Whenever, over these almost forty years, the paper needed an infusion of capital, Parks sold part interests to other community leaders, even bowing out of management for brief periods while others were in charge. A later issue of the *Telegraph* paid this tribute to its co-founder:

> He returned frequently to the editorial control of the paper that the name of the *Telegraph* might not perish from the earth. . . . He viewed the paper as his own child, being childless himself by the death of his only son at a tender age. Editors might weary in the work, lay down the pen and the shears and the paste pot, but Editor Parks was always waiting around ready to step in and fill the gap and continue the paper—always, until death laid its compelling grip upon him and Editor Parks passed to his greatly-looked-for long home.[2]

When death's compelling grip took Parks away, John A. Cousley was there to take up the paste pot and shears. The first of a long line of Cousleys at the *Telegraph,* John Cousley came to Alton in 1850, part of a massive migration of Scots-Irish from Ulster to the New World. Presbyterian "Lowlanders" moved from Scotland to what is now Protestant Northern Ireland and then on to America. One of the main immigrant streams passed through the Cumberland Gap to settle in the hills of Appalachia or further west in the Ozarks. The settlers brought their hatred of Irish Catholics with them.

It was not until eleven years after his arrival in Alton that John Cousley got a job as a printer's devil at the *Telegraph.* He advanced rapidly to print shop foreman, saved his money, and bought an interest in the paper after Park's death. Historian W. T. Norton, who was then the editor, left the newspaper to fill the party patronage job of postmaster of Alton in 1889. The following year, he and others sold a controlling interest in the newspaper company to John Cousley, who promptly made himself the editor and publisher.

It was not unusual in that period for printers to own (and edit) newspapers, just as it was common practice for a partisan newspaper in town to claim the postmastership as its share of the federal patronage spoils. Well into the next century, beginning with Norton, "the *Telegraph* furnished the postmasters for Alton [whenever there was a Republican in the White House] in recognition to the paper for its services to the Republican Party," the paper proudly noted in its seventy-fifth anniversary edition.

There will be ups and downs in every newspaper's life, that article said, so the policy of the *Telegraph* had been "not to gloat over . . . fallen adversar[ies], for the fallen may rise to wreak vengeance, either with coals of fire or vindictive measures." The same story went on to explain: "The *Telegraph* believes in the policy of mercy. If pain or suffering is to be inflicted by the publication of a news item, especially to helpless women or children, or if a good name is to be tarnished, just to satisfy a curiosity for news, the *Telegraph* policy is to blue pencil it."[3]

The truth be known, John Cousley's blue pencil protected not only defenseless women and children. A "dry" Presbyterian like his predecessors, he served as president of the local school board, was an officer of the Masonic Lodge, and was rewarded for his service to the party by an appointment as state civil service commissioner. The news columns of his paper regularly identified whiskey as "the curse of the country." Politicians were reprimanded in print for their drunkenness. Except when moved to predictable partisan fits of irascibility during election campaigns, or to outbursts of indignation over the behavior of sodden public figures, the *Telegraph* was a rather drab product under John Cousley's leadership. He and the Democratic banker-builder-politician Lucas Pfeiffenberger were good friends. Partisan differences aside, they agreed about the need to promote the well-being of the community. While the party papers of that day were daring in their political attacks, they were not inclined to go looking for trouble. The news was generally edited in a way that would not offend the powerful in Alton.

John Cousley's first son, Paul Bliss Cousley, knew as a boy that someday he would take over the paper. He and another youth, John D. McAdams, delivered papers on the same street, Paul carrying the *Telegraph* and John the rival *Daily Republican*. In 1905, by which time young McAdams had acquired a controlling interest in the *Daily Republican,* the two papers merged. To add "Republican" to the name of the *Telegraph* would have been redundant, so the *Evening Telegraph* it remained. McAdams became minority shareholder and business manager, positions he held until his death in 1941.

Paul assumed the editorship in 1913, three years before his father's death. He was a more aggressive editor than his father had been. The *Telegraph* underwent some subtle changes of direction under his control—nothing dramatic, but important nonetheless. The local industries preferred to conduct their business affairs quietly without having to bother with nosy reporters. And they were likely to react explosively to any criticism from anywhere within the community. People in Alton still talk about the time the Illinois Glass Co. couldn't obtain fire insurance because the water pressure was inadequate. What did the glass company do? Why it bought the waterworks, of course, and floated bonds to put up a water tower. Water rates had to be increased in order to pay off the bonds. All hell broke loose when the *Telegraph* ventured to wonder editorially whether working families in Alton should pay for the special problems of the glassworks.

This is not to suggest that Paul was given to needling the glass company or the other magnates in town. He was not. Nor did the *Telegraph* go off crusading for the public park and housing improvements that the consultant Robinson had proposed. It did not. The publisher was very much a part of the city's inner circle.

Contrary to the legends of American journalism, aggressive investigative reporting has never been universally practiced or revered in the newspaper business. Journalists bestow their most prestigious honors on the best examples of courageous investigative enterprise. What is not always understood, however, is that such daring is found almost exclusively in big-city competitive markets, essentially as a form of product differentiation. The reasons for this are more practical than philosophical. Paul Cousley had a domineering personality. Around the newspaper, he was referred to simply as "The Boss." A very judgmental individual, he knew what he liked and what he didn't like, and he wanted you to like what he liked. For all that, he was typical of editors who were more comfortable attacking conditions in some remote location than they were inviting the alienation of advertisers and other important folks at home on Main Street.

The man who had as much as any other to do with the introduction of a new style of independent crusading journalism—one that would "serve no party but the people," a radical notion at the time—was standing at the river dock in East St. Louis, not far from Alton, on the evening of October 10, 1865. His name was Joseph Pulitzer.

A United States Army recruiter enticed young Pulitzer into leaving his native Hungary and coming to fight for the Union during the Civil War. After the war, Pulitzer hitchhiked as far west as East St. Louis. There was no bridge across the river then, and he had no money for the ferry. He could see the gaslights of downtown St. Louis shimmering through the cold misty rain on the other side. Speaking in German to the ferry crew, he offered to fire the boiler on the boat all through the rest of the night in exchange for his passage across the river. Once in St. Louis, he got a job on a German-language paper, the *Westliche Post*. Joey Pulitzer saved his money and in 1878 he bought the *St. Louis Dispatch* at a sheriff's sale.[4]

After its subsequent merger with the *St. Louis Post*, Pulitzer's *Post-Dispatch* went on to become one of the nation's best newspapers. The *P-D* combined tough investigative reporting with a hard-hitting editorial page and thorough if sometimes sensational coverage of the news. Beholden to no party and skeptical of all public officials, the *Post-Dispatch* exercised independent community leadership. Pulitzer saw his newspaper as a vehicle for waging war against "the idle rich" and "the government of the trusts."

Moving east later, as editor of the *New York World*, Pulitzer created what came to be known as "yellow journalism." He believed that the pennies of workingmen would support an urban newspaper that stood up for their welfare even if it meant offending advertisers.

Oliver K. Bovard, the great managing editor of the *Post-Dispatch*, insisted that a "true newspaper" was never content with the surface facts but always dug out the hidden details that would reveal the real meaning of an event. "Never be satisfied with the surface of the news," he told his reporters. "There is a formal and superficial aspect of every news story. It may be a police report, a lawyer's brief, an application for a trolley franchise, or a President's message to Congress. As such it may have a proper place in your story. But to print that alone may result in misleading the reader partially or completely."[5]

The different standards set by the *Post-Dispatch* influenced journalism all over the United States, but all the more so in the St. Louis area. As a cub reporter on the *Alton Telegraph*, James Phelan remembers in his book how inspired he was by the *P-D* style of newspapering:

> The *Post-Dispatch* looked upon the rowdy Illinois East Side as a wayward and intransigent distant cousin whose disreputable life-style was a constant embarrassment, irritant, and challenge. With its strong political clout and staff of good reporters, the *Post-Dispatch* kept St. Louis itself free of the more flagrant vices. This pleased the whorehouse and gambling entrepreneurs across the Mississippi, because anyone looking for action could indulge himself after a short cab ride across the river.[6]

Phelan recounts how Ted Link, one of many talented *P-D* reporters, disclosed "in exact detail, down to the penny," the payoffs that public officials were receiving from the Hyde Park Club in Madison County. "I immediately adopted [Link] as a model of what a reporter should be, and followed his coverage of East Side corruption with awe and envy," Phelan said.

Gambling emporiums, houses of prostitution, prohibition era bootlegging, illegal bookie joints, and other shady diversions were more notable because of the brazenness with which public officials and law enforcement agencies collected payoffs. For many years the elected sheriff was also the recognized slot machine king of Madison

County. The police chief of the city of Madison made no effort to disguise his ownership interest in one of the biggest gambling houses in the county. Although dog racing was banned by state law, dog tracks operated with parimutuel betting, and a circuit judge once issued an injunction barring the police from interfering with the unlawful wagering at the dog races.

In 1951, a committee of the United States Senate spelled out how a national network of terrorist "families" controlled crime and vice in, among other places, Madison and St. Clair counties in Illinois. A former labor union official and bootlegger—Frank "Buster" Wortman—was identified as the Mafia's overseer of the lucrative evil in Metro East. While serving time in a federal penitentiary, Wortman was said to have made the acquaintance of some Mafia figures from Chicago who set him up in business. He was believed to have been blessed thereafter by a special connection to the Chicago criminal organization. "Most shocking in Madison and St. Clair Counties," commented the Senate report, "was the utter blindness of law enforcement officials and the evidence of their unexplained income."[7]

Tolerance of crime and vice on the "East Side" date back long before the first Mafia mobster. Wood River, a neighbor of Alton's in the *Telegraph* circulation territory, grew "rapidly and lawlessly from the time of its incorporation," according to one account, "as hundreds of workers moved in to work at new oil refineries. Liquor, whores, and gambling made early Wood River wilder than most towns of the 'wild' West."[8] Consequently, it was not always easy to tell which of the numerous criminal enterprises were mob affiliated. Nor was it easy to separate criminal groups from ethnic political organizations. When people in Metro East referred to a "Croatian family" or a "Macedonian family," for example, they might be talking about a branch of the Democratic party, a cooperative venture in some brand of vice, an arm of the Mafia, or a fraternal organization.

One student of crime in Madison County said publisher Cousley "was convinced that as long as the gambling interests were local, and kept local by the law enforcement officials, things were all right. He only feared 'gangsters from Chicago.' The outside involvement was apparently well hidden from the *Telegraph*."[9]

When he started working for the *Telegraph* as a $19-a-week reporter in 1941, James Phelan said there were three wide-open gambling joints that had run for years in Alton, one only two blocks from the *Telegraph*'s offices. In his memoirs of an investigative reporter published many years later, Phelan said this:

> When the *Post-Dispatch* would periodically front-page a story on East Side corruption, the *Telegraph* would either ignore it or carry a toned-down version attributed to the St. Louis paper, with no follow-up on its own initiative. I found this puzzling in view of the character of the publisher of the *Telegraph,* a stern, churchgoing Scottish Presbyterian named Paul B. Cousley. He was obviously not a man given to tolerance of whorehouses and crap games. Indeed, he was of such high moral rectitude that he even frowned on beer drinking by his reporters. Most of us, after a hard day of newsgathering, would retire to the Knights of Columbus bar, where Mr. Cousley never intruded. . . .
>
> After I had been on the paper a while, I cautiously raised the issue of the *Telegraph*'s passive tolerance of rampant vice with some of the older reporters. They told me a story that explained why the *Telegraph* persisted in sitting on the East Side compost heap and smelling only roses. Some years earlier Mr. Cousley had launched a *Telegraph* crusade against gambling at the instigation of a woman named Irene Kite. She had sought him out and offered to play the role of a latter-day Carrie Nation, the Kansas temperance reformer who had chopped up bars with an axe. Mrs. Kite had proposed to fare forth with her own axe against the slot machines that were illegally gulping workingmen's wages. Mr. Cousley had rallied church groups and unleashed Mrs. Kite, trailed by his reporters and photographers. Then it had developed that Mrs. Kite was not a true spiritual descendant of Carrie Nation, but the angry wife of a local gambler who had been fired from his job. Her motive had been pure revenge, and the crusade had collapsed into low comedy. Thereafter the *Telegraph* had shunned investigative reporting and had restricted itself to reporting only formal raids against the joints and the arrests of gamblers. Since the law officials never raided the joints, the wide-open gambling was not "news."[10]

The story of Alton's pseudo Carrie Nation is most likely apocryphal. Mr. Phelan tells another tale in his book, though, about a plumber who was beaten by two brothers who ran a gambling joint in East Alton. After the victim was thrown out of the prosecutor's office for insisting that the assailants be arrested on his own sworn complaint, he went to the *Telegraph* reporter, who began looking into the affair, only to be "booted into a roadside ditch" by two men who "put a gun to the back of my head." Phelan then decided to let Mr. Cousley in on what had happened to him. The publisher instructed his reporter to mind his own business and drop the matter, which he did. A short time later, Phelan quit and took a job in California.

Under Mr. Cousley's leadership, the paper would not accept liquor advertising and campaigned vigorously for a local option ban on drinking. In 1932 the *Telegraph* bought out its last remaining competitor, the *Alton Daily Times*. Those *Times* printers who were taken on in the consolidation had been accustomed to "beer breaks" on sweltering summer afternoons. Small buckets of suds were available in the pressroom at ten cents per dip. But Cousley was adamant: no drinking in any manner or form would be tolerated in any part of the plant.[11]

Paul had married well, into the wealthy "flour mill family," the Sparks family. He and his wife had one son—Paul S. Cousley, forever to be known as "Paulie"—and five daughters. A trust was established more than twenty years before Paul Sr.'s death, conveying his majority share of the newspaper to the six children.

The friendships between the Cousley and Pfeiffenberger families were preserved from one generation to the next. The Cousley daughters were best friends of the daughters of Dr. James Mather Pfeiffenberger, the surgeon son of Lucas Pfeiffenberger. The Cousleys and the Pfeiffenbergers sat up front in the same row of pews at the First Presbyterian Church.

For ten years, from 1922 until the inauguration of Franklin D. Roosevelt in 1933, Paul B. Cousley held two jobs—as editor/publisher of the *Telegraph* and as postmaster of Alton. He helped put out the paper in the morning and then moved over to the post office in the afternoon.

Just as his father had known from boyhood that he would one day run the *Telegraph,* so too was it understood that Paulie would one day be chairman of the board of the *Alton Telegraph*. As the only boy in a family of six children, he said he "sort of fell into" a newspaper career. While in grade school, Paulie swept floors and ran errands at the paper. Then he covered student news in Alton High School. After majoring in journalism at the University of Illinois, he started as a reporter of East Alton and Wood River city government and then moved into the office and a variety of assignments.

Paulie married a teacher's daughter from a middle-class section of Alton. He had clearly inherited more of his gentlewomanly mother's sensitivity than his father's aggressiveness. The Cousleys appear to have fit the classic pattern of a son whose father had been a domineering influence in his son's life well into adulthood and who developed a much more subdued personality of his own.

Paul Sr. would not relinquish the title of editor until 1962 when he was eighty-five years old, practically blind, and his son was fifty-five. The old man died the following year, on November 22, 1963, a date made famous by the assassination in Dallas of President John F. Kennedy.

After so many years of waiting, the mantle of leadership did not come easily to Paulie. As the years passed, he often told friends that he would have been happier in a musical career. He had always been devoted to classical music and for many years was a tympanist with the city and county symphony orchestras. He and his wife were disinterested in social climbing or the pomp that went with the power of his job. They preferred sitting home and reading to one another in the evening.

Like his father before him, Paulie was a zealous teetotaler. If his resolve needed any reinforcement, it occurred less than two years after the loss of his father. One Saturday evening in 1965, Paulie was driving a car in which his mother was a passenger on Humbert Road in Alton. Another driver made an unexpected left turn in front of the Cousley vehicle, crashing into it. Mrs. Cousley died of injuries received in the accident. Police said the other driver, who was uninjured, was intoxicated.

5

A True Newspaper in Alton

The *Telegraph* changed into O. K. Bovard's vision of a "true newspaper" in the 1960s. Paulie and his wife had one child, a daughter who was named after her mother, Hope, which in the Cousley tradition became Hopie. Hopie was born on the *Telegraph*'s birthday, an omen of more significance to her grandfather than to her parents. In her teens, she worked summers at the paper, and when the time came Hopie was sent off to the Medill School of Journalism at Northwestern University. At this, one of the nation's premier newspaper training grounds, she had the misfortune of tangling early in her matriculation with a Speed Graphic camera. She enjoyed words and was verbally talented, but the encounter with photojournalism only confirmed what she already knew: that she did not really want a newspaper career; and, furthermore, she did not want to live in Alton or in any other small city. So she changed her major and wound up a librarian in the Chicago suburb of Skokie. Paul B. Cousley's brother, Alex Cousley, had a son, Richard, who became the classified advertising manager of the *Telegraph*. And one of Richard's sons—Stephen—knew as a boy working after schools and summers at the paper that he wanted to be a newspaperman. He majored in journalism and government at Southern Illinois University in Carbondale, where he met a vivacious girl from East St. Louis, his future wife Mary Lou Williamson. Steve started on the *Telegraph* staff as a cub reporter for $100 a week in 1964, just in time to fall under the spell of a new city editor.

His name was Elmer Broz. Paulie was content to look after the editorial page and leave the city editor in charge of the local news operation. An itinerant veteran of the old school—the old St. Louis school—of newspapering, Broz transformed the *Telegraph* almost overnight from community propaganda agency and recorder of history to the Pulitzer-Bovard style of searching journalism.

Broz had worked as a reporter for the St. Louis *Star-Times* (now defunct) and for the United Press news service (now United Press International). He was first hired by the *Telegraph* to cover neighborhood news in Upper Alton, a menial assignment he made the most of by spinning fascinating vignettes out of what would otherwise have been dull three-paragraph items.

Like Bovard and most other good editors of that era, Broz was tyrannical but big-hearted. An excitable, sometimes impetuous executive, ordering his reporters full speed ahead after The Story, he was simultaneously loved and hated by his staff. Around the office, Broz enjoyed playing the part of a character out of *The Front Page*. At the city desk—and just about everyplace else—he sat frozen in a perpetually slouched position as though poised over a smoking typewriter racing the clock to knock out another blockbuster before deadline.

A recovered alcoholic, he occupied his spare hours churning out crime stories for pulp magazines. Like many other metropolitan crime reporters, Broz followed the machinations of the many-familied Mafia with the curiosity and diligence of a birdwatcher. A magazine editor, Sidney Zion, once explained the media's penchant for exhaustive accounts of organized crime with the cynical observation that "the Mafia doesn't advertise."[1]

Otherwise, the paper was Elmer's life. Reporters assigned to cover evening meetings were instructed to call him at home afterward so he could stay on top of the news at all hours. Managing Editor John Focht was not adverse to raising hell in the pages of the *Telegraph,* and Broz assembled a staff of activist reporters who wanted to make a difference. A tall, thin man of Bohemian ancestry, with narrow shoulders and dark, curly hair, Broz loved to drop his chained spectacles onto his chest after the paper had been put to bed, light up a cigar, and chatter on about what newspapering had been like in St. Louis in the good old days when there were several True Newspapers battling for readers.

More often than not, the city editor treated local dignitaries with unaccustomed contempt. Dr. Mather Pfeiffenberger—grandson of Lucas Pfeiffenberger and, like his father, a surgeon in Alton—remembers Broz as an altogether disagreeable fellow who enjoyed insulting Rotarians when Paulie would bring him to the weekly meetings of that esteemed local institution.

As an officer of Piasa Savings and Loan, Dr. Pfeiffenberger also was a community leader protective of the city's image. "Elmer was a total screwball," he remembers. "He had sort of a wild look about him. He was out to stir up headlines, out to downgrade, almost degrade anyone who was successful. The *Telegraph* was the most negative force in the community when it should have been the most positive."

One of his reporters, Joe Melosi, said Broz believed simply that "a reporter should be a reporter and not a stenographer. He thought there's got to be more than those council meeting stories. Find out what's really going on. Enterprising journalism, he called it. He didn't want his reporters buddying up to anybody. 'Don't believe what politicians tell you,' he told us. 'Develop sources on your own. Be hard-nosed. Have integrity.' He didn't care what anybody thought of him. Let the chips fall where they may. When advertisers complained, which they did all the time, he told the advertising department to 'get the hell out of here.'"

Broz turned the *Telegraph* into a paper with hard-nosed reporters who dug beneath the surface of the news. He was ahead of his time deploying reporters to cover news of consumer problems, environmental issues, and regulation of public utilities—all from the point of view of the readers and not the commercial interests involved. One of his favorite subjects was public utility rate setting. Readers were informed in detail how utility rates and policies were determined, and how some industries in the region were polluting the air and water. The *Telegraph* ran a series of stories on child abuse in the community—years before the news media hit upon that topic.

Reporters who worked on these news frontiers knew that their stories would be prominently displayed in the *Telegraph,* much to the consternation of Dr. Pfeiffenberger and his friends.

Though Paulie's editorial columns continued to trumpet the positions of the Republican party, Broz and Focht edited a lively, daring, provocative, reform-minded newspaper that was not afraid to antagonize either the economic leadership of the Alton area or the political leadership of Madison County. Decisions made in the Democratic party clubhouses of the Tri-Cities and in the county courthouse at Edwardsville affected the lives of *Telegraph* readers. Now, for the first time, the *Telegraph* (and also the newspaper in East St. Louis, the *Metro East Journal*) were using vigorous, investigative journalism to try to get at the real stories.

Elmer Broz was both ahead of and behind his time. Later in the 1960s and then in the 1970s consumer affairs reporting would be chic in the most conservative of papers. In another sense, however, the feisty spirit of Pulitzer and Bovard was fading under the onslaught of the chain ownership era. Newspapers were being gobbled up by centrally managed groups guided by corporate comptrollers who understood that bland entertainment could be more profitable than troublesome investigative journalism, particularly in monopoly or nearly monopoly markets.

But Managing Editor Focht believed in what Broz was doing, and Paulie was willing to stand back and let him do his thing his way. More important perhaps than any of that was the presence of the Cousley family heir apparent—Steven Cousley—who was learning about Madison County, its politics, and its newspapers as part of the Broz team. Because Paulie did not have a son, it was widely assumed that Steve was being groomed to take over the news operation eventually. Steve worked for a while in the Wood River bureau and then in the county seat bureau at Edwardsville. In the old Greek revival courthouse in the middle of town, a young reporter could find every conceivable species of political organism. Here, justice, politics, and county government mixed together—in a living laboratory that would make an investigative reporter salivate.

Readers of newspapers the size of the *Telegraph* are well served if the paper assigns a single reporter to the courthouse beat. If the city of publication is not the county seat, the courthouse may not even be covered directly; information may be collected by telephone instead. But by the time Steve was learning to be a reporter, the *Telegraph* deployed three regular reporters in Edwardsville, even though the county seat was several miles removed from the Alton paper's core circulation area.

Partly because of geography, Alton being tucked away in the corner of Madison County as it is, the city's economic prominence did not translate into power in county politics. The Democratic party was dominated by people in Granite City, Madison, and Venice. Alton's political isolation was not helped, of course, by the *Telegraph*'s Republicanism. Peter Simpson, an astute political operative who will figure in our story later, told me this: "Alton has always had a very insular attitude. There was a time when there were enormous riches in Alton. But the leaders there were smug, satisfied, provincial, caring little about the rest of the county. In a sense, Alton's great agony will always be its desire to be eminently respectable." The Broz city editorship represented a belated recognition that, insular though they may be, the lives of *Telegraph* readers were touched by events in the courthouse and elsewhere in the county.

Daily newspapers generally are profitable investments. Though the dispersal of retail trade from "downtown" into outlying shopping centers affected advertising revenues adversely, the daily newspaper is still the primary means of communicating retail shopping information to consumers.

When we talk about high profitability in the newspaper business, what do we mean? By the early 1970s, *Telegraph* circulation stood at just under 40,000. In that 30,000–50,000 circulation range, the profit margin for most papers is between 10 and 20 percent. The Inland Daily Press Association, a newspaper trade association, reported that the typical 50,000-circulation midwestern daily posted a 17.9 percent profit margin in 1979.[2]

With that as a standard, we can make certain generalizations about the *Telegraph* as a newspaper property:

First, its income from advertising and other sources of revenue is less than most newspapers of its size. There is less advertising in the *Telegraph*. This is explained by the economic decline of the area, by the competition for advertising from the free distribution shoppers ringing the entire metro area, and by the fact that the *Telegraph* has never published a Sunday edition. Second, the proportion of its income put back into the news department budget is greater. The *Telegraph* spends proportionally more on the news product. Third, it is considerably less profitable. In 1979, the *Telegraph* brought in about $5.2 million and cost about $5 million to publish—a profit of $207,700 or roughly 4 percent.[3]

In the same year, the typical Inland daily of somewhat greater circulation (50,000) brought in $9.5 million and cost $7.8 million—an operating profit of $1.7 million.

The editorial budget as a percentage of income is one good way to gauge how much a newspaper spends to report the news. In 1979, the average for Inland papers of comparable size was 10.52 percent or a little over ten cents out of a dollar; for the *Telegraph*, it was 13.4 percent or a little over thirteen cents. Another measure is the ratio of editorial budget to the cost of newsprint. How much did the paper spend on news as compared to what it cost to buy the paper upon which to put that news and everything else that goes into the newspaper? The *Telegraph* spent $709,000 for news and $902,000 for paper—a 78 percent ratio. The typical 50,000 circulation daily spent about $1 million on its editorial budget and $1,675 million for paper—a 60 percent ratio reflecting the *Telegraph*'s less than normal advertising volume and number of pages.

The newsroom staff of twenty-eight editors, reporters, and clerks—thirteen of them reporters—is unusually high in relation to the circulation and the profitability of the paper. It was generally understood that a newspaper group owner would undoubtedly prune away some of the staff, beginning with the several old-timers approaching retirement.

Concentration of ownership in the newspaper business followed a general trend after World War II. Just as mom-and-pop grocery stores succumbed to the supermarket chains, father-son-grandson newspapers were taken over by communication groups. In 1979, groups owned 63 percent of the dailies in the United States, representing 74 percent of daily circulation. The process was hurried along in the newspaper business by the operation of the inheritance tax laws. In the same way that farm families find it difficult to pass valuable land from generation to generation because the cash income from the land is not sufficient to pay the estate taxes, so are newspaper properties worth far more than their cash flow would suggest (the *Alton Telegraph* being a good example).

In the Metro East region, individual newspapers were gobbled up by relatively small family-owned groups, which were then purchased by large communications conglomerates and sometimes resold. The *Edwardsville Intelligencer,* for example, was acquired by an essentially in-state group, Lindsay-Schaub Newspapers, Inc., which then sold out to a publicly owned company, Lee Enterprises, which then unloaded the *Intelligencer* on the Hearst group. Of the six most influential newspapers in Metro East, only the *Telegraph* was still locally owned and managed in the 1970s.

Whether to sell the *Telegraph* to a group had been a gnawing source of dissension between the majority owner Cousleys and minority owner McAdamses for many years. In 1979, Paul S. Cousley, the publisher, was being paid an annual salary of $61,630 plus director's fees of $3,000. Steve Cousley, by then the editor, and Peter C. McAdams, forty-two, production and personnel manager (and grandson of John McAdams), both received $54,457 plus the same director's fees. Henry McAdams, Peter's father and John's son, was listed at $52,625 plus director's fees as secretary/treasurer.

Henry McAdams, a gruff, sharp-featured, ascetic looking man of sixty-five, took over as business manager in 1941 when his father was killed in an automobile accident in Florida. Another of Henry's sons, William, then forty, wanted the advertising manager's job that went instead to Steve Cousley's brother David. William had been put in charge of the twice-weekly satellite newspaper that the *Telegraph* published in Jerseyville to the north, but this didn't work out and he finally moved to Idaho.

While the Cousleys were directing the news-editorial operation on the third floor, the McAdamses were entrenched on the second floor. Board meetings were not very congenial. When I had a chat with Henry McAdams in 1982, he minced no words about the deteriorating situation. "A group could do a lot better job with this newspaper than an individual can," he said. "They would put in better management and put out a better paper. We don't make any money. We should easily make 10 percent before taxes, but we don't. We have a good market here. They [the Cousleys] would be happy to have us sell and get out, but they want to pick who we sell to. They want us out. They think they can run this paper better without us. Everything was very calm here until Steve Cousley came in."

It was to be expected, probably, that the Broz style of newspapering as adapted later by Steve Cousley would not have the second floor staff at the *Telegraph* turning handsprings. "The newspaper should be positive whenever possible," Henry told me. "We play up unemployment. Unemployment is with us all right, but I don't think we have to spread big headlines on it. That just scares people. What else can a newspaper do for the community but to build it up? It's to their economic advantage to build it up? They [the news side] are anti-industry. I don't know why."

There is a loose formula for calculating the market value of a paper the size of the *Telegraph:* each reader is said to be worth $500.[4] With circulation down around 35,000, that meant the *Telegraph* would bring in the neighborhood of $17 million to $18 million—this for a property that returned a mere $200,000 profit in 1979.

"They would like to get their money out of the newspaper," Paul Cousley said in 1982, referring to the McAdamses. "Steve and I buck it. We want to keep it. The subject comes up every once in a while. [The groups] know by now how the Cousleys feel about it."

If a newspaper is owned by a group, the managers are usually under more pressure to return an impressive profit. If the managers have no permanent ties to the community, and see the assignment as a stopping place on the way to a better paper, it is especially true. It is even more important—indeed it is essential—if the shareholders buy and sell their stock in the market. The managers of a newspaper owned by the giant of the newspaper chains—the Gannett Co.—would be far less likely to hesitate before trimming one reporter from the courthouse bureau than would the Cousleys. The few members of a family who own a newspaper like the *Telegraph* may be satisfied with a modest return on their investment, whereas the managers of an empire such as Gannett must be concerned about the value of the ownership shares and their attractiveness to investors.

There is another side of this picture, however. A large communications company is likely to be more efficiently managed than the *Telegraph*. The vast resources of Gannett or Hearst are standing behind every individual newspaper. In time of trouble, the corporate lawyers are available to deal with legal problems. Local ownership is identified with a more adventurous editorial style, more dash, more flair, more community involvement, and—if the owners are willing to settle for smaller profits—less attention to the bottom line. But the price of independence can be, and usually is, closer ties to sources of power in the community, a more one-sided view of local affairs, a less well managed operation, and—in time of travail—less economic security.

6

The Memorandum

The best investigative reporters, said *Post-Dispatch* City Editor Ben Reese, are always two parts bastard and one part angel.[1] Journalists who are attracted to that line of work are a special breed. Most of them are quite cynical about the motives of people in the public service. The best of them are more thick-skinned than the typical police officer while being as patient and meticulous as an accountant.

Most of their time is spent either sweet-talking or bullying sources of information. Having no power to subpoena witnesses or records, no authority to compel someone's testimony before a grand jury, no threat of a perjury indictment against a witness who tells less than the whole truth, no right to grant immunity from prosecution as an inducement for a suspect to betray someone higher up, no way of preventing a knowledgeable source from hanging up the phone or walking away from an interview, having none of these tools of the prosecutor at his disposal, the investigative reporter works against long odds.

Yet in a circle of communities like Metro East, where the mayors, county commissioners, sheriffs, police chiefs, prosecutors, and judges all spring from the same tightly controlled stock of political influence, aggressive investigative journalism may be all that keeps self-government from running completely amok.

By the late 1960s, Elmer Broz had assembled a staff of reporters with impressive investigative skills. One of them was Ed Pound, who beat the big Chicago dailies to the punch with a series of stories that led to the resignation of two justices of the Illinois Supreme Court in a scandal involving their ownership of bank stock.[2] Others who had been given the bargain price bank stock included, beside the two Supreme Court justices, the president of the newspaper division of Field Enterprises, owners of the *Sun-Times;* the associate editor of that paper; the political editor of the *Chicago Tribune;* and some prominent crime syndicate hoodlums. Pound later went on to the *Chicago Sun-Times,* the *Washington Star,* the *New York Times,* and the *Wall Street Journal* to become one of the nation's top investigative reporters.

Two others among those in Broz's stable at the *Telegraph* were unalike in almost every respect. Joe Melosi, thirty-five years old in 1968, was hard-boiled, impulsive, emotionally erratic sometimes. His partner, Bill Lhotka, twenty-eight, was more level-headed and less excitable.

Melosi grew up in the little town of Pocahontas in Bond County, which is the next county east of Madison. Until the mines closed down there, his father worked as a coal miner, then in construction. After graduating from Southern Illinois University in Carbondale, Joe owned a weekly newspaper with his brother in Bond county. Later, he worked for a weekly in Wood River, started his own daily in Edwardsville, which soon failed, and then went to Springfield for a year and a half as a reporter for the *State Journal-Register.*

Returning to Madison County, he found a comrade-in-arms in Elmer Broz—his kind of editor. Broz installed Melosi as the Wood River bureau chief and told him to look into reports that the carpenters, pipefitters, and other construction trade unions had been infiltrated by mobsters.

His partner in the labor union racketeering investigation was to be Lhotka. In contrast to Melosi's Italian coal mining family background in rural southern Illinois, Lhotka came from a Bohemian neighborhood in Cicero, the city just west of Chicago made famous as the home base of Al Capone. Bill's father, Tony Lhotka, worked as a warehouseman for the Railway Express Co. Bill majored in history at Quincy College in downstate Illinois, was hired as a sportswriter for the *Telegraph* before being drafted into the Army for two years and then went back to the *Telegraph* in the Edwardsville county government bureau.

One of Melosi's sources was a carpenters union officer named Bill Harder. Harder told the reporters he had been involved in the torching of houses built with nonunion labor. Before agreeing to a story in the *Telegraph* about these activities, Harder asked Melosi to arrange a meeting with federal prosecutors attached to the Justice Department's "strike force" on organized crime, then encamped in St. Louis.

Harder lived in a mobile home in Chouteau Slough near the Chain of Rocks Bridge. Two days before his date with the federal investigators, he heard someone start the power mower outside. Going to the door to investigate, he was shot and killed by a shotgun blast.

Melosi and another *Telegraph* reporter, Ande Yakstis, had escorted other sources to meetings with federal authorities across the river, and this time they went to talk with special prosecutor Brian Conboy about the murder of Harder. Two carpenters local union officials were later indicted for the murder but never brought to trial. After that, Melosi said he started receiving phone calls warning that he would wind up in a ditch with his throat cut if the labor racketeering stories continued.

Reporters assigned to a particular "beat" often form special relationships with trusted news sources. Almost always, these are symbiotic relationships that benefit both the giver and receiver of hard-to-get information. Reporters learn which informants are both knowledgeable and reliable. And it is to the source's advantage, either directly or indirectly, for the information to become known. Sometimes it's as simple as the anticipation of being treated kindly by the newspaper in the future. Seldom though do sources divulge valuable information because they admire the color of the reporter's eyes or, still less, because they believe the public has a right to know.

The newsgathering process is an uncertain, tentative, groping procedure that can misfire as easily as not. Without this subterranean flow of news tips and gossip, and the exchange of favors for reasons not always revealed to the reader, the gathering of news would be confined mainly to news releases and official pronouncements. These may be part of the story, the great O. K. Bovard cautioned, but to be "satisfied with the surface of the news" is to fail the reporter's responsibility to his or her readers.

Nor is it uncommon for reporters to deliver unverified tips to prosecutors and other government authorities with the understanding that their news organization will be given an advance break on any resulting news developments, such as the announcement of an arrest or indictment. When the *Chicago Sun-Times* prepared a friend-of-the-court brief for the appeal in the *Telegraph* case, A. Daniel Feldman, counsel for the *Sun-Times*, sought to explain that relationship this way:

> The relationship between reporters and law enforcement officials is ambiguous but understood by both: Police and reporters work the same territory but with different objectives. They meet at the scene of crimes, sometimes drink in the same bars and cannot avoid talking shop to each other. . . . The [decision in the *Telegraph* case] implies that this kind of communication is somehow wrong and that police who talk to reporters become in some magic way the reporters' agents. The voluntary exchange of information between journalists and law enforcement authorities is natural and inevitable.[3]

Not all journalists would endorse Mr. Feldman's rendition of journalistic ethics. After the death of the longtime director of the Federal Bureau of Investigation, J. Edgar Hoover, the FBI was disclosed to have abused its powers, which caused some news organizations to reconsider their collaboration with law enforcement agencies.

Nevertheless, Seymour Hersh, Pulitzer Prize winning reporter and author of *The Prince of Power*, a critical book about Henry Kissinger, was quoted in 1984 as saying: "I can't sit in judgment of someone who took a dive for a good story. A lot of federal prosecutors won't talk to you unless you deal with them." "Taking a dive" is journalistic parlance for overlooking something unfavorable by a valued source of information. To which Clark Mollenhoff, the elder statesman of investigative reporters, added: "Of course reporters should cooperate. We have to cooperate. Anyone who says he doesn't cooperate at all is a damned fool. Anyone who cooperates all the time is a damned fool."[4]

For better or worse, Joe Melosi got to know and trust a former sheriff of Madison County—Barney Fraundorf—at the same time that Bill Lhotka was establishing a similar relationship with the current sheriff's chief investigator, a veteran policeman named Demos Nicholas.

Fraundorf and Nicholas both were products of the Democratic organization in the city of Madison. Fraundorf had disappointed some of the party leaders by being an honest police chief in Madison and one of them told me later that his endorsement for sheriff was primarily to get him out of their hair. He enjoyed sitting on a bench in the lobby of the courthouse outside his office and chatting with reporters. After serving his one term as sheriff (1962–66), he maintained his contacts with the newspeople while working as a security officer for a trucking company. Nicholas was also a former Madison city policeman who aspired to become sheriff himself by taking advantage of the factional rivalries within the party organization.

Through their separate contacts with the two sources, Melosi and Lhotka became aware of the $1.5 million in construction loans by Piasa to Hazel. This, they were told, was happening at a time when other contractors were having difficulty borrowing money. After checking the recording of the Hazel mortgages in the courthouse, the two reporters wrote stories in the *Telegraph* about the extent of the real estate development loans to an ex-convict.

The newsworthiness of an investigative story is enhanced by the presence of a timely "news peg" upon which to hang a running story, and the *Telegraph* had theirs when Hazel and two companions savagely beat two other men in a tavern in Cottage Hills, for which they were charged with aggravated battery. Hazel pleaded guilty to a reduced charge of battery and was fined $500. When Jim Green was asked later in one of the court proceedings about the trouble resulting from these stories in 1967, he said, rather too nonchalantly, it would seem, that "Don had gotten into a scrap in a tavern and it came out in the paper."

DeGrand and Wuellner were then in the position of having to deal with the public knowledge that Piasa's preferred loan customer was a man with a criminal past who had become one of the area's leading real estate developers. The shareholders in a savings and loan association can take their passbook deposits out as quickly as they put them in, of course, which explains why Piasa's officers had to be alarmed by the publicity. An S & L can be severely damaged by news or gossip that triggers a mass withdrawal of savings.

The two men at Piasa came up with a solution to the Hazel public relations problem. They arranged for Jim Green to buy out Hazel's interest in two large apartment complexes that Hazel had built: Kingston Estates in Bethalto and Wood River Gardens in Wood River. The deal also included fifty houses and a large tract of undeveloped land owned by Hazel in Bethalto. Green relied on Piasa's legal advice, agreeing to the terms without having his own lawyer. The inducement for him to relieve Piasa of the Hazel problem, according to later testimony, was the promise of more financing for Green to develop the Hazel land.

Although Green had to keep borrowing more to pay off his earlier debts, he kept plunging ahead. He purchased still more land at the Lake of Seven Fingers near Staunton in the rural northeastern corner of Madison County. There he planned to build a mobile home park and vacation site, more four-apartment buildings, and a theater, again anticipating more loans from Piasa. Piasa had acquired the Staunton tract by foreclosing on a loan to someone else and then making a $150,000 profit by selling it to Green for $525,000.

It was assumed then by both Green and DeGrand, though without any written commitment, that Piasa's loan spigot would stay turned on indefinitely. Piasa's board approved the transfer of Hazel's holdings (and his debts on those holdings) to Green, although it became clear later that only DeGrand understood the full extent of Green's borrowing and the use of straw parties to muddle the financing picture. What was already a confusing trail of conveyances and reconveyances among individuals, some of whom were known by reporters and in some cases by police as shady figures, was now further complicated by the flurry of recorded transfers from Hazel to Green.

To anyone who already thought Green was a front man for Hazel, what was happening now looked mighty suspicious. Nor, apparently, did the directors of Piasa give adequate thought to what should have been obvious—that from now on Piasa's well-being would be tied to that of Green's construction business.

On toward the end of 1968, a period when Green's financial problems were getting no better, the *Telegraph* reporters kept scratching for something that would keep the story alive. According to Melosi and Lhotka, Fraundorf and Nicholas had told them separately that they suspected "Mafia rackets money from Chicago" of having been put into Piasa to finance legitimate ventures such as the real estate development.

Later, the two reporters would cite a third source—Robert Trone, an assistant state's attorney in Madison County—as one who had mentioned a possible Piasa-Mafia connection. When the *Telegraph* case came to trial, Trone remembered Melosi and Nicholas having suggested a grand jury investigation of the matter but insisted he had contributed no information of his own and said he rejected the grand jury request. He did recall that Nicholas had said the only builders who could obtain construction loans at Piasa were Hazel and his subcontractors. Another contractor, never identified by the two reporters, was also cited as a source. Melosi testified at the trial that he forgot the name "on purpose" because of the danger of retaliation against the man.

The essence of Nicholas' theory floated before Lhotka, duplicated essentially by what Fraundorf was telling Melosi, was that Green was a front man for Hazel and that the cash in the pledged accounts "had all the earmarks," as Melosi and Lhotka would put it, of a kickback involving Piasa and Green.

The Mafia has always had the problem, made more ominous by the activities of the Internal Revenue Service, of how to "launder" its millions of ill-gotten dollars through legitimate financial institutions, thereby putting this wealth to work earning income in more conventional ways. Because enormous sums of cash flow through S & Ls—insured by Uncle Sam, no less—S & Ls are known by the FHLBB to be a lucrative opportunity for such laundered investments. Which helps to explain the excitement in the Washington offices of the board when the Justice Department invited them in on a gang-busting adventure which we'll get to shortly.

(In this case, however, the purported Mafia money link to Piasa [and its related enrichment of some of the characters in this story] would be investigated over the next five years by various federal agencies, and by a grand jury in Springfield, Illinois, without any indictments being returned. Allowing for a certain blurring of the distinctions between organized and unorganized crime, there is no evidence on the public record of any Piasa involvement with "Mafia money.")

But what were Melosi and Lhotka to do? They had received tips from two local law enforcement officials who were in a position to know at least something about which they were talking. The tips were that a prominent financial institution in the community and two of the biggest builders in the region were tied in some uncertain way to organized crime. Hazel's criminal record and his reputation in the eyes of local law enforcement agencies were matters of fact. Hazel's favored status as a Piasa borrower was a matter of fact. So was Green's. So were the connections between Hazel and Green and the others. So were the "mob" influences in the carpenters and other building trade unions. But what of this Mafia business?

The Mafia does not retain a public relations counselor on its payroll to answer inquiries from the press. The Alton reporters had no ready contacts in Chicago law enforcement. How to check the story further? Would it have helped to phone Green or DeGrand? And ask them what? If they were associated with the Mafia? Not only would that have been absurd at that stage of the investigation, but the reporters reasoned that it could have blown whatever might be forthcoming later by alerting the guilty to cover their tracks. Investigative journalists are far more vulnerable to an evasive coverup than are the police and prosecutors.

Years later, when all this was aired in the courts, the reporters insisted that it would have been naïve to call DeGrand or Wuellner or Dr. Pfeiffenberger (a Piasa board member friendly with the Cousley family) and inquire whether any of the rumors about Piasa were true. Elmer Broz, the city editor, knew what *he* wanted to do. According to Lhotka, who was keeping his editor informed of the progress of the investigation, Broz suggested the publication of a story with the new tips based on anonymous sources. Lhotka said he advised strongly against that, pointing out that there simply was not enough verified information to print anything.

The two Justice Department attorneys Melosi had met with after the Harder murder were still in St. Louis overseeing a "strike force" investigation of labor racketeering and organized crime. The two men—Brian Conboy and David H. Martin—made a practice of trading for investigative leads by promising reporters a head start on the news of any federal action stemming from the tips. Melosi had even been given Conboy's private phone numbeer in his Washington office. As they moved around the country trying to uncover evidence of criminal activity, the outsiders lacked the background understanding of local conditions and sometimes discovered that local authorities were protecting Mafia figures.

So in February of 1969, just after a new President (Richard M. Nixon) and a new Attorney General (John N. Mitchell) had taken office, Melosi and Lhotka made arrangements to see Conboy and Martin at the Bismarck Cafe on 12th Street in downtown St. Louis. Following lunch, the conversation shifted to Conboy's room at the Sheraton Jefferson hotel.

The two reporters laid out what they knew and what they had been told but could not confirm. They told of their suspicion that Don Hazel, Jim Green, and Bob DeGrand were the beneficiaries of a system of channeling Mafia cash from Chicago through Piasa in Alton. When the meeting ended, Conboy asked them to check their information as thoroughly as they could and then send a written confidential memo to him at his office in Washington, where he would soon be returning.

"I thought the information [from the sources] was on the level," Melosi recalled many years later. "I thought it was fact. These guys [the former sheriff, the chief investigator for the present sheriff, and an assistant state's attorney] were credible sources. They had been involved in investigating criminal activity in Madison County for years. I thought they had informants among the hoods. We went as far as we could and sent off the memo because it was virtually impossible for us to check the veracity of the information. We wanted people with more resources to check the charges because the charges were pretty severe."

If the charges were true, Melosi and Lhotka thought the FBI and other federal agencies might be able to check out the funds at their source in Chicago. There was no way the records in the courthouse at Edwardsville, or anywhere else, would tell them of a Mafia involvement in the affairs of the Piasa First Federal Savings and Loan Association.

On March 26, 1969, Melosi sat at his typewriter in the *Telegraph* office and wrote the following memo:

Confidential Memo to Brian Conboy

Here is the report of a possible link between the Chicago family of the Cosa Nostra and Piasa First Federal Savings and Loan Association, Alton, Ill., and of some of the principal characters involved.

Piasa, an investigator told us, gets vast sums of money from Chicago via Southern Illinois. A "vicious" hood, Stanley Kowalski, is reported to be the bag-man. Kowalski, 50, known as "Ski" or "Big Ski," deposited $2–3 million at Piasa in December, our sources say. It is believed to be Mafia rackets money with which to finance legitimate and illegal enterprises in Madison County. The bulk of it is reportedly earmarked for building new homes, apartments and business places.

Piasa, according to county records, has made a number of loans to Don Hazel, 44, a close associate of known hoodlums Terry Thweatt and Luther Harris.

Hazel, reportedly the No. 2 crime boss in the county, is connected with James Green Construction Co., a multimillion dollar operation. Green, at one time a pipefitter, has become a major contractor since his association with Hazel. Hazel is a silent partner on some of Green's biggest apartment projects.

Green deals solely with Piasa. He is also involved with other firms which also do a big business with Piasa, firms like the John Sobol Realty Co., Fairway Estates, Inc., James Green Development Co., Green Highlight Association, Village Green Mobile Home Park, Howard Steel Construction Co., Wayside Development Co., Inc., and Creative Homes, Inc.

Records show there are about 100 land transactions between Piasa and Green and about the same number between Piasa and Hazel. (We plan to spend the next three weeks going through all land deals.)

Some contractors are irked by favoritism shown by Piasa toward Green and Hazel. And some bankers are hot about some "pledge" deals between Piasa and Green and a man by the name of Ray Kozielek. Kozielek, a Madison city councilman, rose in two years time from a "jackleg" electrician to half-partnership in Sobol Realty Co.

Briefly, a "pledge" has all the earmarks of a kickback from Piasa to favored contractors, like Green. Green has bragged that he has over $1 million in pledges coming to him over the next five or six years from Piasa. Pledges amount to about 10 percent of actual building cost. (A $45,000 apartment project is inflated to a $50,000 loan, with the $5,000 set aside in escrow for later payment to the contractor, who ultimately sells the apartment to a third party, through a realtor like Sobol.) Piasa also can use the escrow money for investment while sale of the apartment is pending.

Hazel or Green do not directly withdraw money, because it would be too obvious. Loans also [blank] as a cover.

Not too long ago Hazel, Green, and Kozielek were "small timers." Today they are giants in the building industry in the county.

Piasa is reportedly ready to foot the entire bill on a big commercial-residential complex for Kozielek.

It is unclear as to how these men are connected with the Mafia. But all are associates of hoods formerly aligned with Buster Wortman.

Background Notes

Hazel has come on strong since the death of Dominic Todaro, a convicted gambler, once believed to be a downstate lieutenant for the Chicago family of the Mafia. Todaro died in December, 1967. Hazel fell heir to Todaro's fortunes—the bail bond business, vending machines and some real estate.

(On July 23 and Oct. 22, both in 1964, carpenter William Harder filed a Mechanic's Lien against Hazel for payment of wages. Later, Harder was deeded some property by Terry Thweatt, to satisfy the demands of the lien. Harder was murdered in September 1967 after talking to reporters about hoodlum activity in the carpenters union. Landon "Pug" Fisher and Thweatt were indicted for the murder. The indictment is still pending today. Hazel owns the mortgage on Thweatt's property and posted the property bond on Fisher.)

Hazel at one time worked for Bob Leu, a former gambling casino operator and a Big Time developer, now in "semi-retirement."

Leu is rated confidentially as the rackets boss in the county. He uses guys like Hazel, Green and Kozielek, Thweatt, et al., as frontmen.

Leu's past activities were varied. He ran the notorious "200 Club" in Madison in the 1950's and knew Sandra O'Day, one of the principals in the famous Greenlease kidnap case.

Leu's "200 Club," a casino, was closed down after a State Police raid ordered by the Governor because local police had failed to act.

About the same time, Leu developed Sunny Dell subdivision on property owned by the city of Madison. No records are on file showing any land transfer on the property.

The city of Madison is run by Mayor Stephen Maeras, a top boss in the powerful Madison-Venice Democratic Party Machine.

We have found no connection between Leu and Green in regard to residential developments near Leu's home territory of fast growing Mitchell-Pontoon Beach, but there is an indirect connection through Hazel.

Hazel's police record—Indicted Feb. 5, 1965, by a Madison County Grand Jury for aggravated battery, along with Bert Simpson and Eugene Sullivan, the hoods associated with Thweatt, in connection with the Dec. 18, 1964, beating of Jewel Sims and Eliza Beaver in a Cottage Hills Tavern. The charges were later reduced to battery. Hazel pleaded guilty and paid a $500 fine. The other two were placed on probation.

The status on Luther Harris—He was recently convicted on a car theft charge and sentence is pending. He was one of six who gang-clobbered carpenter Pete Klader in 1966, but was acquitted.

Thweatt was also in on the beating and pleaded guilty to a reduced charge of disorderly conduct, now faces trial on a charge of aggravated battery in the pistol beating of Bobby Wallace, brother of Shelby Wallace, who was acquitted in the fatal shooting of Terry Thweatt's son.

The principal characters involved here—Leu, Hazel, Thweatt, Harris, Fisher and a Leon Kohler, a "health food" salesman traveling frequently to California, all figure in a criminal network which includes sale of narcotics, car theft, burglary, prostitution, gambling, fencing stolen merchandise, primarily guns and TV sets, and other illegal interstate activity.

Unions, like Pipefitters Local 553, Carpenters Local 1808 and Laborers Local 338, provide cover jobs for most hoods who also act as enforcers when union members or contractors step out of line.

There are a number of specialists working in these unions—"burners," dynamiters, hit-men, etc.

> In summary, a criminal conglomerate appears to be flourishing unchecked in Madison County. No one has been able to put all the pieces together. But we may be able to, with your help.
>
> Please do not assign any resident FBI agents out of the Alton office. The few local authorities in whom we have confidence distrust the senior agent, for reasons too sensitive to mention here.[5]

Melosi and Lhotka signed the single-spaced three-page memo, each page of which was marked "Confidential Memo" at the top. It was then mailed to Conboy in Washington. The reference in the last paragraph reflected the suspicion of Fraundorf and Nicholas that the agent in charge of the Alton office of the FBI might himself be controlled by hoodlums.

The memo represented a mixture of some of what Melosi and Lhotka knew journalistically about crime in Madison County (Bob Leu's gambling casino past, for example, and his reputed status as "rackets boss in the county"); some details from the public record (the land transactions between Piasa and Green/Hazel); some oversimplified laymen's interpretations of real estate finance (the nature of pledged accounts, for example); some conjecture (Hazel's standing in the organized crime hierarchy of the county); and a frank admission that "no one has been able to put all the pieces together."

All journalistic inquiry begins with the reporter's preconceptions of what the story is likely to be. These preconceptions of the likely dimensions of the story determine the questions the reporter begins with. If the subject is complicated, the reporter is handicapped by his generalist's background preparation, which is necessarily limited; by the fragmentary nature of the details he attempts to piece together; by the potentially misleading nature of the separate pieces; and ultimately by the fact that he can seldom be certain he has gotten to the bottom of anything.

Melosi wrote a short note that was sent along with the memo to Conboy:

> Brian:
> Here is the memo I promised. It's a bit windy. But we need to know

where this big money is coming from. All our sources indicate it is rackets money earned by the Chicago family of the Mafia.

Could you please reply, either by mail or telephone. My number is 618-259-0027. Address for our bureau is *Alton Evening Telegraph*, Broadway and Main, East Alton.

Joe Melosi

7

The Fall of Piasa

A few days after the memo arrived at his office in Washington, Brian Conboy left his job in the Justice Department for a new position as administrative assistant to a Republican member of the United States Senate, Charles E. Goodell of New York.

Back in Alton, the reporters were unaware of Conboy's plans to change jobs. Without giving it much thought, they assumed all along that their message would be handled personally by the man they had dealt with in St. Louis. Melosi and Lhotka had visions of a discreet query to the FBI in Chicago while the memo was kept stashed away in Conboy's office safe. Had they known that the contents of the memo were about to be set adrift in the federal bureaucracy, they might not have been so cavalier about the epistle from Alton. Their letter lay in a stack of unfinished business turned over to Conboy's associate David Martin. Martin had been present at the conversations in St. Louis, but he too would resign from the Justice Department a short time later for the job of chief counsel to the United States Secret Service.

No one else at the *Telegraph* saw the memo. Elmer Broz knew about it, but did not read it. Steve Cousley had become an assistant to the publisher by then. He was generally familiar with the Hazel-Piasa investigation but was not told about the letter to Washington. Paulie was only vaguely aware of an ongoing inquiry that he knew involved Piasa.

On June 3, 1969, a little over two months after the mailing of the memo, the assistant attorney general in charge of the criminal division wrote a letter to Frank Dorer, the regional supervisor of the Federal Home Loan Bank Board in Washington. After summarizing the allegations contained in a communication from a "confidential informant" who was not identified, the letter requested "an examination of the records of Piasa."

A little over a month after that, on July 10, 1969, Dorer wrote to Victor S. Meller, chief examiner for the FHLBB in Chicago. A copy of the letter from the Justice Department (but not the memo itself, which Dorer never saw) was attached to Dorer's letter to Meller, which said, in part:

> . . . as you know, this is the first instance where the organized crime section has brought us into the picture as a participant and we are hopeful that our conduct of this assignment will be such as will result in our active participation with that unit in the future.
>
> While I most assuredly am not promoting any form of "witch hunt," I do believe that the examiners' approach to this examination should be different from that normally employed in dealing with an association with a "one" rating.[1]

A "one" rating means that the affairs of the association appear to be in good order—the outcome of the previous year's routine examination at Piasa.

A portrait of Benjamin Franklin, the father of the "thrift industry" in the United States, hangs at the entrance to the Federal Home Loan Bank of Chicago in an office building on the south bank of the Chicago River just off Michigan Avenue. The S & L bureaucracy is made up of numbers specialists, not gumshoes. Flattered as they undoubtedly were by the invitation to enter the foggy labyrinth of federal gang busters, most of the savings and loan examiners were more adept at leafing through deposit slips in the basement vault of an S & L than they were at penetrating the alliances of organized crime in Madison County, Illinois.

Except for "Mac" Christie. The assignment in Madison County was a natural for Clarence McCord Christie. More than once he had used different poses to try to get "inside" a sedate S & L and worm the real story out of a secretary or clerk. A crusty, naturally suspicious individual, Christie enjoyed using undercover sleuthing tactics that infuriated the association executives and made his bosses uneasy.

But the mission in Alton was right down Mac Christie's alley, and it was he who led the team from Chicago for the six weeks of poring through Piasa's records in August and September. DeGrand said later that Christie told other Piasa employees that they were looking for "gangster money"[2] DeGrand said he was given to understand that there was Mafia money in Piasa and that Christie had had some contact with whomever this source of information was. Later, DeGrand complained of surreptitious midnight meetings in hotel parking lots between the would-be James Bonds from Chicago and employees of the S & L.

Keeping secrets did not come easy to Mr. Christie. Eventually, either this year or next, although neither Christie nor anyone else at the FHLBB had seen the memo, DeGrand learned from Christie that the inquiry had somehow involved a written memo from Joe Melosi at the *Telegraph*.

Christie's crew did not find what they were looking for. But the more searching review than would otherwise have been conducted did uncover some serious problems that had gone undetected in previous examinations. The report that the examiners wrote described "numerous regulatory violations and inadequacies" in Piasa's lending practices, including a concentraton of speculative construction loans to Jim Green's corporations and a group of seven other borrowers. The other seven included John Sobol, Raymond Kozielek, and Mike Sasyk—men with whom Green had been associated in real estate deals and each of whose indebtedness to Piasa exceeded $1 million at the time of the audit.

Nearly half of Piasa's loans were for construction, the examiners noted, and almost half of the construction loans were secured by pledged savings accounts without an adequate down payment from the builder. The report also criticized appraisals based solely on expected costs rather than the sale value of what was being built; loan payouts without inspections of building progress; and a policy of permitting the builder to delay the first payments on the loan until the project was finished.

Having belatedly discovered the heavy concentration of loans to Green and his associates, the FHLBB expressed "serious reservations about [Piasa's] overall lending practices." Then, a few days after that, the federal agency ordered Piasa temporarily to stop lending any more money to Green. The letter came from Edward A. Eckert, one of three supervisory agents in Chicago and the examinations chief.

At about this time, Henry Wuellner, Piasa's president, apparently began to have doubts about Bob DeGrand's honesty. According to later testimony by Green, DeGrand told him that "the old man thinks you're paying me off." DeGrand recalled that Wuellner said to him that "not only he but everybody else at Piasa thought that I was on Jim Green's payroll and that someway I had my hand in Jim Green's pocket."

Following a board meeting in early November, which was attended by FHLBB officials from Chicago, the directors volunteered to limit any one borrower's loan debt to one percent of assets—or $1 million. Green was then $3,873,569 in debt to Piasa; he had just been saddled with Hazel's debt; he had six projects of his own only partially completed; he needed more than $13 million to complete them; and there would be no more money coming from Piasa until the money owed Piasa was brought under $1 million—not a very promising outlook.

One of the top county Democratic leaders, Mike Sasyk, had a $150,000 development loan on some farmland. He made arrangements to increase the loan to $300,000 and lend the additional to Green, but the feds told DeGrand that the transaction could not be made because the property was not being improved.

By the end of the year Green was behind in his loan payments. He could not go ahead with his projects, or pay his suppliers and subcontractors what they were due, or pay withheld income taxes or social security taxes, whereupon the Internal Revenue Service filed a $150,000 lien against him. Without the additional financing that DeGrand had promised Green when the Hazel transaction was made, Green was sinking fast. So, to a lesser extent, was Piasa. Although there were no news stories in the *Telegraph* about Piasa's troubles with the FHLBB, rumors of the search for "gangster money" did circulate in the community. Instead of continuing to grow as they had before, deposits were withdrawn from the savings and loan—a net withdrawal of $2.5 million in the ten months following the audit.

In 1970, meanwhile, Steven Cousley became editor of the *Telegraph,* a promotion that everybody considered inevitable; everybody, that is, except Elmer Broz, who thought he deserved the job. Whatever power struggle there was was over in a hurry. If a Cousley is in line to be editor of the *Telegraph,* the chances are good that he will reach the head of the line in due course.

Under Steve's leadership, the paper continued the vigorous journalism that Broz so admired. In a vocation branded with cynicism, Steve is idealistic, principled, ingenuous. There is an Eagle Scoutish quality about him, both in his boyish appearance and his soft-spoken, straight-arrow manner. He projects a stern Puritanical unexcitability, a remarkable absence of visible emotion. One of his relatives told me she had never seen Steve visibly angry. He is the first of the Cousley editors known to sip alcoholic beverages now and then.

When asked later whether he had informed himself of Melosi's and Lhotka's sources during the Hazel-Piasa stories, Steven explained: "No, I don't ask any reporters who their sources are. There is sort of a code in the news business, especially where you're dealing with characters like this, you keep your sources confidential."[3]

As adapted to the new editor's preferences, the Broz style of enterprising journalism kept pushing for news that would shake people up. The *Telegraph* poked into the connections between the Democratic organization, the judiciary, and real estate development, for example. In July of 1969, Lhotka disclosed that Circuit Court Judge William Beatty and John E. Lee, a "major cog in the Tri-Cities political machine," were partners in another land venture, the Bethalto Hills Development Co. Lhotka pointed out in his story that Beatty had been elected to the bench with the endorsement of the "Tri-City dominated Democrat machine in which 'Doc' Lee, the mayor of Venice, is a leader."[4]

In the judicial elections of 1970, a judge named Joseph H. Goldenhersh ran for the Illinois Supreme Court from the district that included Metro East and all of southern Illinois. Before his advancement in 1964 to the state Appellate court—the intermediate appellate branch between the trial courts and the Supreme Court—Goldenhersh had been the attorney for the East Side Levee and Sanitary District.

On October 27, 1970, just before the Supreme Court election, Melosi wrote a story in the *Telegraph* which started: "The patronage-packed East Side Levee and Sanitary District paid the law firm of Goldenhersh and Goldenhersh bond issue fees of $32,000 which were triple the limit allowed by the Illinois State Bar Association's rate schedule, the *Telegraph* found today."

Melosi pointed out in his story that the payments were made to the firm in which Goldenhersh's brother Marvin was a partner shortly after Joe's elevaton to the Appellate court. Goldenhersh's Republican opponent circulated copies of Melosi's story through the judicial district. Goldenhersh won anyhow and on election night he encountered Melosi in the vote tally room at the courthouse in Edwardsville. Despite the flush of victory, the justice-elect was not in a mellow mood. He walked up to Melosi and told him, in Steven Cousley's presence, that "I'm going to nail you one of these days."

In the meantime, unless he miraculously struck it rich with one of his projects, Jim Green was in no condition to make his $74,000 a month in loan payments to Piasa. He had counted on the S & L continuing to feed him more money to pay back what he had already borrowed. When Piasa's board turned off the supply of more credit, voluntarily but under the prodding of the federal regulators, Green was in a pickle and so were DeGrand and Wuellner.

Once the mortgages were delinquent, Piasa could have moved to foreclose on them and claim Green's properties. But it is very expensive in Illinois to initiate foreclosure proceedings in court, even if DeGrand and Piasa's board had wanted to do so.

What happened instead was a complicated debt restructuring agreement worked out by the lender and the debtor. Essentially, the Base Agreement, as it was titled, did this:

Piasa established a subsidiary—PSL Realty Co.—which took title to Green's properties.

In addition to $811,000 of Green's savings accounts pledged against the loan, Piasa contributed $750,000 of its own to help reduce the debt.

In turn, PSL Realty contracted with a new partnership—Granite Investment Co., of which Green was principal partner—to manage the properties.

The provision that would later incite ten years of litigation called for 80 percent of the rents to be used to pay off the debt, leaving the other 20 percent for a "rental service fund" that would pay Granite's operating expenses. If and when the loans were no longer delinquent, Granite would regain ownership of the properties.

Green was represented during these negotiations by a St. Louis lawyer named Mark Gale. Green, of course, had no money to pay a lawyer. So, in lieu of fees, Gale's firm acquired a 25 percent interest in Green's 55 percent interest in Granite Investment Co. Gale and his law partners were able to use their interest in the company as a tax shelter.[5] In 1971, for example, according to testimony in subsequent legal proceedings, Gale reported a $27,000 loss on his own interest in Granite, which enabled him to reduce his personal federal income taxes by half of that, or $13,500.

One of the purposes of the agreement was to give Green a chance to complete the construction of his pending projects and make them income earners. His rental units continued to lose money, however, and subcontractors, suppliers, and others soon were clamoring for the $930,000 owed them. The situation got worse instead of better.

Even before the agreement had been worked out, the FHLBB representatives from Chicago informed Piasa's directors that the FBI was looking into possible Mafia connections with the association. Rumors found their way "onto the street," as several of the principals would later describe it. Savers began withdrawing their deposits. By the end of 1969, Piasa reported reserves and surplus of a little over $4 million, or about 5 percent of the $81.5 million in savings, which was well below the 8.3 percent average in federally insured S & L's.

DeGrand's once close relationship with Wuellner deteriorated in step with Piasa's declining financial health. When the federal auditors returned for their 1970 examination, they went over the books again and found that the concentration of loans to Green and his associates was considerably greater than they had thought in 1969. The FHLBB suggested that DeGrand be asked to resign.

On October 5, 1970, DeGrand was called back from a trip to Maryland, where he and his wife were visiting two married daughters, to submit his resignation. His letter referred to "personal reasons." He said later that he deliberately waited until Saturday afternoon to notify the *Telegraph* of his resignation so there would be plenty of time Sunday for the newspaper to ask for an elaboration of his reasons before the story on Monday. He said he was "stunned" by the reporters' failure to contact him for his comments.[6]

The story by Melosi and Yakstis pointed out in the opening paragraph that Piasa "has been under federal investigation for more than a year because of some transactions with [Green's company]." Green had borrowed more than $15 million from Piasa until "falling into financial straits last spring," the story recounted. Sources were quoted as reporting that loans to Green had been made above the appraised value of the property.

Eckert's decision to send one of his assistants to manage Piasa for a couple of months after DeGrand's forced resignation prompted some second thoughts in the Washington offices of the FHLBB about how the Piasa matter had been handled. Eckert and the top supervisory agent, Albion Fenderson, were called to Washington to explain how the many Green loan improprieties had gone undiscovered before the 1969 audit. As a consequence, Eckert was transferred to the applications division and a new supervisory agent was sent to Chicago.

Not long after that, Wuellner also resigned because of ill health. Dr. Mather Pfeiffenberger and two other officials of Piasa walked over to Paulie Cousley's office at the *Telegraph* to see what could be done about enlisting the newspaper's support of the new management. Dr. Pfeiffenberger said later (in a court deposition) that he had not believed the meeting would accomplish anything.[7]

"Q—Why did you feel that it would accomplish no good?"

"A—Because I felt that the *Telegraph* had made—we were pretty certain now of the source of the accusations which had caused

Piasa's problems, in our opinion, and I felt that someone who had known me all my life, who had known my father all his life, whose father I had operated on, who I saw weekly at church, whose mother was my mother's best friend, whose sisters were my sisters' best friends, who would make an accusation such as he had made against me, was not my friend."

"Q—What accusations had they made against you?"

"A—That the officers of Piasa were Mafia connected. I was an officer."

Later in the deposition, Dr. Pfeiffenberger recalled one day he met "Mr. Henry McAdams out on the sidewalk in front of the First National Bank and told him that I thought what his fellow directors and associates at the *Alton Telegraph* had done to Piasa was, in my opinion, the most dishonorable, treacherous, and un-Christian thing I had ever known of one institution doing to another in the city of Alton, and I hoped he conveyed my sentiments to Paul and Steve Cousley. [Another time] standing outside the Stratford Hotel, talking with Charley Norman, and Steve Cousley turned around and said 'hello, Mather,' and I said, 'who have you been bearing false witness against lately?' And he blushed and left, and that is the last conversation I had with him."

"Q—I take it from your attitude and cryptic comments . . ."

"A—You are correct. I have more respect for a prostitute or a highwayman because they are honest about what they are doing."

Whether a more protective attitude by the *Telegraph* would have restored public confidence in Piasa is doubtful. Newspapers that try to shield important political and economic institutions from criticism usually develop a credibility problem. Readers begin to wonder whether they can believe any of what they read. The movement of rumors "on the street" can be devastating under such circumstances.

By March of 1971—five months after DeGrand's departure—savings in Piasa had dwindled from $100 million to $72 million. Piasa's officers feared that an even bigger "run" was about to occur on the withdrawal windows. On March 14, the FHLBB invoked its powers to arrange a "supervisory merger" of Piasa and a smaller S & L in East St. Louis—Illini Federal Savings and Loan Association. In effect, Illini Federal, with savings of about $65 million, swallowed the larger but critically wounded Piasa. Almost one-fourth of Piasa's $100 million in loans were delinquent, of which Green's amounted to between $14 and $16 million. Piasa could not have paid its March 31 quarterly dividend. Therefore, the merger agreement with Illini Federal included the promise of a continuing FSLIC subsidy to help cover the bad loans, beginning with a payment of $6 million.

The *Telegraph*'s news story said the details of the merger were "unveiled" by FHLBB officials at a motel room meeting with Steve Cousley and reporters Melosi, Lhotka, and Yakstis. The story recapitulated Piasa's problems with the FHLBB, noting that "an exhaustive *Telegraph* investigation into the holdings of builder James Green and Don Hazel in the spring of 1969 led to the federal inquiry."[8] The article went on to retell how Hazel, who was "dealing with area hoodlums, including bailing some of them out of jail," had "borrowed freely" from Piasa; and how Green "from a start in 1964 built a $15 million empire." Reappraisals of mortgaged properties revealed in mid-February, the story reported, that Piasa was "hopelessly insolvent."

In the same edition, on March 15, the newspaper published an editorial entitled: "Faith Must be Restored." "The story of the rise and fall of Piasa Savings and Loan had to be told. . . . Too many local citizens' life savings, home loans and business loans were involved for those responsible to continue to ignore informing the many publics," the editorial began. It went on to say:

> Beginning in mid-1969 exhaustive investigation by a skilled *Telegraph* investigative reporting team including Bill Lhotka, Ande Yakstis and Joe Melosi produced a confusing array of evidence. . . .
>
> The weight of decision making on how to handle news stories was heavy on the shoulders of many as the stories broke.
>
> The *Telegraph,* banking experts and officials of the institution knew there would be loss of faith by depositors and a resulting "run" on the institution. Millions of dollars flowed out after the first resignation was announced and the federal government stepped in. . . .

Inept management practices, faulty flow of information to the board of directors, poor judgment on loans, and a variety of complex inner workings were unraveled through the tedious months.

Meanwhile, shared confidences with federal officials the past few months produced a tense waiting period preceding further stories in the *Telegraph*.

Premature, speculative or inaccurate news accounts could have blown merger search efforts to pieces. . . .

"Many lives have been affected by the Piasa story, "the newspaper commented, and "many careers have changed drastically."

"We hope," the editorial concluded, "the merger assists in restoring public confidence and calmness on the severely shaken *Telegraph* area financial scene as the job of rebuilding begins."

In Washington, the chairman of the FHLBB, Preston Martin, wrote a letter praising the *Telegraph* "for the responsible way in which you handled the developing story of the problems of Piasa First Federal Savings and Loan Association. The people of Alton and the surrounding area are fortunate to have such a responsible newspaper as the *Telegraph*."[9]

Branching policy implications, which the editorial also discussed, referred to the FHLBB's practice of honoring state law on branches. The Illinois legislature had steadfastly resisted branches because of the fear of financial institutions downstate that the huge Chicago banks and S & L's would spread over the entire state. Now, by the back door, the federal agency had permitted an institution in a depressed city (East St. Louis) to operate a branch office in the seemingly more economically viable Alton market—the first time this had happened in Illinois. Illini Federal, which had been in East St. Louis since 1894, welcomed the chance to reach out beyond the increasingly dilapidated (and increasingly black) city.

In April the *Post-Dispatch* assigned a reporter to prepare a series of three stories about the demise of Piasa. DeGrand told the reporter that Christie's examining team "came to Alton already convinced there was crime syndicate money in Piasa."

"Employees of the bank, including clerks and tellers, were told the team was looking for syndicate money. 'It didn't take much time for the information to get on the street,' DeGrand said. . . . 'Savings were down and we couldn't control the rumors,' DeGrand said. 'The Chicago Home Loan Bank was convinced that we had syndicate money [and] that I was connected with the Mafia."[10]

The reporter, William H. Dunlap, went on to say:

". . . Federal officials attribute the association's problems to 'gross mismanagement on Green's part.' Other observers of Piasa's activities are critical of different aspects of the association's lending and of the operations of Green's construction company. To a man, however, they said they did not know of, nor did they suspect, any organized criminal activity in Piasa or the Green construction companies. One observer, who asked not to be identified, said he believed Green had overbuilt in some areas, including Bethalto, and because of the surplus of apartments was unable to fill his units at the expected rentals. With the resulting low cash flow from these projects, he was unable to make a profit or maintain the repayment schedule on his loans."

Dunlap's story became especially important later because of another quote from DeGrand:

"According to DeGrand, Piasa's difficulties began in the summer of 1969 with a letter from Joe Melosi, a reporter on the Alton newspaper, to the United States Department of Justice alleging that there was crime syndicate money involved in Piasa. The Justice department began an investigation then and passed the letter on to the Federal Home Loan Bank Board, the regulatory agency that supervises the nation's federally chartered savings and loan associations."

The quote indicates that on that date (April 25, 1971), DeGrand knew of the existence of the memo, but does not establish that he had seen a copy. The statute of limitations for the filing of a libel action in Illinois is one year after the plaintiff knew or should have known about the allegedly libelous material. The purpose of such a statute is to settle such controversies while witnesses are still alive, their memories fresh, and evidence available.

With Illini Federal's marriage to Piasa came some stepchildren: the subsidiary PSL Realty Co., the forty-eight mortgages on Green's properties, and the problem of what to do about them. The man who was given the responsibility for taking care of this mess was

John Hackmann, forty-two, the executive vice president and chief operating officer of Illini. Hackmann had been a display advertising salesman for the (then) *East St. Louis Journal* before going to law school and then taking a job with the S & L.

By that summer he knew the full dimensions of the problem: There were $12 million in loan balances on Green's real estate valued by Illini's appraisers at $6 million to $8 million.[11] Granite Investment was losing $30,000 a month on the properties. They were only 60 percent occupied. Vacant buildings were not properly boarded up. Trash was scattered about the grounds. The rental income was barely sufficient to pay the operating expenses, leaving little for taxes and insurance, and nothing to reduce the principal on the debt.

Under the terms of the earlier "Base Agreement" between Green and Piasa, Green's company—Granite Investment—was obliged to collect the rents and turn them over to PSL Realty, which now meant Illini Federal. An audit of Granite's books at the end of 1971 convinced Hackmann, according to his later testimony, that Green had held back, or "skimmed," $162,730 in rents during that calendar year.[12] Green considered it unfair for him to get nothing out of his business at the same time that nothing was being applied to reduce the debt.

Hackmann and Richard McGovern, general counsel for Illini Federal, thought they had two alternatives.[13] One was to exercise their right to forfeit the contract because of Granite's noncompliance with its end of the deal, take the considerable losses, and wash their hands of Jim Green's real estate empire. The other was to continue working with Granite, but with Green out. They met with Mark Gale, who was Granite's lawyer (and a 25 percent owner of the business), to see whether something could be worked out.

Illini Federal had no way of knowing who the 600 tenants were in the projects or who had paid how much. A request that someone from Illini be stationed in Granite's offices to watch what was happening was refused. So, after conferring with FHLBB officials in Washington, Hackmann and McGovern arranged a meeting at the Media Club in St. Louis on March 21, 1972, with Green, Gale, and another Granite partner, Darrell Layman.

There, and at another meeting a week later, Hackmann wanted to discuss the orderly takeover of the rental properties with Illini Federal as the managers and rent collectors. Before doing that, Green demanded between $25,000 and $100,000 for his interest in the business, but Hackmann maintained that there was no way Green could be paid anything because his creditors would grab it. Green had separated from his wife Shirley, who happened to be a partner in his real estate ventures, so the list of creditors included her at the top.

Green insisted that he be given the money as a "stake" with which to start over in another state.

At one point in the conversation, Green suggested that he be allowed to "steal a few months rent." He allowed as to how he intended to take the money anyhow, with or without permission. Asked about this later in court, Green admitted having used the word "steal" but said he was only jesting.

According to Green's later testimony, McGovern told him: "Jim, your back is up against the wall; I'm coming after you."[14]

"Come and get me," Green said he replied.

At this most inopportune moment, Green's partner Mark Gale withdrew as his lawyer, leaving his client in the lurch. Later, Gale explained that because of his interest in the company he might be called as a witness in a legal proceeding and would thus have an unethical conflict.

The rent money then stopped coming altogether from Granite to Illini Federal.

Uncertain what to do, Illini Federal tried to deliver notices to the anonymous tenants instructing them to send the money to them.

Green's new lawyer Terryl Francis wrote letters telling the tenants to keep doing as they had been before, and to pay no heed to the "outside forces" trying to interfere.

Some of the befuddled tenants told Illini they weren't paying anything to anybody until the matter got settled.

Green, meanwhile, had "backed out" (the term he used later) of any involvement in Granite and was staying at a motel across the river in St. Louis, where he was visited periodically by Layman, outside the jurisdiction of Illinois courts.

On April 11, Illini Federal's lawyers went before Judge William Beatty in Madison County Circuit Court seeking two things: one, an injunction to force Green to turn over the rental records and stop interfering with the proper collection of the rents; and, second, the issuance of a writ of ne exeat republica, in effect to prevent someone from "exiting" the jurisdiction. Both were granted.

Green turned himself in at eleven o'clock that night and was lodged in the Madison County jail in Edwardsville. He was released at one o'clock the next afternoon, having posted a $50,000 bond to guarantee his appearance in court.

PSL Realty, now part of Illini Federal and holder of title to Green's properties under the Base Agreement, served notice of default and forfeiture of the contract, which in this case means the agreement. The legal dispute here is fairly clearcut: Because the "second chance" agreement did not pan out, and the Green properties were dropping farther and farther behind in their overdue loan payments, the successors to Piasa claimed the right to exercise control. Green, on the other hand, argued that the S & L people had no authority under the agreement to take over the management of the properties and to disburse what income there was as they wished. "They want to walk off with our property, some $13 million of it," Darrell Layman told Joe Melosi on May 10, "and not give us a damn thing for it. We have worked for 10 years to build up this company and someone walked in and took it away from us."[15]

On April 28, another Madison County Circuit Judge, Joseph Barr, denied Granite's motion to dissolve the injunction and appointed the FSLIC receiver of the properties in question. FSLIC then designated Illini Federal as its local agent to collect rents, pay bills, and manage the properties. By taking this legal route, Illini Federal (and the FHLBB-FSLIC in the wings) had elected to assert its right to control of the properties by contract forfeiture rather than by foreclosure of the mortgages. Green had been seemingly guileless in his court appearances. He said he had gone to St. Louis because he heard that Illini Federal wanted him arrested. He said he wanted the S & L to "buy me out so I would have money to start over." He vowed, however, to do everything possible to resist the takeover in court, telling Illini's lawyer: "We feel we can beat you people."

To carry on the fight, Terryl Francis put Jim Green in touch with a well-known lawyer in East St. Louis—Rex Carr.

Carr's willingness to accept the case raised eyebrows all over Metro East—and in the offices of the FHLBB in Chicago. His reputation as a very skilled and very wealthy plaintiff's counsellor had spread beyond Madison and St. Clair counties. But how would he be paid? Green was broke. That complication was handled by the creation of yet another partnership—Green Investors Associates—to hold two-thirds of Green's interest in Granite Investment. Forty-five percent of Green Investors was signed over to Rex Carr's law firm. So now two lawyers held an interest in the financially beached construction company.

Beached but still breathing. By challenging the legality of the forefeiture of the contract, Carr hoped to have the properties returned to Granite Investment. He likened his financial interest in his client's company to a contingency fee. A lawyer takes such a case with his fee being contingent upon a successful outcome, whereupon he pockets a percentage (usually one-third) of the award as his fee. If his client loses, the lawyer receives little or nothing. Here, however, Carr did not have to win to be paid. As long as the issue could be kept open in the courts, he and his firm could claim a continuing tax loss on their interest in Granite to be written off on their income taxes, just as Mark Gale was doing.[16]

8

Jury Selection in Metro East

Many reporters and editors are my friends, but I really wouldn't want my daughter to marry one. That's because they are basically so poorly paid. But we [lawyers] are perceived by society as being worth more than journalists. We're not really.[1]

—*Rex Carr*

Downtown East St. Louis has a bombed-out look about it, resembling the contested zone of downtown Beirut. In the midst of the rubble stands a modern brick building, the offices of one of the most accomplished personal injury trial lawyers in America—Rex Carr. In a typical recent year, Carr earned personal income in excess of $1 million.

He is a short man, about five feet, four inches tall. Except for a shallow cleft in his chin, his face is smooth and unlined. His eyes are a cold, unblinking blue gray. He has complete faith in his brilliance before a jury. By his own tabulation, Carr has lost only 10 of some 300 trials and thousands of cases; never, he says, because of his own mistakes.[2]

One summer afternoon when the temperature outside was 104 degrees, he wore his suit jacket while talking to me in his office. I chanced to ask him about adverse decisions by the 7th Circuit United States Court of Appeals and the Illinois Supreme Court on one of the issues involved in this story. He locked me in his icy stare and disposed of the matter with this simple declaration: "They were both wrong."

He uses his imperious, overbearing manner to intimidate witnesses, opposing lawyers, and judges. An attorney with one of the big Chicago firms who tangled with him during the many years of litigation involved in this story remembers "one of the toughest, most imaginative and resourceful lawyers I have ever known." Carr works alone in the courtroom, without assistants. He is able to do this because of his uncanny memory, his exceptional ability to organize the elements of a complicated medical malpractice case in his mind, for example, and to keep the parts tied together coherently in the minds of the jury. Everyone's awareness that his cases are meticulously prepared has something to do with the intimidation, too.

Carr can shed tears before a jury, and frequently does, but his style is more tyrannical than flamboyant. "Witnesses may not evade questions, they may not cry their way out of it," he insists. "Many lawyers let up. I don't. I'll persist until I get what I'm entitled to.... There is no limit to how far I'll go to get the truth."[3]

"This is an arena, it's combat, me against the other lawyers," he said on another occasion.

Unlike most of the other princes of the Metro East personal injury litigation empire, Carr is not publicity shy. In his early years, he relied on publicity to get clients. In those days, the *East Louis Journal* was published in a building directly across Missouri Avenue from his office—an abandoned building Carr's firm now owns. At the end of the day he would stop by Keiflien's saloon, a workingman's bar, to drink with the printers and newsroom employees.

"There's real satisfaction in doing something good for some guy who's been hurt, recognizing that this guy who's been crapped upon by society in one way or another gets some fair compensation," he told me. But another time he told a reporter for the *Belleville News-Democrat*: "I'm not doing these things out of some philosophic summum bonum [highest good]. I think that is the way the human animal is. If there is a God, I think that is the way He makes us. I don't think that is cynical. I think it's fine. I think it speaks very well for human beings that we can get good feelings from doing good. What if we got feelings of gratification from being cruel?... I don't want to put on any airs that I'm doing it for the good of humanity. Bull... I'm doing it for the good of Rex Carr."[4]

In 1968, while representing the teachers union of East St. Louis in acrimonious contract negotiations with the school board, Carr was accused of being a disruptive influence. "I follow the trouble, the trouble doesn't follow me," he responded. When the teachers went out on strike, Carr added this comment: "Basically, this is a world where the strong feed upon the weak. Anything anyone gets, he has to stand up and get it."[5]

It is not hard to understand how he came to that view of life. His parents moved to East St. Louis from the far tip of southern Illinois known as "Egypt." The region wedged in among the rivers is said to have acquired that name because, like the biblical Egypt, it supplied grain for the rest of Illinois during the hard winters of the 1830s. When Rex was five years old, his railroad fireman father deserted the family. This left his mother Madge, to raise the five boys. She had the father (who married five times in all) jailed periodically for nonsupport, but to no avail. The family survived the Depression on relief. Rex can remember his mother walking across the "free bridge" to sell pencils in downtown St. Louis.

All five sons worked their way through college with no help from home. After serving in the Navy, Rex graduated second in his University of Illinois College of Law class in 1949. He hitchhiked home weekends for a part-time job chopping ice for the railroad cars at the stockyards in National City. Returning to practice law in East St. Louis in 1950, Carr could not find a job with a firm. So he borrowed a judge's office in the morning while the judge was on the bench, grossing $500 in his first year of practice.

His career improved as the young lawyer identified himself with the often controversial local underdog causes (such as the teachers union). He was chairman of the East St. Louis Human Relations Commission and counsel to the local National Association for the Advancement of Colored People (NAACP). The firm that he helped organize was dissolved in 1967 over his refusal to fire a black secretary who had been hired.

The key to success in Metro East, however, lay in breaking into the railroad and barge worker injury litigation trade. Federal laws enacted in 1908 and 1918 specifically made it possible for railroad workers to sue their employers any place the railroad has tracks, and barge line employees any place the river runs by. The legal doctrine of *forum non conveniens* is generally intended to prevent litigators from suing someplace so inconvenient that the other side's witnesses can't be produced. This exception to that doctrine represented a political decision by Congress that railroading and barge jobs were so dangerous then, and the transportation industry had such a stranglehold on most judges, that special measures had to be enacted.

Chicago was the center of railroad damage claims until the 1940s. Then Pinky Lee, a railroad brotherhood union official in Cleveland, began steering cases to an East St. Louis attorney, Joseph B. McGlynn, who had his office in the *Journal* building. McGlynn worked out the "ticket" system of referrals whereby unions referred all their injured workers to him in exchange for a reduced contingency fee (25 percent) and his promise to kick back 5 percent to the union legal defense fund.[6]

After McGlynn's death, several Metro East lawyers began sharing transportation union "tickets." The results in East St. Louis and Granite City courts were fabulously successful. "The railroads were unpopular then," Carr has remarked. "They belched out smoke and grit, and blocked crossings, and didn't give a damn about people at all. They had no public relations. It was easy to get good results from juries in this industrial area."

Carr's big chance occurred in 1955 when he persuaded a jury to award $85,000 to a railroad worker with a ruptured disc injury. He had offered to settle for $20,000. The railroad lawyer laughed and said $5,000. It was then the biggest ruptured disc award in Illinois. Later, in the 1960s, Carr obtained a $121,000 ruptured disc award from a jury in Dallas, Texas.

If you're beginning to suspect that the game may be fixed in Metro East, it must be pointed out that some of Carr's big winnings have been elsewhere. He won a $7 million judgment (later reduced by the judge) in the District of Columbia for a Madison youth who was injured in a diving board accident at a Washington hotel swimming pool while attending a Boy Scout convention.

Back home, he won a $5.7 million verdict against an Alton hospital for the unintended removal of a woman's small intestine during a routine gynecological examination. The municipality of Alton had to issue bonds to pay off another settlement of a Carr-represented case involving allegations of police brutality.

He drives a $35,000 BMW 733i which is equipped with a radar detector to warn of state police speed checks. The license plates on the car, which is parked in a secure garage under the law firm building and well away from the local chop shop entrepreneurs, reads simply: REX. Until recently, Carr owned a sailing vessel in Florida that he used for journeys to the Bahamas and thereabouts. Now he makes do with a twenty-six-foot sailboat in Lake Carlyle, a short drive east of his home of Belleville. The Carrs charter a bigger boat for their annual sailing vacations in the Caribbean. He also owns an interest in the eighteenth-century chateau Cezy, ninety miles southwest of Paris, France, where guests can charter a six-person "gourmet barge" for $6,000 a week, meals and wines included, or soar in a fleet of hot air balloons. Not all the proceeds of the lawyering industry trickle down into Metro East, it turns out.

One of the three children from his first marriage is a missionary in Colombia. Carr told a reporter for the *New York Times Magazine* that the son's activities are "a filial response to [Rex's] atheism." His second wife, Edna, is his former secretary. They have a seventeen-year-old son.

Carr is one of four lawyers from Metro East who are members of an exclusive national all-male fraternity called the Inner Circle of Advocates. The 100 members of the club meet every year in some warm weather spa to gloat and exchange trade secrets. To be eligible for initiation, one must have tried at least fifty personal injury cases and cashed in on at least one million-dollar judgment. The logo for the club is the numeral 7, presumably representing the number of digits in a million.

Another of the Metro East initiates into the Inner Circle is Morris Chapman of Granite City, in whose firm Judge Charles Chapman once worked. Morris Chapman is not pleased by all the attention Carr has brought to Metro East. "Guys like Rex are bad for the profession," he said recently. "How much money does he need beyond a certain point? I've always taken the position that you've got to live within the system. And if you go out and get these $20 million verdicts for a guy from Podunk, you're going to kill the Golden Goose."[7]

Most of the business of Carr, Korein, Kunin, Schlicter & Brennan is contingency fee work—the Golden Goose of torts—accident negligence, product liability, medical malpractice. His partner, Sandor Korein, who also earned an income of $1 million in 1983, represents the National Maritime Workers Union in suits against the barge lines. There are seven other partners and nine lawyer associates in the firm. Their support staff includes three investigators, a photo lab technician, and a fulltime pilot for the firm's airplane.

The contingency fee system has come under attack lately from, among others, the then Chief Justice of the United States and the president of Harvard University. Warren E. Burger said the United States is the only country in the common-law world that uses it.[8] Derek C. Bok of Harvard criticized the emphasis on costly conflict in legal education instead of "the gentler arts of reconciliation and accommodation."[9]

The argument usually raised in defense of contingent fees likes to portray the system as "the poor man's key to the courthouse." Without the occasional windfall profits of an easy case, the personal injury lawyer could not gamble his time and skill on losers—or so goes the argument.

The problem with that argument is that Rex Carr takes only cases he thinks he can win—and cases where there's lots of money to be recovered, either from an insurance company or a wealthy defendant. Otherwise, "the poor sucker goes without," he told the *New York Times Magazine* writer. "What good would it do for me to help him? I can't make money for him. He's out of luck."[10] As for the way the system works in Metro East, Carr says any criticism can be traced to "sour grapes from defense lawyers."

"[Plaintiffs'] lawyers in Madison and St. Clair Counties know how to sell a personal injury case to a jury. They're not afraid to go to court. Also, this is not a silk stocking sort of place, and you get a good cross-section (on the juries). Most of the judges here were plaintiffs' lawyers. What the layman doesn't understand though is that the judge does the plaintiff a disservice if he gives erroneous rulings in a trial and then it [the judgment] is taken away on appeal.

The plaintiff's lawyer is a fool if he utilizes that inclination, because he's going to get reversed. You don't make any money trying the same god-damned case over and over again."

Madison County is decidedly not a "silk stocking sort of place," and what silk stockings there are somehow do not often walk their way onto the juries. Carr says he tries to avoid having "big shots" on juries, people who "don't have a heart." "Poor people would just as soon give away somebody else's money as anybody," he has observed.

The theory of the jury system is that the pool of prospective jurors shall be representative of all of the citizens in the community.

Illinois law requires that jurors be of voting age, "in the possession of their natural faculties and not infirm or decrepit, of fair character, of approved integrity, of sound judgment, well informed, and understand the English language." In Madison County, the lists are drawn from voter registration records. Postcard questionnaires are then mailed to the names and addresses randomly selected from the lists. Until this point, the process is automatic.

The next stage is not automatic. On the third Wednesday of every month, the three jury commissioners meet in a tiny office in the bank building across from the courthouse to go through the cards and sometimes the letters submitted in response to the questionnaires. The commissioners are appointed by the Circuit judges. Their job is to decide which of the names shall next go on the active list from which the panels of prospective jurors are chosen as the need arises.

What is distinctive about the Madison County system is one question on the postcard: "Circle level of educaton—grade school/high school/college." The other questions are fairly standard in all the counties of Illinois—occupation, physical impairments, ever been convicted of a felony, etc. (Certain occupations are exempt from jury duty, including lawyers and newspaper editorial and mechanical employees.)

But so far as I was able to tell, Madison is the only county that asks jurors *before* they are put on the active eligible list what their level of education is. An administrator of the jury office in Cook County (Chicago) told me: "There is no reason to ask that. How far you've gone in school has nothing to do with your eligibility to serve on a jury."

When I asked Nina Henkhaus in the jury office in Madison County why the question was included, she replied: "More or less to make a good selection."

A "good selection" in Madison County means panels of prospective jurors in which educational level is a consideration. After the presiding judge has excused potential jurors "for cause"—the cause usually being an expression of partiality for one or the other side in the case—the lawyers have an opportunity to exercise a certain number of what are called "peremptory challenges." This is the game the lawyers play as they try to guess which potential jurors are likely to be against them.

If the number of college-educated citizens on a panel is kept small, the plaintiff's lawyer can use his challenges to eliminate all or most of them. The educational level in Madison County is below the statewide average. But there were (in the 1980 census) 34,741 with some college experience living in the county—which is 23.66 percent of the twenty-five-and-over population, compared to 31.32 percent for the entire state.

Although England and most other Western nations have discontinued the use of juries in civil cases, it is deeply ingrained in the United States legal system. If there is a problem, it is usually understood to be the underrepresentation of racial minorities and low-income citizens generally on juries. Until 1968, the federal courts used a "key man" selection system that deliberately put "big shots" on juries. The daily fee for jury service is small ($10 in Madison County), and in most communities hourly-paid laborers argue strenuously to avoid their civic duty.

It seems obvious, however, that juries consisting predominantly of lesser educated people "with a heart" (or at least with no disinclination toward transferring wealth from insurance companies to the lower socioeconomic classes) are crucial to the extraordinary success of complicated damage suits in Madison County.

The controls on the referrals for jury service of college educated residents is one peculiarity in the system there. There are others. For example:

One of the cases to be described in detail later involved the five-week trial of a damage suit brought by Carr for Jim Green against Illini Federal in connection with Green's overnight jailing under a writ of ne exeat republica.

Midway through that trial, the following exchange took place (according to the official transcript) in the chambers of the presiding judge, Victor J. Mosele:

"W. Stanley Walch [attorney for Illini Federal]: Counsel have agreed, subject to the approval of the Court, that the Court ascertain the amount of lost wages that will be involved in the jurors presently serving, including wages lost to date. . . ."

"Rex Carr: Sure. Absolutely."

"Mr. Walch: Including wages lost to date, and when that amount is ascertained, each side will deposit immediately one-half of the amount in a special fund to be disbursed to the Court by the County or through the Clerk of the Circuit Court in such method as the Court may determine, to those jurors who are losing compensation as a result of the length of this trial; and Counsel have further agreed that the Court should instruct . . . or request the Court to instruct that this money is coming out of a special fund out of the County; and Counsel further agree that neither side will raise this as an element as a point of error in this case or any subsequent appeal in this litigation."

"Mr. Carr: It is so stipulated."[11]

What is happening here is the two sides in this lawsuit have agreed to supplement the fees paid the jurors by the county with their own subsidy, though the jurors are not to be told some of the money is coming from some place other than the public treasury, namely out of the pockets of the competing parties.

When I asked Walch years later if this was a common practice in Madison County, he replied: "Payment of lost wages is most unusual. It is not standard practice and was done in the Green case solely because of the length of the trial and the fear by counsel for both parties that a juror who suffered significant financial loss during the trial could become biased against whichever side he felt was responsible for the delay."

Once the shock of his removal from Piasa subsided, Bob DeGrand was at first devastated by the experience and then obsessed by an all-consuming desire for revenge. He could not find another job for seven months. He could not keep up the payments on the big house, and the family had to rent a smaller place in Upper Alton. "This was what the family talked about, thought about, lived with for twelve years," his son Luke recalled later. "It became the focus of his life and the life of the family [there were then seven children living at home]. He began drinking some. I can remember his walking around the house talking to himself and saying spiteful oaths under his breath. My mother told him he had to stop showing such bitterness, and then he'd claim he'd been praying. One night there was an electrical storm and the power went out. All nine of us [children] were there. We sat around the fireplace and he decided he wanted to tell us what had happened. He said he didn't want us to hang our heads in shame. He told us there was a point when he would have sold his soul to extricate himself from all this. He had a hard time living with the fact that he couldn't provide for his family. Mom hadn't asked for any of this and, to a certain degree, she got tired of living with it."

DeGrand trudged to lawyer after lawyer—Rex Carr among them—but they all told him that the FHLBB was immune from civil suits and there appeared to be no other feasible legal remedy. DeGrand blamed the *Telegraph,* Christie and "Chicago" (meaning the Federal Home Loan Bank of Chicago), the FHLBB in Washington, the directors of Piasa (for making him a scapegoat, he thought), and some of the lawyers for Piasa. The more he reflected, the more he became convinced that the whole affair had been "prearranged" to benefit Illini Federal. In a rambling fifty-nine-page typed statement, he said: "I have talked to several law firms regarding this matter. Unfortunately the statute of limitations protected the *Telegraph*. I was unaware there was a statute of limitations in cases such as this or I would have acted sooner." Elsewhere in the statement, DeGrand said: "A good question might be asked, if you knew the *Telegraph* and Federal Home Loan Bank of Chicago created this problem, why didn't you stay and fight instead of resigning? The answer is that I had no one to fight with me. . . . I fully realize that what the *Alton Telegraph* and the Federal Home Loan Bank of Chicago did to Piasa I cannot change. However, they can be fully assured that until the day I die I won't stop fighting to clear my name publicly regardless of what the odds are."

He made periodic trips to the Springfield office of Democratic Sen. Adlai E. Stevenson trying to trigger a Senate investigation of the FHLBB's handling of the Piasa matter. One of Stevenson's former staff members said that "the Roman Catholic hierarchy," presumably at the diocesan level in Belleville, had been involved in the attempt to bring about an undoing of what DeGrand considered an injustice against him.

By this time DeGrand had made contact with politician/ghostwriter/free-lance writer Pete Simpson. Peter Lawton Simpson is a former English instructor and poet whose ghostwriting career began as a sophomore at Notre Dame writing term papers for football players. He was elected to one term as an alderman in St. Louis and then worked on the staff of St. Louis Mayor A. J. Cervantes. In 1972 DeGrand was looking for someone who could piece together the story of the death of Piasa from his perspective and sell an article to some national magazine. Then an assistant to the president of Southern Illinois University at Edwardsville, Pete Simpson was typical of the many professionals who inhabit the world of politics and function out of public view. The Democratic organization in Madison County needed a few articulate sophisticated operators like him to give the machine a certain gloss. "Poets are people whose words are good," he once confided. "My fictive heroes are Huckleberry Finn, who was full of hilariously mischievous wonder, and Odysseus, who could put both alien royalty and young ladies caught in the buff on a beach at their ease."

Apart from his possible interest in free-lancing an article, Simpson's assignment provided the perfect cover for trying to penetrate both the Chicago FHLB and the *Telegraph*. "DeGrand had heard about the memo and wanted me to shake it loose," Simpson said later. "He gave me $500. I said I'll go in the watermelon patch and see if there's any watermelon. I found a watermelon and broke it up and there were just too many seeds. It was beyond my scope. I didn't have the resources to track down this kind of story."

In his role as seemingly objective free-lance journalist, Simpson interviewed Melosi (Lhotka had taken a job with the *Post-Dispatch* by now) and the FHLB officials in Chicago. Then he took tapes of the interviews to DeGrand. Simpson told me his "impression" was that he had been given a copy of the memo by Melosi and had delivered it to DeGrand, but Melosi does not remember that happening.

In any event, Simpson, who had gotten DeGrand a job in the business office at the regional university in Edwardsville, went with DeGrand to try to persuade the *Post-Dispatch* to do a story about what they construed as the FHLBB's abuse of power in the Piasa case. Also, an investigation of Green and DeGrand by the FBI and the Internal Revenue Service was well under way, starting with the information in the Melosi-Lhotka memo. Nothing came of either the congressional investigation or the coverage by the *Post-Dispatch*.

However, when Lhotka, who was working in the Jefferson City state capital bureau, heard about the visit to the newspaper in St. Louis, he called his former partner Melosi to tell him that Senator Stevenson might set off a Senate probe.

Melosi smelled a story for the *Telegraph*. The Nixon administration was in power in Washington. Could it be that the FHLBB had somehow conspired to snatch Piasa away from its rightful managers? How was Illini Federal tapped as the merger beneficiary? Could it be that we, the *Telegraph,* were used? Why not give DeGrand his turn at bat? Journalists think of "the news" as a swift-flowing stream. Today's flotsam drifts by and is gone. Tomorrow there will be something different, something "new." This produces a strange discontinuity in the portrayal of events that nonjournalists have difficulty appreciating. Could there, after all, be a new angle to the Piasa story?

The DeGrands were sitting around the living room saying the rosary on the evening of February 16, 1974, when they were interrupted by the ringing telephone. It was Joe Melosi calling to tell Bob DeGrand that he would like to interview him for DeGrand's side of the Piasa story. Four days later, Melosi met DeGrand for the first time. Both men tape-recorded the conversation in DeGrand's home.

Out of this and later conversations came an agreement that DeGrand would give Melosi a copy of the statement he was sending to Stevenson's office, presenting DeGrand's side of the story, in exchange for a copy of the Melosi-Lhotka memo. Melosi actually signed a paper promising to publish a story in the *Telegraph* explaining DeGrand's defense. Some idea of Melosi's thought process at this time is revealed by his remark in a subsequent written report to Steve Cousley of his contacts with DeGrand that "DeGrand admitted [*sic*] in the February 25 meeting that if the feds had not mishandled the August 1969 examination and started rumors about gangster money, Piasa would still be alive today." Steve was not pleased by his reporter's signed commitment on behalf of the *Telegraph* and refused to print the story.

The exact date DeGrand first saw the contents of the memo is extremely important for libel statute of limitations purposes. If DeGrand had already been shown a copy of the memo by Simpson, as Simpson says, then the eventual filing date of DeGrand's libel suit against the *Telegraph*—on February 13, 1975—did not fall within the one-year statute of limitations and should have been thrown out.

Notwithstanding that complication, one lawyer agreed to take DeGrand's libel case on a contingency fee basis. His name was Dick Mudge. While Mudge was an undergraduate at Harvard, he met a fellow student who made a lasting impression—John F. Kennedy. Mudge patterned his reform campaign for state's attorney (the elected county prosecutor in Illinois) after the Kennedy style. He was a handsome, vigorous young man who looked and acted like another Kennedy brother, just at the time John and his brother Robert were entering the national stage. Mudge had flown eighty missions as a fighter pilot in World War II before being shot down and imprisoned in Germany. Searching for a way to publicize his campaign in Madison County, he donned his old aviator's helmet and flew a chartered Piper Cub over the Club Prevue, a well known gambling house near Collinsville, which he "bombed" with 8,000 leaflets vowing to shut it down. "In order to eliminate the source of money by which a small group of politicians controls a corrupt government, you've got to stop gambling," he proclaimed. He beat the Democratic organization in the primary and was elected in 1956 and reelected in 1960.

Finishing his two terms in office, Mudge then returned to the practice of law in Edwardsville. He had gotten caught up in the civil rights and antiwar movements, marching with Martin Luther King in Birmingham and going to Vietnam on his own fact-finding mission. In one memorable occasion at the caucus of Illinois delegates to the 1968 Democratic convention in Chicago, Mayor Richard J. Daley, who was famous for his malapropian speech and liked deliberately to mangle the names of his enemies, recognized the critical delegate from downstate as "Mr. Sludge."

Paulie Cousley had been editorially enthusiastic about Mudge at the outset, but was disappointed by his performance in office. That helps to explain why a liberal reformer would tilt at the windmill in Alton, beside which the *Telegraph*'s Republicanism grated on him.

Merely having a copy of the memo was not enough, of course. Mudge had to prove its connection with the Piasa audits. DeGrand had tried unsuccessfully earlier to learn about what happened in the Justice Department by asking Sen. Ralph T. Smith (who had been appointed to the seat vacated by the death of Everett McKinley Dirksen) to intervene with Atty. Gen. John Mitchell.

Dr. Pfeiffenberger, who now bitterly regretted not having resisted the Piasma merger, agreed to help DeGrand and Mudge. He prevailed upon the Republican congressman from the district, Paul Findley of Pittsfield, to help obtain the documents, but Findley, a former small-town weekly newspaper editor, dragged his feet. Findley did discuss the matter with presidential chief of staff Donald Rumsfeld on a campaign visit to Alton, but nothing came of that either.

Rex Carr, in the meantime, had started Green's counterattack by filing a bewildering flurry of law suits in the Circuit Courts of St. Clair and Madison Counties. He alleged a civil conspiracy between the FHLBB and Illini Federal to wrest Green's properties from him. The feds could not be sued, but Illini Federal could, and sue Carr did, on several different fronts, in several different courts, seeking vast financial damages and the return of the properties to Granite Investment Co.

While this was going on, Green was in Cape Girardeau, Missouri, "pounding nails," the expression he used later in court to describe his job as a carpenter. He had divorced his wife Shirley, and was making frequent involuntary trips to Springfield, Illinois, where the United States Attorney had referred the FBI-IRS investigation that began with the Melosi-Lhotka memo to a grand jury.

9

The Law of Libel

The existence of the confidential memo from the two reporters had been revealed willy-nilly by a crew of savings and loan gumshoes whose investigative ardor exceeded their professionalism. The exact contents of the memo were made known subsequently by one of the reporters who willingly turned over a copy either to DeGrand's undercover agent or later to DeGrand himself. Why in the world, one might ask, would Joe Melosi have done that? In Melosi's mind, the message to the Justice Department was ancient history by then. Journalists are today- and tomorrow-oriented. They don't give much thought to the slowly unwinding continuum of events. Melosi was off sniffing new stories, and new angles to old stories. Another reason is that he never dreamed a confidential communication to a law enforcement official that never resulted in a single published word in the newspaper could be actionable in a court of law—certainly not *five years* later. Certainly not by someone whose name was not even mentioned in the memo. Melosi may or may not have been aware of the one-year statute of limitations for libel in Illinois, but he never remotely thought of the letter as libelous. Who would? Most journalists go about their workaday lives soothed by an inchoate sense of immunity from the complexities of such things, thanks to the mystical aura of The First Amendment.

It is, all lawyers know, one thing to bring a lawsuit, another to make it fly. The break Mudge needed to move the DeGrand suit forward occurred ironically through the workings of a federal statute that journalists lobbied for: A law that gave them access to public records—the Freedom of Information Act of 1966. The libel complaint filed in Madison County Circuit Court February 13, 1975, sought $1,170,000 in compensatory damages and an additional $1 million in punitive damages. In a civil suit, the request for punitive damages on top of the alleged financial loss incurred by the plaintiff is intended to punish the defendant and make sure he doesn't do it again. Any money awarded for punitive damages goes to the plaintiff (and his lawyer) along with the compensation for proven financial injury (which can include loss of prestige and emotional well-being as well as income). Melosi and Lhotka, named as codefendants with the *Telegraph,* were accused in the complaint of "composing and publishing said letter with such a reckless disregard and carelessness as to its truth or falsity as to indicate an utter disregard of the rights of the plaintiff."

In order to be covered by the law of libel, a written statement must identify the defamed individual, injure that person's reputation, and be "published to a third party." In a newspaper story, of course, there are many third parties—namely, all the readers. The "publication" in this case had to be the communication to the Justice Department, the "republication" occurring later without the newspaper's knowledge.

Mudge filed a demand under the FOI Act for copies of the correspondence within and between the Justice Department and the FHLBB. The Republican administration of Gerald R. Ford complied, but with all the names blotted out, making the documents useless as evidence. When the Democratic administration of Jimmy Carter took office, Atty. Gen. Griffin Bell reconsidered the request and opened the complete file of correspondence to Mudge's inspection. Thus the plaintiff was able to construct a bridge of evidence between Washington and Chicago leading to the audit in Madison County.

The *Telegraph,* meanwhile, answered the complaint in court and moved for dismissal of the suit. A report of a possible violation of the law given to a law enforcement agency is "privileged absolutely," the newspaper argued, meaning that it was automatically protected against legal attack. The defense also raised the statute of limitations issue, pointing out that DeGrand had undeniably known about the memo at the time of the *Post-Dispatch* story in April of 1971, almost four years before the libel suit was initiated.

Barney Fraundorf and Demos Nicholas, identified in the *Telegraph*'s answer as the two principal sources of the allegations in the memo, had both died in the intervening years. So had Henry Wuellner, the former president of Piasa and DeGrand's boss. So, a few months later, in February of 1976, would Elmer Broz, the city editor under whose command Melosi and Lhotka had carried out their assignments.

Judge Beatty, the former personal injury lawyer in Granite City whose real estate development partnership with one of the top Democratic party leaders had been the subject of a story by Lhotka in the *Telegraph,* denied the newspaper's motion to dismiss the case.

A majority of libel suits are decided at this early stage by what is called "summary judgment." The judge reads the pleadings—the statements of what the two sides believe they can prove—and then decides "summarily" that the probable outcome is so clear in advance that the time and expense of a trial are unnecessary.

Here, however, Judge Beatty held that the "good faith" of the reporters was at issue. He said the absolute privilege did not apply because "it is questionable whether there was a real desire *primarily* to report a crime." On the statute of limitations issue, the judge said there was a factual dispute over when the plaintiff had knowledge or should have had knowledge of the memo, and therefore it was a matter to be decided by the jury. DeGrand contended that he did not know about the memo until a few days less than one year before the libel suit was filed.

With the passing months and years, DeGrand's hatred of the *Telegraph* and the savings and loan regulators in Chicago boiled and churned within him. He developed a nervous tic in one eye. He talked of little else. He wanted more than monetary compensation for the damage to his reputation. He wanted vengeance against the *Telegraph*. So DeGrand and Mudge made the rounds of the others whose names were in the memo, urging them to join the procession and sue the *Telegraph* for libel.

Jim Green would later testify that he had not known about the existence of the memo until DeGrand visited him in Cape Girardeau a few days less than one year before Carr filed a libel suit in Green's behalf January 26, 1977—almost eight years after the sending of the memo. By now Carr was engaged in an extremely intricate dance of litigation with the lawyers for the FHLBB and Illini Federal in several different state and federal courts. The libel suit was merely another step in the dance that Carr hoped would one day lead to the return of the properties to Granite Investment (of which he was now a partner).

Within a few months, lawyers in Madison County filed libel suits against the *Telegraph* and the two reporters by:

—Ray Kozielek, described in the memo as a Madison City councilman who had been a "jackleg electrician" and was involved in "pledge deals" with Green.

—John Sobol, owner of a realty company in Granite City that had dealings with Green.

—Don Hazel, described as a close associate of known hoodlums and "reportedly the No. 2 crime boss in the county."

—Stanley Kowalski, depicted as "Big Ski, a vicious hood, and a bagman."

—Elvin "Bert" Simpson, described as a "hood."

The men asked for amounts ranging from a modest $1.5 million to Bert Simpson's more expansive $12.4 million.[1]

As all of these cases skipped across the various dockets of the Circuit Court, the *Telegraph* was obliged to pay lawyers to prepare and submit the necessary answers, motions, depositions, and assorted other pieces of paper that make the multibillion dollar legal industry chug along in the United States.

The specter of libel is always there looking over the editor's shoulder in the newsroom. It has been said many times that a newspaper that does not commit libel fairly regularly is not doing its job. Anything that makes others think less of a person is libel. What matters to journalists, of course, is to have a *defense* against libel—truth being the most utilitarian defense.

Gossip is as old as mankind. Human beings were telling tales on their neighbors as soon as they learned to use language. Penalties for defamation were in the common law of the western world long before the invention of the printing press. In the Law of Twelve Tables, written 300 years after the founding of ancient Rome, slanderers were to be beaten with a club. At the end of the ninth century, under Alfred the Great, king of the Saxons, the punishment for slander was "no lighter penalty than the cutting off of his tongue." In seventeenth-century England, judges not only fined and imprisoned defamers but ordered them whipped or their ears cut off.[2]

The divine right of kings made it possible for monarchs and the established church to punish their subjects for criminal libel threatening their security. Seditious libel disappeared from American law by the start of the nineteenth century. Truth was not a defense against a charge of libel, however, until the trial of John Peter Zenger in colonial New York. Until then the mere fact of publication was sufficient to convict.

The words of the First Amendment—"Congress shall make no law . . . abridging the freedom of speech, or of the press"—do not absolve the press from accountability under the law. The government cannot censor the press. It cannot ban the publication of something objectionable. Beyond that, however, the news media can be made to answer for what they have published in almost any way legislators and judges decree.

What happened in Alton a century and a half ago—when Elijah Lovejoy was murdered and his press thrown in the river—would seem to dramatize society's need for some peaceful means of redressing grievances against the press. Fred W. Friendly, the former president of CBS News who is now a professor emeritus at the Columbia Graduate School of Journalism, put it this way: "There has to be some kind of redress—a tort law called libel—if we are not to kill people and break the presses or tear down the television transmitter."[3]

The word *libel* itself is believed to derive from two Anglo-Saxon roots—*lye* (to speak falsely) and *bell* (loud). There have always been fewer libel suits in the United States than in England, some say because of the greater mobility of Americans. Americans are more inclined to move on than to try to rehabilitate a bad reputation. (Jim

Green's first impulse was to acquire a financial "stake" so he could move to another state and start over after the collapse of his real estate business.) There are many libel suits in France, but the maximum recovery is the equivalent of $2,500. French courts can compel the printing of a retraction and even order the libeler to buy space in other publications for retraction notices. That would violate the First Amendment in this country. Just as the state cannot stop the printing of something, so can it not force a publisher to print something involuntarily.[4]

The common law sufficed here until 1964 when the United States Supreme Court made a distinction between the libeling of public figures and others. In *Sullivan* v. *New York Times,* the court overturned an Alabama jury's award to a police commissioner who claimed he had been libeled in an advertisement placed in the *Times* by a civil rights organization. For public figures (such as the police commissioner), the offending statement must have been made with "actual malice," a term the justices defined as knowledge of its falsity or reckless disregard of whether it was false or not. Because they had not thrust themselves into the public eye, as a police commissioner or other public official (or entertainer or athlete) does, DeGrand and Green were not considered public figures.

In another case ten years after that, the Supreme Court ruled that states may not "impose liability without fault" where nonpublic figures are involved. In other words, a private individual must prove "fault," which is defined as unreasonable or negligent conduct. One of the effects of that decision was to make the easily misunderstood processes of newsgathering the business of libel juries. Did the newsroom staff exercise the proper caution in reporting the story? The 1974 case also held that damages beyond the costs of reputational injury can be imposed to punish the libeler only if the private individual has proven "actual malice"—that is, only if there is clear and convincing evidence that the libeler seriously doubted the truth of what was written.

(More recently, in 1985 and 1986, the Supreme Court established in two 5-to-4 decisions that non-public figures seeking damages for libel on "matters of public concern" have the burden of proving that the statements were false; but that they may collect punitive damages without proving actual malice if the subject of the libel was something other than a matter of public concern.)

Punitive damages unrelated to the financial harm sustained by the victim of a libel are a powerful invitation for juries to discipline controversial "hell-raising" newspapers. Between 1978 and 1982, juries awarded damages in forty-seven out of fifty-four libel cases tried in the United States, including punitive damages in thirty of those trials. The first $1 million libel verdict was not returned until 1976, and by 1982 there were six others that large or larger. Through the 1970s, the largest newspaper libel judgment ever paid was $250,000, reduced on appeal from $750,000 in 1973. The largest settlement out of court was $600,000 paid in 1976 by the *San Francisco Chronicle* to the religious sect Synanon.

Twenty-eight states (Illinois not among them) do not allow insurance companies to cover punitive damages in libel suits. In these places, newspapers may be insured against compensatory damages but not punitive damages.

Many of the most prominent news organizations are big enough and rich enough to absorb libel judgments without insurance. The *New York Times,* for example, does not carry libel insurance and does not settle libel cases out of court. In 1963, the general counsel of the American Newspaper Publishers Association—Arthur B. (Tim) Hanson—instigated libel insurance for less affluent newspapers under the auspices of the Mutual Insurance Group of Bermuda, which he served as United States general counsel. In the late 1960s and early 1970s, the *Telegraph* was protected by a $1 million "umbrella" libel policy and another for reimbursement of up to $200,000 in legal fees, both arranged by Hanson's group.

Any analysis of the politics of libel policy in Illinois must begin with, first, the influence of the *Chicago Tribune* and, second, the regional tensions that have existed throughout the state's history between the Chicago metropolis and downstate.

Down through the years, the *Tribune* wielded enormous political influence in the state capital in Springfield. Many news organizations, sensitive to the conflicts between their journalistic and business functions, are reluctant to throw their weight around except on their editorial pages. But not the *Tribune* in the era of publisher

Robert R. McCormick and immediately thereafter. The *Tribune* used its clout to inspire the Illinois Supreme Court to fashion an "innocent construction rule" for libel suits. This strange rule required that if an allegedly libelous statement could be construed in two or more ways, one of them not libelous, it must be read the innocent way.[5] Partly because of this unique rule, before 1981 ninety-three percent of all libel cases in Illinois were decided in favor of the press.

The *Tribune*'s power was responsible for another important feature of the law of libel in Illinois. Especially during the many years when the malapportioned state legislature was dominated by downstaters, crusading Chicago newspapers ran the risk of angering downstate politicians with their aggressive reporting of state government. State law required, however, thanks again to the *Tribune*, that the venue (place of trial) in a libel case must be in the county of the defendant newspaper's publication. If there is to be a legal tussle with some country bumpkin downstate, the *Tribune* would deal with it in Cook County, where the *Tribune*'s power was well understood by the judiciary. The considerable practical significance of this for the *Telegraph* was that the newspaper could not ask for a transfer of its libel problems to a more neutral venue by claiming Madison County judicial bias.

As it happened, the cases against the *Telegraph* bounced around Madison County from one judge to another. Having perturbed most of the judges at one time or another, the newspaper had reason to request the disqualification of most of the judges upon whose dockets the libel cases appeared.

The Green libel case and those of the others who were prompted by DeGrand and Mudge to file their own suits presented special statute of limitation problems. Green's case, for example, was not filed until almost two years after Mudge had sued in behalf of DeGrand. The jury would be asked to believe that Jim Green did not know of the existence of the memo in which his name figured so prominently at the time of the bringing of a libel suit based on the memo by a man (DeGrand) who was not even mentioned in the memo.

By early 1979, the DeGrand case had landed on the docket of a relatively acceptable (to the *Telegraph*) judge—Phillip Rarick—and the parties were ready to go to trial. The months and months of taking discovery depositions from prospective witnesses by the lawyers for both sides were over. One final motion by the *Telegraph* to dismiss the case on innocent construction grounds was denied by Judge Rarick. The trial that Dick Mudge had been working toward since 1974 was about to begin.

Through a stroke of fate that could not have been foreseen, however, on August 28, 1979, less than three months from the DeGrand libel trial date, Mudge suffered a heart attack while driving his car.

Nancy DeGrand turned pale when she answered the phone at home a couple of hours later.

"It's about Dick Mudge," she told her husband.

"He's dead, isn't he?" DeGrand said.

"Yes," she replied, and left the room.

DeGrand flew into a rage, pounding his fists on the wall and cursing this yet another accursed turn of fate.[6]

Mudge, the quixotic figure who was to have led him by the hand to the sweet well of revenge, was gone. Without him, DeGrand knew there would be no trial of his libel suit.

10

An Odyssean Journey

DeGrand's seething sense of frustration was compounded by his awareness that earlier in the summer of Mudge's death Jim Green's counselor Rex Carr had succeeded in bringing to trial a $6 million damage suit seeking compensation for Green's one night in jail in 1972.

The Madison County Circuit Court's designation of the Federal Savings and Loan Insurance Corporation as receiver for Green's properties meant that the FSLIC and Illini Federal Savings and Loan Association, now vastly enlarged by the FSLIC-arranged absorption of Piasa, had the unobstructed right to collect the rents and manage the real estate while the ultimate status of the properties was being fought over in the courts.

The improper jailing litigation, and the $10,545,000 libel suit filed on Green's behalf in 1977, were only two of the multiple thrusts by the imaginative Mr. Carr. Beginning with his agreement in 1972 to represent Green in exchange for an interest in Green's investment company, the lawyer-knights for the opposing interests jousted hither and yon across the judicial landscape of Illinois. The shared objectives of FSLIC and Illini Federal (who, it will be remembered, had signed a "contribution agreement" at the time of the Piasa merger to guard Illini against losses resulting from the Green debts) were to cut their losses and realize the best financial deal they could out of the delinquent mortgages. Carr on the other hand, argued in as many different forums as he could find that the taking of the mortgaged properties from Green and their subsequent management had been improper under the agreement worked out previously by the lender Piasa and the borrower Green.

As the several prongs of the litigation evolved, the state appellate court in southern Illinois vigorously took Carr's side and the federal courts took the other side with equal determination. When this conflict reached the intermediate federal appellate court—the 7th Circuit United States Court of Appeals sitting in Chicago—Judge William J. Bauer began the court's opinion with a sardonic prelude:

"These consolidated appeals present for review a decade of litigation, whose Odyssean journey through the various state and federal courts sitting in Illinois was ultimately destined on a collision course between the two court systems and which achieved that destiny in a rather dramatic interim finale when on October 2, 1979, the United States District for the Southern District of Illinois invoked its injunctive powers to enjoin the Illinois state courts from further interference with its jurisdiction over certain property subject to a mortgage foreclosure action instituted in the district court nearly four years earlier.

". . . Although the final chapter of this case remains to be written, its history stands as a compelling testimonial to the maximum utilization of the American jurisprudential system, embracing as it does both the state and federal trial and appellate courts as well as the federal bankruptcy courts."[1]

Before his appointment to the federal court by a Republican president a few years before, Judge Bauer had been a Republican leader of the biggest and wealthiest Republican county in Illinois— exurban DuPage County, west of Chicago.

The confrontation of which he spoke, between the state and federal judicial system, can be personified by the principal judges who were involved: Charles E. Jones of the state Appellate Court in southern Illinois, which sits in Mount Vernon; and J. Waldo Ackerman of the United States District Court for the Southern District of Illinois, sitting in Springfield.

Since the rural and urban counties of the region were joined in an appellate district in 1964, only one candidate from the rural section has been able to win a primary election against the Madison and St. Clair Democratic organizations. That man was Charlies Jones from

McLeansboro, a town of a little over 2,000 citizens in the far southern tip of the state. He practiced law for only four years before running for county judge at the age of thirty and later for the appellate bench.

Ackerman had a different background. A few wealthy old families who had been in Springfield since Lincoln's time were still calling signals from the sidelines, but after World War II the Republican party fell into the hands of a group of young progressive attorneys who had moved to the state capital because they thought it would be a good place to practice law. Wally Ackerman, a "Percy-Rockfeller Republican," worked his way up from assistant state's attorney to election as state's attorney, to circuit judge in the Sangamon County circuit, and then to a lifetime appointment to the federal trial court in the district that includes Springfield and Metro East.

A complete record of the legal skirmishes over the control of Green's apartment buildings would fill a bar journal, but would be of interest, if at all, to lawyers. When it was all over, Carr estimated that he had devoted at least one-third of his working hours to Green-related matters. His principal antagonist during much of this time was a corporate lawyer from Chicago who was representing the FSLIC—one Robert W. Patterson. Law firms in Chicago usually are known for their affinity either to the local Democratic organization, which selects most of the judges, or to the Republican party and its connections with the business and financial community. A tall, ultrasuave buttoned-down type, Patterson is one of ninety-five lawyers in the Republican firm of Hopkins, Sutter. His forty-second-floor office across from the First National Bank building has a lovely view of Lake Michigan beyond the Loop.

After the various lawsuits had been kicking around for a while, Patterson dispatched a letter to Carr telling him, as a professional courtesy, that he was about to request an advisory ruling by the state's Attorney Registration and Disciplinary Commission based on a set of hypothetical facts.

Real estate developer defaults on mortgages . . . forms limited partnership to try to regain properties . . . lawyer retained who is assigned 60 percent of partnership interest . . . lawyer takes depreciation deduction against his personal income on the real estate in which the partnership has a contingent interest . . . foreclosure proceeding started . . . foreclosure challenged by the attorney, who continues to take depreciation against the real estate on his tax return.

Before Patterson could send off his "hypothetical" complaint, Carr beat him to the punch by filing his own complaint accusing Patterson of improperly trying to coerce Green into settling the litigation.

The commision issued an advisory opinion stating that the circumstances constituted a "clear violation" of the rule prohibiting lawyers from acquiring a proprietary interest in the subject matter of litigation. An exception is made, the opinion pointed out, permitting a lawyer to "contract with a client for a reasonable contingent fee in a civil case."

"The fact, here, that substantial tax disadvantages compound the potential loss of the litigation and its termination, of course, has no bearing on the evils inherent in the type of fee arrangement described," the opinion went to explain. "It was and is professionally improper for the lawyer to purchase (with his services) or otherwise acquire the 60 percent interest in the general partnership."[2]

Patterson did not press his complaint against Carr, nor did Carr his against his adversary. Another lawyer, Stanley Walch of St. Louis, sought unsuccessfully to bring before the jury the fact of Carr's interest in Green's company during the ne exeat damage trial in 1979. Carr explained in the chambers of Judge Mosele, according to the trial transcript, that Green had no other assets with which to retain an attorney and, therefore, had no choice but to sign over part of his interest in the partnership, first to Mark Gale and then to Carr. It was the same as a contingency contract, he argued, to which Walch responded that it was not the same in that the benefits were not contingent upon an award of damages by the jury. Judge Mosele, agreeing with Carr that the information was immaterial and irrelevant, refused to permit it to be mentioned in the presence of the jury.

Going back to 1972, Carr's first move for Green was to file an "interlocutory" appeal with the state appellate court in Mount Vernon of the original decision by Judge Joseph J. Barr appointing the receiver and removing Granite Investment from any management role. An interlocutory decree by an appellate court is usually to decide some preliminary or subordinate issue before a case is tried. In his petition for such a ruling, Carr challenged the injunction against Green and the naming of the FSLIC as receiver.³

Three of the five elected justices of the 5th District Appellate Court in Mount Vernon are from Madison and St. Clair counties. The other two are from small towns in "Egypt." The clerk of the court is a former Democratic chairman of Madison County. The *American Lawyer*'s previously cited article on the "plaintiffs' paradise" in Madison County described the appellate court in Mount Vernon as "extremely hospitable to plaintiffs' claims," a fair if understated assessment of its reputation in Illinois.

Nothing happened to the appeal for four years—until 1976. In May of 1973, meanwhile, Carr filed two suits in his home county of St. Clair seeking $31 million in actual and punitive damages for Green from Illini Federal. One of the cases alleged a civil conspiracy to violate the original "Base Agreement" between Piasa and Green and to forfeit the contracts, the legal step whereupon the new lender Illini took over the properties. The second had to do with an apartment project in Springfield that got lumped into the Green properties through unusual circumstances. Green and a Madison County builder named Howard Steele had been partners in a $2.5 million apartment project in Springfield called Spencer Gardens and also financed by Piasa. Green sold his interest to Steele at the time he was trying to reduce his Piasa debt in order to qualify for additional borrowing. Then, when the Base Agreement was being prepared, Green and Piasa offered Steele an interest in Granite Investment if he would deed the property to Granite Investment, which he did. Spencer Gardens, later renamed McArthur Park, caught Carr's attention because it was one of the former Green projects earning more than it cost to operate. Carr accused Illini Federal of diverting the income to shore up the losers instead of using it to pay off the mortgage on the Springfield buildings so they could be returned to their owners—according to Carr, in violation of the agreement.

Throughout 1974 and 1975, the attorneys put their lances down and talked about a settlement. But in 1976 the state Appellate Court ordered the receivership dissolved, whereupon the FSLIC purchased the Green mortgages from Illini Federal for $10,673,000 and sued in federal court for foreclosure. During the period of the receivership, the FSLIC and Illini collected $5.7 million in rents and spent $4.1 million of that for the maintenance and improvement of the properties, leaving little for debt reduction.[4] The debt was then estimated at about $14 million on real estate with a market value of about $9 million.

Carr went back to the state court and alleged mismanagement of the properties by the receiver, which he said entitled Green to possession. On the same day, the FSLIC asked Judge Ackerman for an order authorizing it to remain in possession, which the judge granted.

Then the state court ordered the FSLIC not to proceed with the foreclosure in federal court. But the federal judge rejected Carr's contention that the state courts had exclusive jurisdiction over the properties. To the contrary, said Judge Ackerman, he had exclusive jurisdiction.

The state Appellate Court then met in special session to consider Carr's request that the FSLIC be held in contempt for purchasing the mortgages *and* fined $10 million *plus $1 million a day* if it continued to pursue the foreclosure in federal court.

Judge Ackerman then issued an injunction of his own forbidding the justices of the state Appellate Court *and* all the judges of all the state courts in Illinois from interfering with his jurisdiction in the case. In a memorandum accompanying the injunction, the federal judge said: "I believe there is a serious question as to whether, after the outlay of millions of dollars, the FSLIC could, even if it so desired, simply walk away from this action and thereby, in effect, forfeit the properties to the parties who are alleged to be in default under the mortgages."

On the very day scheduled for trial of the foreclosure proceeding in Judge Ackerman's court, Granite Investment filed a petition to reorganize under Chapter 11 of the federal Bankruptcy Act. This had the automatic effect of removing the foreclosure from the United States Bankruptcy Court and suspending all pending litigation.

In the meantime, Carr had filed a new suit in St. Clair County seeking "specific performance" of the Piasa-Green contracts and $15 million in damages against Illini Federal for, among other things, selling the mortgages to FSLIC.

Early in 1980, a judge in St. Clair County set that case for trial. The FSLIC then reminded the state judge that the federal court had enjoined the state courts from interfering with its custody of the very property at issue in the specific performance case. But the federal bankruptcy judge, James D. Trabue of East St. Louis, said he had jurisdiction now, not the federal district court, and *he* said it was okay to go ahead with the trial in St. Clair County.

The FSLIC returned to Judge Ackerman with a request that Carr, Green, and the St. Clair judge, Thomas P. O'Donnell, be held in federal contempt.

At this point, cooler heads prevailed. Judges Ackerman and O'Donnell agreed to keep quiet and do nothing more until the 7th Circuit Court in Chicago could rule on Carr's appeal of Ackerman's actions.

Who will prevail? Will the state court system face down the federal court system? Will the Illinois Supreme Court accede to the wisdom of the federal court in Chicago? Will the FSLIC and Illini lose their shirts? Who will eventually be declared the rightful owners of the properties?

In the midst of all this, Carr did succeed in bringing to trial in Madison County the ne exeat damage suit, which sought $6 million in actual and punitive damages for what he alleged had been the malicious issuance of the writ against Green.

The lawyers for the Illini Federal thought they had a fairly straightforward answer to the complaint in the wrongful imprisonment suit: Jim Green had skimmed the rent money—money that didn't belong to him—and had made known his intention of continuing to do so until he had enough to go off somewhere else and start over. The savings and loan association that had acquired his bad debts was justified, therefore, in asking the court to prevent Green from leaving the jurisdiction. This was done through the issuance of a writ of ne exeat republic, under which he was lodged in the Madison County jail overnight until he posted a $50,000 bond as assurance that he would remain in the area.

The lawyers for Illini Federal were mistaken.

For five weeks, beginning in early May of 1979, Judge Victor J. Mosele permitted Carr to put Illini—and, more importantly, the FSLIC—on trial for their handling of the Green real estate problems following the merger with Piasa. As the trial unfolded before the jury, the central issue became the propriety of Illini's forfeiture of the contracts for ownership of the properties.[5]

At one point, Carr asked the witness Richard McGovern, general counsel for Illini and a codefendant in the case: "Isn't it true that you thought if you had Green arrested on a writ of ne exeat, he would leave the area without a fight and you could get these properties without a fight?"

McGovern said, no it was not true.

Contrary to the impression sometimes given in movies and television dramas, the jury's only function in a trial is to decide questions of fact. Who is telling the truth? The responsibility for seeing that justice is done is the judge's. This time Judge Mosele allowed Carr to go far beyond the ne exeat issue and lay out before the jurors his interpretations of the highly complicated "workout" agreement and its later implementation.

His first witness—DeGrand—began by describing the origins of the agreement. DeGrand conceded that most of the Green mortgages were seriously delinquent and that Green was in precarious financial condition.

A brief review is in order here. Except for the enormous size of Green's debt, the arrangement wasn't all that different from what might happen if a homeowner fell way behind on his mortgage payments. The lender puts up some money (in this case $750,000) to go along with the borrower's "pledged" savings accounts. Ownership of the property is given to the lender (in this case a special subsidiary, PSL Realty Co.), which then issues "contracts for deed" to the borrower's newly formed investment company, which will continue to manage the properties. Someone who buys a house "on contract" does not acquire actual ownership until it's paid for—which is essentially what was to happen in this case. The agreement provided that the managers were to be allowed 20 percent of the rents for operating expenses with the rest to go to pay off the overdue loans. But Green testified that the properties were still losing $30,000 a month at the time of the jailing. The new owners of PSL Realty (Illini Federal) then took steps to "forfeit" the contracts. Here the word "forfeit" is used to mean the loss of property for failure to comply with the terms of the contract, requiring in this case progress toward paying off the debts.

The issue Carr argued through day after day of grilling witnesses and offering page after page of baffling financial records was his contention that Illini had no right to take over the properties and deprive Green of his 20 percent cut when it did. Illini's lawyer, W. Stanley Walch of the St. Louis firm of Thompson and Mitchell, insisted that Illini had the right under the Base Agreement to stop the hemorrhaging of funds caused by a debt greater than what the properties could conceivably be worth.

Walch found himself in the position of having to prove Green's mismanagement, Piasa's extraordinary lending generosity, and the deceptions which the FSLIC claimed had occurred. In the course of the testimony, Piasa's appraisal practices were attacked. One of the critical FSLIC reappraisers—Clarence Bruckner of Glen Ellyn in DuPage County—let slip his animosity toward the "motorcycle types" who lived in some of Green's apartments.

Carr chewed on that one over and over.

"Carr: When you said they were the motorcycle type, I had two sons that had motorcycles; one of them has long hair and is studying to be a minister. Is he in the category you mentioned?"

Bruckner tried to explain that what he really meant was what he called "greaseballs."

"Carr: What is a greaseball, Mr. Bruckner?"

"Bruckner: I call a greaseball a man or woman who's unkempt bodily."

"Carr: How many tenants did you see that you would call greaseballs in this project of young married couples?"

"Bruckner: Certainly more than a couple . . . I saw the motorcycles in the hallways."

While Carr was given free rein to hammer away at Bruckner and McGovern and the other defense witnesses, Mosele restricted Walch's questions carefully. Walch was ordered not to question

Green about the pending libel suit against the *Telegraph,* or about any of the several other lawsuits that had been filed in his behalf and which offered different theories of the causes of his alleged loss of income other than those propounded in this case. Judge Mosele said the contradictions were not relevant. Raymond Kosielek's testimony that he had been a "straw party" for Green loans was ruled inadmissable. An officer of another savings and loan association would have testified that Green's credit reputation had been destroyed before the issuance of the writ, but was disqualified by the judge at Carr's urging.

The jurors must have been perplexed by Carr's calculation of $3 million in lost investment income—representing what Carr hypothesized Green would have received after the date of the jailing had it not been for the jailing. Walch could not mention the fact of the receivership before the jury, although any losses had to have been entirely conjectural inasmuch as Green did not have possession of the real estate. The defense attorney also pointed out in his questioning that Illini Federal had been required to post its own $50,000 bond when it requested the writ of ne exeat against Green, and that Green had not filed a claim against the bond.

In his closing argument to the jury, Carr said the defendants' case had been "a combination of lies and slander" against Green, and that the ne exeat writ had been "a lie to the court." He told the jurors they should do more than just compensate Green for his lost income by also awarding a large amount of punitive damages because they were "for the benefit of and would go to the public." Punitive damages are "for the ultimate benefit of the public," he repeated. In no way do punitive damages or "exemplary damages," as they are called, benefit anyone other than the plaintiff into whose pocket they go (after the lawyer has taken his one-third).

Carr was also permitted to inform the jury that the FSLIC would pay any judgment against Illini. "They could pay us the bloody national debt and still have money left," he assured the jurors. His theory throughout had been that the taking of Green's properties was part of a "Watergate syndrome" and a "coverup," having happened at roughly the same time as the Watergate scandal.

The statement to which Walch objected most strenuously in his posttrial motion (and which he described as "incredible") was Carr's assertion before the jury that "the Court will tell you that we are entitled to a verdict in this case."

The jury retired to begin its deliberations at 4:45 P.M. on June 6, 1979. One of the few college-educated voters of Madison County who had somehow survived the jury selection system and been seated on the jury—a high school teacher from Edwardsville—was excused from completing the trial, with the approval of both lawyers, because he said some high school seniors would not graduate unless he were available to process their end-of-semester grades. The two sides agreed that the trial would continue with only eleven jurors. This is the trial mentioned previously in which the two sides agreed secretly to reimburse the jurors out of their clients' pockets for lost wages.

At 9:30 P.M. the jurors went home for the night without reaching a verdict. They resumed at 9:30 the next morning, and made their decision at 7:30 that evening: $3 million in actual damages for Jim Green, without any punitive damages.

It was, Carr commented to reporters, "a tremendous vindication of Green."[6]

"This is the first chance an impartial jury has had to hear both sides," he said. "What the jury did was compensate Green for his personal losses over the last seven years."

Walch filed a sixty-eight-page motion requesting that the verdict be overturned by Judge Mosele. The motion raised these allegations:

1. The plaintiff failed to prove damages for one night in jail. "The meager evidence on reduced wages and income from investments could not possibly support a verdict in excess of $100,000."

2. The trial, "largely due to plaintiff's counsel's tactics, got totally out of hand and the jury and the court were totally misled." This started, according to Walch, when Carr was permitted "to turn this into a trial to construe the basic agreement and determine if the contracts for deed had been wrongfully forfeited."

3. Carr's closing argument was "outrageous." At a hearing on the motion in November, Walch argued that "the Court was biased in favor of the plaintiff" and "totally lost control of the trial with

highly prejudicial consequences to the defendants." The calculation of Green's damages was an "insidious deception" by his lawyer, Walch contended.

Carr responded that the evidence supported a finding of wrongful motive and ulterior purpose for the issuance of the writ. He expressed his evaluation of Walch's sixty-eight pages by telling the judge at the outset: "Your Honor, I'm not going to attempt to answer all the assertions and allegations made in the post-trial motion. As a matter of fact, I've not been able to finish reading the entire thing. I just scanned it." He said he remained confident that there was "no error that would be considered reversible" in the trial record.

A short while later, Judge Mosele denied the defense motion and Walch served notice of his intent to bring an appeal before the appellate court in Mount Vernon. Until the appeal was disposed of, Green would see none of the $3 million that a jury of his peers had decided to give him for his night in the county jail.

11

Give Him the Money

On April 28, 1980—four months after the denial of Walch's motion to reduce the $3 million verdict in the ne exeat case—Steve Cousley walked into a small room on the third floor of the city hall in downtown Granite City to watch the selection of the jury in the trial of Jim Green's libel suit against the *Telegraph*. Never, in the eleven years since the reporters had written their memo to the Justice Department in Washington, had Cousley thought this day would come and the libel case would actually go to trial.

Flashing back to the endorsement solicitation visit by Judge Chapman, there could be nothing reassuring in Steve's awareness that Charles W. Chapman, the trial judge, was now, unexpectedly, a lame-duck judge.

Having been appointed the previous November by the Illinois Supreme Court, at Justice Goldenhersh's bidding, to a vacancy on the Circuit Court, Chapman had run for nomination to a full six-year term. Much to everyone's surprise, he was defeated by Andreas Matoesian in the Democratic primary election the month before. Chapman had coughed up his $10,000 for the Democratic organization's support, only to lose at the polls. He would leave the bench and hang up his black robes at the end of November. During the primary campaign, the *Telegraph* gave its editorial endorsement to neither Chapman nor Matoesian, but did run news stories that were critical of Chapman's campaign promises to labor union audiences.

Until December, Judge Chapman would continue to preside in

the branch courtroom of the Circuit Court of Madison County across the city hall rotunda from the mayor's office. The steel mills, so vital to the city's economic well-being, are a few blocks away. A photo mural in the hall outside the courtroom depicts the fiery blast furnaces and other steelmaking scenes in this old soot-sprinkled community below the bluff. A plaque in the first floor lobby honors the memory of Granite City steel tycoon George W. Niedringhaus ("an employer of many . . ."). The courtroom is large enough for six rows of pewlike benches. On the side walls hang framed copies of the judge's code of ethics and the oath of admission to the bar, courtesy of the Madison County Bar Association.

Finding a lawyer to represent the *Telegraph* was not an easy task. Many of Alton's best known barristers—beginning with the newspaper's regular firm of Schlafly, Godfrey, Fitzgerald—discovered conflicts when they heard that Rex Carr would be on the other side. The policy of the libel insurers organized by the newspaper publishers association is to entrust local attorneys with the conduct of the trial while general counsel Tim Hanson is available for expert consultation in Washington.

While preparing earlier for the DeGrand case, the *Telegraph* finally came up with William M. Cox, whose offices were in East Alton, as the lead attorney, and Steve Cousley's brother-in-law, Charles Williamson of Belleville (Mary Lou Cousley's brother), as the backup technically representing the two reporters.

Bill Cox, fifty-seven, had settled a few minor libel problems for the *Telegraph* in the past but was not an experienced trial lawyer and had never tried a libel case of any kind for anyone. His father had been state's attorney in Calhoun County, a tiny, apple-growing county wedged between the Illinois and Mississippi rivers north of Alton and distinguished chiefly as the only county in Illinois that never had any railroad tracks. Bill flunked out of the University of Illinois and then out of Illinois College before joining the Navy Air Corps in 1942. Serving as a signal officer on an aircraft carrier, he caught bomb fragments in one leg and was hospitalized for nine months recovering. After the war, he graduated from Shurtleff College and in 1949 the Washington University Law School. One of his early accounts was as a lobbyist in Springfield for the chiropractors of Illinois. There is a rustic, folksy air about him which belies his three decades of experience in the Madison County politico-judicial system, which he, as most others, describes with the single word "peculiar." He drives a car with vanity license plates—B COX. A handsome man with shimmering blue eyes, his genial manner covers a hardened cynicism about how things get done in Metro East.

My first meeting with Bill Cox following the trial tells a lot about the bar culture in this region of confirmed suers. I stopped by his office wanting to talk about the *Telegraph* libel case, but he jumped up suddenly from his desk and reached into a corner for a bottle of wine sitting on the floor—"pure grape wine," the label said. It turns out that he had unsuccessfully defended a man in a particularly sordid rape case in an adjoining county. His defense had been that the rapist was so drunk he didn't know what he was doing. The defendant had been convicted and put away in the penitentiary, but Cox's heart was already in the next phase of the case. He pointed to the small print on the label, which indicated that the alcoholic content of the fortified wine was extremely high—about 18 percent. An obvious case of false labeling, said Cox, who was eagerly planning to sue the wine company on behalf of the convict's dependents, alleging that the misleading beverage was really responsible for the terrible things that had happened. Here in Madison County even defense lawyers get really excited thinking about suing people who have money.

The original plan had been for Cox to handle the DeGrand case defense and Charlie Williamson to be in charge of the Green case. Williamson made a good living defending insurance companies, but had never been associated with a libel case and would almost certainly not have been retained for this assignment had it not been for his Cousley family connection. In any event, the two lawyers switched roles and Cox took over the primary trial responsibility. Joe Melosi, volatile and undaunted as ever, did not like Cox's tactical planning and at one point, according to Cox, threatened to file a complaint with the bar association against Cox, which did not contribute much to the stability of the defense team on the eve of the trial. When it was all over, ANPA lawyer Tim Hanson said publicly on more than one occasion that the co-counsel were "not knowing in the field of libel and that hurt us."[1]

The trial itself is almost an anticlimax in most lawsuits. The questioning of witnesses, the dredging for evidence, the work of gathering depositions and "discovering" the facts had been going on in this case since the filing of DeGrand's suit by Dick Mudge.

In one of the early depositions, Paulie Cousley made this statement to Mudge:

"Mudge: Are you telling me that [Melosi] acted outside the scope of his authority when he wrote that letter to Mr. Conboy?"

"Paul Cousley: Let's put it this way. I think, if he had consulted us, we would have either suggested he not write it or write it in a less objectionable form, more purely inquiring than accusing."[2]

Although this was Paulie's view then and in some but not all of his later statements, it was not shared by Steve Cousley. Through all the years of turmoil, Steve never wavered in his conviction that Melosi and Lhotka had done nothing wrong trying to check the facts in a story which, if true, would have been news of importance to the people of Madison County. He never seriously considered the possibility of trying to appease the various plaintiffs with the publication of some sort of apology.

By now the investigation by the FBI and the Internal Revenue Service, which included the presentation of evidence to a federal grand jury in Springfield, had been concluded with no criminal indictments against Green or DeGrand. Albion Fenderson, senior vice president and general counsel of the Chicago Federal Home Loan Bank, wrote to Senator Stevenson's staff that his agency's files "contain no information which would substantiate any allegations in the local Alton press of any criminal conduct on the part of Mr. DeGrand."[3]

Embroiled in their own fight with Carr over the disposition of Green's properties, the FSLIC and FHLBB were not very enthusiastic about coming to the aid of the *Telegraph* in the libel case. Before the DeGrand case had been put on the shelf, lawyer Cox wrote to a FHLBB official in Washington complaining about the "bureaucratic wall of silence" and threatening to "contact Senator Percy and my good friend [Congressman] Melvin Price and see what leverage, if any, they can apply." A few days later, the Chicago bank promised to supply Fenderson, Eckert, Christie, and others as witnesses.[4]

Looking back much later, one of the top executives of the FSLIC in Chicago offered this retrospective view: "As far as these [federal] agencies were concerned it was the wrong case in the wrong court with the wrong lawyers. The *Telegraph* didn't realize the seriousness of its problem until it was too late. It was the wrong court because the state courts are subject to political influence. Carr was a master showman with political connections. We were very, very concerned."

The Cousleys may not have initially realized the seriousness of their problem, but they knew now that a loss to Green would be followed by demands for settlement or trial of the claims by DeGrand and the others. One of the other plaintiffs, Don Hazel, died in Springfield in 1979 at age forty-four. Pending libel actions die with the plaintiff in Illinois, so the Hazel suit was later dismissed. But the others were waiting in the wings.

Just before the trial was to begin, Cox wrote a letter to Carr requesting "a figure or demand of settlement"—lawyerese for "can we settle?"

Back came the reply:

My client James C. Green will settle his claim against the *Alton Telegraph* for the amount of insurance available, which I understand is $1,000,000.
                    Yours very truly,
                    Rx[5]

The thought of paying $1 million—the largest settlement ever of a libel suit in the United States—appalled the Cousleys. So Carr's proposition was quickly rejected. Any possibility of compromise disappeared. The preparations for the trial went on.

Like the managers who meet with the umpires at home plate before a game, the judge and the lawyers talk about the ground rules *in limine,* "at the outset" of a trial. Judge Chapman's preliminary rulings were both important and damaging to the *Telegraph*'s case. Cox and Williamson had decided that it would be fruitless to try to prove the truth of many of the allegations in the memo or to portray Green as an associate of dishonorable people. DeGrand instead was to be pictured as a moderately villainous figure who led the builder into precarious financial waters for his own ulterior motives.

The strategy of the defense was to show how Piasa had connived to sucker the inexperienced Green beyond the federal agencies' borrowing limits until he could not possibly keep his enterprise afloat. This would require showing that the FHLBB had good reason to stop the drainage of Piasa money into Green's operations. However, Carr argued, and Judge Chapman agreed, that the defense should be permitted to bring up only what happened before the date late in 1969 when Piasa imposed its voluntary restrictions on individual borrowing, thus turning off Green's supply of credit. The 1969 FHLBB audit could be mentioned, but not the 1970 audit. It was the 1970 audit that uncovered many of the straw party and other hidden loans to reveal, according to the federal agencies, that Green and his associates had exceeded the federal regulations. But Judge Chapman said the defense lawyers could not refer to the 1970 audit nor to letters from DeGrand to the FHLBB that tended to confirm Green's excessive borrowing.

To bring in what had become known after Green was deprived of additional loans from Piasa would, Carr contended, "unduly complicate this trial and make it extremely difficult for the jury to understand."

"Our whole case," Cox answered, "is that the lending practices and the loan concentrations" were the reason for the loan cutoff to Green. The piecing together of the facts of the relationship between Piasa and Green was, he maintained, an ongoing process that did not end when Christie's team departed Alton.

A second blow to the defense case occurred when the judge decided there could be no mention of the $3 million verdict in the ne exeat case or of any of the pending suits brought elsewhere by Green. If another jury in another courtroom decided that the false imprisonment and the foul deeds of the FSLIC and Illini Federal had been responsible for financial losses calculated by Green at $3 million, how, Cox asked, can the same plaintiff now turn around and offer an entirely different theory blaming the newspaper for the loss of the same $3 million? Still other lawsuits were pending in which Green accused the FHLBB of conspiring with Illini Federal to cheat Green out of his properties by improperly forfeiting the contracts. But Judge Chapman agreed with Carr that Cox should not be permitted to question Green about his inconsistent testimony in various of these proceedings. Time enough later, Carr remarked in the judge's chambers during the libel trial, to reconcile the various claims when they are actually collected.

In yet another crucial decision at the outset of the trial, the judge disposed of a complication for Carr by holding that, despite Illinois case law to the contrary, Green could collect damages suffered by a corporation, the James Green Construction Co.[6] The company had been a plaintiff in the original libel complaint until someone looked at an Illinois law that says a corporation cannot sue more than two years after it has been dissolved. "If the Court rules we're not entitled to damages on Jim Green's ownership of the corporation, you might as well dismiss the law suit," Carr told the judge, "because we have no damages except as how it affected his ownership and operation of the businesses." He need not have worried. Judge Chapman ruled in his favor.

Because the regular pool of prospective jurors had been emptied, the judge obtained the approval of the lawyers to use a special selection. The circuit clerk telephoned potential jurors on a list provided by the jury commission, ordering those who could be reached by phone to report for possible service on this specific jury.

By the time the twelfth juror was seated on the second day of questioning by the judge and attorneys, thirty-eight had been called into the courtroom. Three of the thirty-eight were college graduates, all schoolteachers, all excused by the exercise of one of Carr's challenges. None of the four from Alton, or three from East Alton, or two from Wood River were chosen for the jury. Four of those selected for the jury were from Granite City, one from Roxana (next to Wood River below the bluff), one from Edwardsville and one from Collinsville (above the bluff), and the other five were from the growing communities around Alton such as Bethalto (where some of Green's projects were built). Seven were men, five were women. Two of the twelve had not gone to high school, the others had. Four identified themselves as readers of the *Alton Telegraph*.

Apart from the legal issues, the comments during the questioning period could not have been very reassuring to the editors of the

Telegraph. A materials review engineer at McDonnell Douglas who was seated on the jury said, "the only thing I read is the sports and the funnies." A mother who worked part-time tending bar (and was not selected) said she bought a newspaper only during the school term and "strictly for the school lunch menus." Another woman who was excused said she read "the ads and the garage sales" in the *Telegraph*. "If I read it once a week, I'm lucky," remarked a teacher's wife who was excused by Carr. "I'll remember Ann Landers, and that's about it."

A coil blancher operator with an eighth grade education was excused by the judge after he responded to a question by speculating about the meaning of the First Amendment and its application to lawsuits against newspapers. However, the brother-in-law of Howard Steele, a partner in Granite Investment, had to be challenged by Williamson. Another defense challenge was used to excuse a man who said he "knew Mike Sasyk [the political leader who was a partner of Green's] well."

Among those chosen early for the jury were a Japanese war bride whose husband was a metallurgist at Granite City Steel; a retired welder at the Shell Oil refinery; two other McDonnell Douglas employees; a divorcee who supported her six children working in Papa Kay's pizza parlor in Bethalto; and a woman whose leukemia was in remission and who dozed through much of the trial.

The last two to be seated on the jury were Jerome Pragacz and Helen Toncoff, who lived within a few blocks of one another in Granite City not far from Green's Gaslight Walk apartments in the town of Pontoon Beach.

Jerry Pragacz, fifty, was the son of Polish immigrants who settled in St. Louis. His father was a foundry worker. As a boy Jerry dreamed of being a policeman. He joined a suburban St. Louis police department, worked himself up to the rank of chief before getting a job as a security officer at the General Motors plant in St. Louis. Except for the industrial fumes that foul the air and aggravate his bronchial asthma, Pragacz enjoys living in Granite City. He and his second wife Martha each have three children from previous marriages.

Until recently his wife had worked as a secretary in John Sobol's real estate office, two blocks from the Pragacz residence. When the judge heard this news, he said "oh" and went on to question the next person in the jury box. Cox and Williamson asked in more detail about the Sobol relationship, satisfying themselves, possibly because their preemptory challenges were running short, that Pragacz would be an impartial juror. Not only did Jerry Pragacz not subscribe to the *Telegraph,* but he told the judge he had "never heard of" that newspaper. He told me later that he was "not much of a reader of anything. My wife gets very upset with me. A lot of times we'll get something and it has to be put together. She says 'now make sure you read the instructions.' I tell her 'I'll put it together. I'll read the instructions when I get around to it.' I don't have time to read it. In fact I don't understand it when I do read it. About the most things I'll read in the newspaper is 'Ziggy,' the horoscope, some of the comic strips, and maybe a couple of the headlines. My wife gets the [St. Louis] *Globe-Democrat* in the morning and the *Granite City Press-Record.* I don't even look at 'em. The only thing I do is pick 'em up in the yard and bring 'em in here. I like to watch television for my news. I get all I want out of it. I watch Channel 2, that's my favorite one. They've got this gal who goes investigating this action stuff. A lot of that stuff wouldn't surface if they didn't dig into it. But they'll get a little carried away. I've had experiences when I was on the police department where they print what they want to write. You tell 'em the story, and they'll write it the way they want to. But I like to read the *National Enquirer.* A lot of people think it's junk, my wife for one. They call it a scandal sheet, but I like it."

The last to take her place on the jury was Helen Marcovsky Toncoff, sixty-one, wife of the Granite City High School football coach. Her father owned a grocery store in Granite City. She knew that Judge Chapman's wife was of Macedonian background, the same as her parents. John Toncoff, her husband, played professional baseball in the New York Giants organization before returning to Granite City as a coach in 1955. Helen worked for many years in the office at one of the junior high schools in town.

On each of the twenty-four days spread over the next six weeks,

Helen and Jerry sat side by side in the front row of the jury box listening to the evidence in *Green* v. *Alton Telegraph*. In the relatively drab lives of most of the jurors, the trial was an exciting interlude. People gaped at them as they were being shepherded about the city hall. By displaying a card marked "Official Juror" on the inside of their car windshields each morning when they returned, they could park at a meter without paying. Bailiffs looked after their needs. Cautioned not to talk about the case during the frequent prolonged interruptions while the lawyers were arguing points of law in the judge's chambers, the jurors necessarily became thoroughly acquainted with the families, jobs, medical histories, emotional hangups, miscellaneous interests, and even some of the moral values of their newfound comrades.

Judge Chapman did his part to enhance the social experience. He brought homemade sausage one morning for the jury's midmorning recess. Another day his wife baked a cake for the jurors. Through his culinary surprises, the judge shared their sense of togetherness.

A dreary gray pall drops over the industrial bottoms of Metro East in the winter months. Smoke from the mills and refineries clings close to the rooftops under the heavy cover of dark clouds. When it snows, the whiteness is quickly sullied. Spring is the most cheerful season in Granite City, and as the trial moved into May, the sun shone, the ice was gone from the river, the weather turned suddenly warm, the flowers began to bloom, and the downtown area put on its brightest face for the unlikely cast of characters assembled for this courtroom showdown.

Dapper in a blue double-knit polyester leisure suit, with his graying hair combed down over his forehead, Jim Green attended every session in the company of the new wife he had married a short time before. When the jurors were in the room, he appeared uncharacteristically subdued.

Steve Cousley, outwardly stoical, came every day too. Melosi and Lhotka had both left the employ of the *Telegraph* by now, though the Cousleys assured them that all their legal expenses would be borne by the newspaper. Melosi, who had undertaken several ventures, including the curious purchase of a minor league baseball franchise in Florida, fidgeted uncomfortably through the trial. Lhotka, still on the staff of the *Post-Dispatch,* did not have much of an appetite and lost twelve pounds by the time it was over.

Bob DeGrand attended almost every session, accompanied on the most crucial days of the trial by all nine of his children, including Robert, Jr., in his priestly attire.

Attorney Robert Patterson escorted the FHLBB-FSLIC delegation of witnesses from Chicago, led by Albion Fenderson and Ed Eckert. The Chicago contingent, which stayed at a top-rate hotel across the river in downtown St. Louis, arrived in Granite City thinking their role would be quick and simple, not knowing that Carr had them down as the villains in his script.

There were two notable absences on the list of witnesses. Neither side cared to subpoena the unpredictable Mac Christie, who had since successfully sued the FHLBB for discrimination in promotions. Nor did Carr call Dr. Pfeiffenberger as a witness. With the passing months and years, Mather Pfeiffenberger's anger at the Cousleys intensified until Carr probably was uncertain what his appearance on the witness stand would be like.

Before the opening statements by the lawyers, the judge told the jurors that they could not take notes. "It may seem a little unfair," he agreed, "but the rules of the Court forbid it and so you have to rely on what you hear." (Three years later, the state legislature passed a law requiring that Circuit Courts in Illinois permit jurors to take notes during a trial.)

In their opening statements, the opposing attorneys explain to the jury what the case is about and what they intend to prove, thus establishing the framework for the disjointed evidence that will follow.

Carr began by relating the story of Green's association with Piasa. Everything was going fine, he said, until the *Telegraph* published stories "calling Don Hazel a hoodlum and things of that sort . . . and challenging the propriety of financing somebody by the name of Don Hazel. Of course, there are no laws that say a man that has a police record is not entitled to own a home or apartment buildings or to get them financed."

He carried the narrative on through the FHLBB audit of 1969 at a time, he said, when Green was "operating at full blast through his companies and through associates, and he was successful in all his operations. He was working many, many hours a day to be successful."

"He had big things in the works," Carr continued, but after the federal audit "it was common knowledge in Alton that Piasa was being investigated because it had Mafia money in it."

Carr then read portions of the memo to the jury, interjecting at one point, "what a horrible thing to say."

Although evidence of lie detector tests is clearly inadmissible in Illinois, Carr went on to say: "He [Green] had been investigated by the FBI following these things that occurred in 1969. He took a lie detector test. He has been given a clean bill of health. He passed the lie detector test. His life has been and is an open book."

Cox did not object to the lie detector reference. When I asked Carr later about this, he said he knew that Cox would not do anything the jury would construe as an attack upon Green.

"This is the first opportunity we have had to face our accusers," Carr informed the jury. "The bad thing about aspects of this case that still affect us today is that some fine people say you should report suspicions to law enforcement agencies. I have heard it in this courtroom, and maybe in Nazi Germany. . . . They [Melosi and Lhotka] wanted to get a story for the newspaper and, therefore, they created a story to get a story. They wanted to put in the newspaper, because of the vendetta they have had against the Piasa Savings and Loan, that Piasa was being investigated. They wanted to get a story.

"Now, I don't have any problem in knowing that you are going to bring in a compensatory verdict for Jim Green because of what happened to him, and the dollars and cents are on paper. . . . You should (also) bring in a verdict for punitive damages, a substantial sum of money, to let the *Alton Telegraph* know and not just the *Alton Telegraph* but the rest of the newspaper world know that you shall not damage somebody facelessly. . . . I will ask you not just to restore to Jim that which was taken from him but to assess a verdict that will serve as a warning to others and to deter the *Alton Telegraph:* Don't do this again."

As if to confirm Carr's understanding of the defense strategy, Cox emphasized in his opening statement that the federal examiners found many irregularities, "but not a Mafia connection—not one sentence of that letter influenced the FHLBB to shut off credit to James Green."

"Much of Green's dilemma was caused by his domination by DeGrand and Wuellner. Jim Green is a nice guy. I like him. I have had hours in his company since these cases were filed. . . . You will see that Robert DeGrand misrepresented or concealed things from his own board."

Referring to "the corrupt management of Piasa," Cox said "they led Green down the primrose path."

As for the letter, once it was sent confidentially, it was out of the reporters' hands, the lawyer said, pointing out that the FBI investigation did not occur until 1973, four years later.

Williamson, in his brief opening, agreed that publication of a news story about the allegations in the memo would have been malicious. But the reporters had never met Green or DeGrand, had no reason to want to malign them in any way, and "I am sure you will conclude that if he is entitled to recovery from anyone it certainly is neither the *Telegraph* nor Mr. Lhotka nor Mr. Melosi."

That last remark raised some eyebrows in the FHLBB corner of the courtroom. The defense had embarked on a strategy of conceding Green's goodness and trying to show that DeGrand was responsible for the ruination of both Green and Piasa.

As the plaintiff's first witness, Green was questioned by Carr.

"Q—Now, Mr. Green, have you ever withdrawn any Mafia money from Piasa?"

"A—No."

"Q—Have you ever heard of any Mafia money, outside of this memo, being in Piasa?"

"A—On the streets . . . no."

He said he had never had any connection with Buster Wortman or Terry Thweatt, individuals named as gang figures in the memo.

"Q—Were you ever part of a criminal conglomerate flourishing unchecked in Madison County?"

"A—No."

"Q—Were you ever part of any criminal association or group at anytime, anyplace, anywhere?"

"A—No."

Green then recalled being present when Wuellner asked DeGrand: "Why do you worry about Jim Green so much?" He said DeGrand told him a short time later that "the old man thinks you're paying me off."

"Q—Tell me, Jim, in point of fact, had you ever given Bob DeGrand anything of value at any time in your years of association with him and Piasa?"

"A—Not one penny, never."

"Q—Did you ever offer anything?"

"A—Never."

He said FBI agents had questioned him several times, but "I took a lie detector test and passed it."

"Q—What did the FBI ask you about when they interviewed you?"

"A—About connections with DeGrand, with Hazel. They were very interested—did I have any money hidden in any bank accounts overseas; did I have any hidden trusts?"

"Q—What did they want to know about Don Hazel and you?"

"A—Whether or not he was backing me in any of my projects; whether he and I were in any hidden businesses and so forth."

"Q—What did they want to know about DeGrand?"

"A—Whether or not I had paid him any money; whether I had given him any kickbacks and such."

Green said he was also subpoenaed to appear before a grand jury in Springfield in late 1972 or early 1973.

"Q—What did they inquire of you there?"

"A—The same thing, about Hazel."

"Q—Did they ask you anything about whether or not you had any connections with the Mafia?"

"A—Yes."

"Q—Did they ask you about any improper connections with Bob DeGrand?"

"A—Yes. They were interested in the loans that Bob had made to me; whether they were proper loans; whether I had paid him any money."

"Q—Did you respond truthfully to those questions?"

"A—That is correct."

When the witness was turned over to Cox for cross-examination, the judge permitted Carr to interject frequently with corrections and other comments that muddled whatever it was Cox was trying to get at.

Green, for example, told Cox that "A little bit of a cold feeling" had developed toward DeGrand when the credit crisis occurred.

"Cox—Irritation?"

"Green—To a degree."

"Cox—Irritation to the extent that you distrusted . . ."

"Carr—He didn't say that."

"Green—Well, it agitated me a little bit, yes."

"Cox—You became aggravated with him?"

"Carr—He just said agitated."

"Green—I don't know to what degree of agitation you're talking about. I wouldn't have shot him, no."

Given the defense's theory of the case, Cox almost had to make some dents in the testimony of Carr's second witness—DeGrand. Except for bringing out the ownership by DeGrand and Wuellner's son of a separate credit insurance agency at Piasa which produced $25,000 a year of extra income for DeGrand and to which Piasa home mortgage customers were steered, Cox scored few significant points. It is not unusual for savings and loan executives to peddle credit insurance on the side. DeGrand denied that he had ever led Green down a primrose path. He said he was "110 percent positive" there was no Mafia money in Piasa. And he said the reason why he had not resisted more strenuously his removal from Piasa was that he had been "scared to death" by the reports of a Justice Department Investigation.

Again Carr objected constantly to Cox's line of questions. During one conference in the judge's chambers, the judge upheld Carr's objections and then Carr explained to Cox what the ruling meant.

In his own questioning of DeGrand, Carr maneuvered him into blaming the *Telegraph* for the loss of his job and a health hazard caused by the incompletion of a sewage lagoon at the Gaslight Walk apartments near Granite City.

The two reporters were then summoned as "adverse" witnesses by Carr. This exchange occurred with Lhotka:

"Q—Weren't you, in fact, Mr. Lhotka, sending this information to Mr. Conboy and Mr. Martin to get them to do the legwork of a reporter, that is to check on the facts in a story?"

"A—Yes sir, to some extent."

"Q—And weren't you sending it to them in the hope or in the expectation that if they checked it out and found any of the contents to be true that you would have an exclusive story?"

"A—Yes, most newspapers like to be first."

Adopting DeGrand in effect as honorary co-plaintiff, Carr asked Lhotka if he ever attempted to find out whether DeGrand was a religious man or whether DeGrand's son was a priest.

Melosi turned out to be a far more hostile witness. Carr asked him about an anonymous local contractor who he said had also told him about Piasa's preferential treatment of Green and Hazel.

"Q—Why don't you know [his name]?"

"A—Because I forgot it—on purpose."

"Q—You forgot it on purpose?"

"A—Yes sir."

"Q—You wiped that from your mind?"

"A—Yes, I did. I didn't want to endanger the man's life. He would have more to lose than me."

"Q—More to lose than Jim Green has lost?"

"A—Yes."

"Q—More to lose than the *Alton Telegraph* is going to lose?"

"A—Yes, his life."

"Q—Because Jim Green is connected with the Mafia?"

"A—It's possible."

"Q—Are you going to repeat that here today, Mr. Melosi?"

"A—I don't know."

A moment later, Carr said:

"You are a person skilled in the use of words. You know how Goebbels of the Nazi Party made the science of the big lie a real skill and a real science to repeat it so that people will believe the grossest kind of lie? The Nazis proved you could repeat the grossest kind of lie and people will believe it. You knew that. You learned that in journalism school, didn't you, sir?"

"No, I didn't," Melosi replied.

"You didn't learn that in journalism school? You did not learn how Goebbels manipulated the press in Germany to change an entire country's minds and attitudes?"

Once, when Melosi endeavored to explain a yes-or-no answer, Carr said: "I did not ask you 'because,' Mr. Melosi."

After Cox complained that the witness was entitled to explain his answer, Carr shot back:

"In a word, like hell he is, Mr. Cox. He's entitled to answer my question."

Robert Trone, the former assistant state's attorney who had been named by the reporters as another of their sources, recalled conversations with Demos Nicholas and Melosi about the two men's impressions that Hazel had a special connection at Piasa, but denied contributing any specific information to Melosi.

The next "adverse" witness—Paulie Cousley—stepped into the witness chair intent upon stonewalling Carr's assaults—with results adverse to his newspaper. He came through to the jury as a stubborn, crusty, curmudgeonly figure quite unlike the real Paulie.

He told Carr he knew DeGrand "because he lived about a block up the street from my parents for a long time. As a matter of fact, my father was a member of the [Piasa] board of directors that hired him."

"Was DeGrand's reputation, prior to 1969, that of a decent and honorable man?" Carr wanted to know.

"When you're talking about a decent and honorable man, you're talking about a rare specimen."

A minute later, Carr inquired whether Paulie knew Dr. Pfeiffenberger well enough to ask him "a few frank questions" on the phone.

"Well, like I say," replied Cousley, "all my sisters and his sisters kind of grew up together. I never felt that I could call on Math for any personal advice or anything unless I needed some with regard to my health."

"You knew that [Melosi and Lhotka] were working on a particular story that involved Piasa?" he was asked.

"That's the catch," he answered. "I didn't. I just barely had a few hints of it."

Carr made the most of the different statements Paulie had made in different depositions about the authorization for the reporters' memo. In one of the statements, he said he "was naturally dependent upon my reporters to do that part of the work" and his knowledge of the Piasa inquiry "made me regret deeply that they [Piasa] were headed for any kind of trouble."

At the trial, this exchange occurred:

"Q—When these reporters wrote to Mr. Conboy, they were working for the *Telegraph,* weren't they, sir?"

"A—I wouldn't characterize it as such, no."

"Q—They were working under [the editors'] control and direction, weren't they, sir?"

"A—How much control and how much direction was used, I'm not sure."

"Q—I'm not sure, either, Mr. Cousley. They were in fact so working, weren't they, sir?"

"A—Theoretically, sure."

Steve Cousley, who came next, said the reporters were acting "fully and completely" as employees of the *Telegraph*.

As assistant to the publisher, he said he knew of the "ongoing investigation" but did not know about "the specifics of writing the Justice Department."

"Q—And they of course had the authority to write the letter to the Justice Department?"

"A—We didn't have any rules that said you can't write to someone."

"Q—Was it the belief in the Alton community that [Piasa] had the reputation of being tied in with the underworld before August, 1969?"

"A—Yes sir."

"Q—Now, upon what basis did the community come to that belief?"

"A.—There were rumors afloat in the community for several years."

"Q—And from whom did you hear those rumors?"

"A—Real estate people, savings and loan people."

"Q—Could you name those people?"

"A—No sir, I don't remember."

"Q—When did you first hear that?"

"A—May I tell you how my understanding evolved, or do you really want to know?"

He then said he had first heard it in the mid-1960s. "The Hazel information was about in the community and had been for several years."

"Q—What did you do about ascertaining whether or not the information was true?"

"A—I covered stories relating to Don Hazel that broke in the courthouse."

"Q—What else did you do?"

"A—I don't know what else."

"Q—Did you call anybody at Piasa to ask them about the truthfulness of the story?"

"A—No sir."

Later, the eyes of most of the jurors glazed over while the plaintiff tried to reconstruct the financial losses he claimed to have suffered because of the memo sent by the reporters to a Justice Department attorney, after which:

the statements in the memo were relayed to the FHLBB in Washington and

then to the FHLBB in Chicago; and the Chicago examining team investigated the allegations as part of its annual audit of Piasa; and

the federal auditors found lending practice irregularities, but no evidence of the allegations in the memo; and

Piasa's board reacted to the FHLBB report by prohibiting loans of more than $1 million to one borrower; and

Green was unable to borrow more money from Piasa because he already owed almost $4 million; and

his inability to obtain additional loans caused him to fall farther behind on his existing mortgage payments and his enterprise to collapse.

Listening in the jury box, unable to take notes, jurors with a far greater financial background than the twelve good and true citizens on this jury would have been hard put to make sense of the bits and pieces of financial damage evidence.

Green claimed the following damages:

1. Profits of $3,431,000 from the sale of seven real estate developments that were either partially completed (as in the case of Gaslight Walk, where 400 of the 900 planned units were finished) or he said were planned for the future;

2. His equity in properties financed by Piasa estimated at $1,621,000;

3. Savings accounts pledged to Piasa as security for the Green loans and applied to his debts under the Base Agreement—$933,000;

4. Injury to his reputation worth $1,000,000.

Total actual damages: $7,045,000.

On May 9—after nine days—Carr rested the plaintiff's case. The first phase of the trial had not gone well for the newspaper. Green and DeGrand weathered the cross-examination without significant harm. Melosi and Paulie Cousley were belligerent witnesses. The reporter appeared nervous, fidgety, uncomfortable; the publisher had been unwilling, quite simply, knowingly to utter one word that could conceivably be of comfort to his inquisitor.

Later, when it was over, juror Jerry Pragacz offered these observations:

About Green—"He was being honest."

About DeGrand—"A beautiful person. He was an honest man. You could tell he was hurt. Being a big executive of a firm and then lose your job overnight and not know why."

About Paulie—"The old man was very arrogant. He impressed me as saying, 'let's get all this bullshit out of the way and get it over with.' Like, 'you guys are wrong and I'm right.'"

About Melosi—"I look at it . . . if a guy can't look you square in the eyes he's not to be trusted. And his eyes were shifting around all the time. That's my personal feeling. Even when he talked to his attorney he would turn his eyes. Just didn't impress me one bit."

The next phase would be crucial. Cox's job for the defense would be somehow to convince the jury that Green's business had been a mess, DeGrand had irrationally kept pouring Piasa's money down a hole, and the FHLBB had been justified in doing what it did, even if the Mafia money question had never arisen.

His key witness, to this end, was the senior vice president and chief operating officer of the Federal Home Loan Bank in Chicago, the visibly aristocratic Albion Fenderson.

Fenderson's father and grandfather were small town county seat lawyers in northern Maine. After answering the call to service in the Air Force (as a photographer), Al Fenderson wrote to the Harvard Law School and asked if he could enter with only three prewar undergraduate years at the University of Maine. For a veteran, Harvard was willing to waive its regular eligibility rules. Upon his admission to the bar, Fenderson returned to Maine to practice in a small town. Two years later, the big textile mill in town fled to the lower labor costs in the South, crippling the local economy and inspiring the young lawyer to leave New England. After three years at the Justice Department, litigating the claims of foreign nationals who were trying to recover property that had been seized during the war, he joined the FHLBB as a lawyer in 1956. In 1964, Fenderson moved to Chicago as general counsel and second in command of the bank there.

Bob Patterson, the attorney in the FSLIC's years of litigation on the Green matter, helped Cox prepare the savings and loan aspects of the case and conferred with Fenderson, Eckert, and the others from Chicago about their testimony. But, sitting in the tiny courtroom as Fenderson took the stand, Patterson knew all too well that Rex Carr had, by his own estimate, devoted the better part of one-third of the last eight years to familiarizing himself with the details of the federal agencies' actions in the Piasa-Green affair.

As it turned out, Fenderson was on the stand for nine grueling days. Fenderson told Cox that he had noted the unusual concentration of loans at Piasa but attached no particular significance to it before the 1969 audit. He repeated the agencies' critical concern about the alleged overappraisals of Green's properties and what he described as the "bootstrapping" process whereby pledged savings accounts made it possible for Green to keep on borrowing without putting much or any of his own money in a project.

This exchange then occurred:

"Cox—Did [anything] in the letters [from FHLBB officials in Washington] have any effect on the supervisory action that was taken by you in regard to Piasa in 1969?"

"Fenderson—None whatsoever."

"Cox—Can you explain that, please."

"Fenderson—Once it was reported that examiners had found nothing to substantiate any of the allegations made in these documents, then the matter was not considered by me any further. It had nothing to do with further action."

Cox tried to bring in correspondence between DeGrand and the FHLBB after 1969 that appeared to show that loans made secretly to Green in the names of others (and not discovered previously by the auditors) had raised Green's loans beyond the legal limit, but the judge enforced his order barring such evidence.

At one point in Carr's cross-examination, he made a mistake by phrasing a question: "No examiner or no examination report *ever* found that Piasa had violated the lending limitations relating to one borrower . . . isn't that correct, sir?"

"It was established in later reports," Fenderson replied, "that in fact they had . . ."

Carr tried to stop him, and Williamson said: "Rex, you asked him that. . . . The question was asked and he is entitled to answer it."

For Carr, it was a rare slip. Judge Chapman hastened to the rescue by saying: "Mr. Carr, would you rephrase your question?"

Out of the jury's hearing, Williamson complained to the judge at the bench: "I don't think the Court has an obligation, nor do I think it has the right, to correct any error in questioning of the cross-examiner . . ."

Even before then, Carr and the witness had been locked in tense combat. Fenderson's upper New England twang and his severe Ivy League gray flannel appearance made him a prop for Carr's sarcasm.

Early on, Fenderson complained that "you are not letting me answer the question."

"You are a lawyer, aren't you, a Harvard grad?" Carr responded.

"And you should give me an opportunity to answer," the witness said.

"You are a Harvard grad, aren't you?"

"Yes."

While the jurors looked on with amusement, the attorney from East St. Louis then proceeded to deliver a short lecture to the "Harvard grad" on proper courtroom procedures.

Whatever civility existed between the two professionals at the start soon disappeared. Here was a typical exchange:

"Q—When you made decisions relative to these associations worth millions and millions of dollars, you used the same knowledge that you have exhibited here today, or the same lack of knowledge, haven't you, sir?"

"A—No sir."

"Q—You have not?"

"A—No sir."

"Q—You used some greater knowledge?"

"A—No sir, I used my knowledge, not my lack of knowledge."

Later, Fenderson reiterated, "I can state very decisively that I was not in any way influenced by the allegations [in the memo] that had been proven, as far as we were concerned, to be unfounded."

On May 20, Fenderson's fifth day of cross-examination, Carr suddenly turned to the bench and said:

"Your Honor, Mr. Patterson continues to signal the witness!"

From his seat in the courtroom, Patterson said: "Your Honor, I have not . . ."

"Again, I know he is," Carr interrupted. "I saw you this time. It has been reported to me by other people that you have been signaling the witness. I have seen the witness look to you for direction."

Judge Chapman recessed the trial and summoned the lawyers to his chambers. Patterson insisted he had done nothing of the kind.

"That is a damned lie," Carr exclaimed.

Patterson then accused Carr of deliberately misleading the jury and "browbeating my client to death."

"Mr. Patterson, respectfully, butt out," Carr suggested.

"No, I'm not going to butt out," Patterson said. "My responsibility is to my client. I would like you to respond."

"My response is: Go to hell, butt out, get lost, disappear, quit screwin' up the law suit!"

Williamson and Cox moved for a mistrial because of the exchange in the courtroom, a motion denied by the judge.

A little later, back in the courtroom, Carr asked Fenderson to explain the FHLBB criteria for evaluating the propriety of construction loans.

After Fenderson answered, Carr said:

"Your Honor, the witness is absolutely lying to me."

Another time, in the presence of the jury, Carr said:

"Mr. Fenderson is now lying, Your Honor."

Each time, the lawyers for the defense moved for a mistrial.

Arguing against the second motion in the judge's chambers, Carr said: "If I was the judge, the witness would be in jail now. I'm not going to point a finger at the judge. He's a calm, dispassionate figure in the courtroom and he remains so. I don't think either side should criticize him for being calm and dispassionate, and not being dramatic. The last thing we want in this case is a dramatic, upstaging judge."

The calm, dispassionate judge bid the trial continue, which it did.

One of the jurors, Helen Toncoff, as a girl working in her father's grocery store in Granite City, learned six languages indigenous to the neighborhood, one of them being Polish. Each morning when they took their places in the jury box, Jerry Pragacz greeted her in Polish with "Good morning, how are you?" and she answered in Polish. Toward the end of Fenderson's testimony, he would mutter to her, under his breath but loud enough for her to bear, in Polish, "you liar, you liar, just a bunch of lies." Long after the trial was over, I asked Jerry Pragacz for his recollections of that portion of the experience.

"The one I really got aggravated with was this guy from the FHLBB [Fenderson] and the cheating—he was getting signals from another attorney that was sitting out there. To me, as a law officer, I—he impressed me that he was making a mockery of the court system. . . . The attorney caught him at it, and put a blackboard to block his view. I thought, this was an educated man, a scholar. I meant he went to Yale and he bragged on how intelligent he was, and I sat there and I says, man, if that's what intelligence is, I'm glad I'm stupid. And, really, I think all the jurors felt the same. We were starting to get aggravated at that, because it was the same—I mean, I don't have the education that a lot of people have. But I know common sense, that when you say 'hypothetical question,' which means it doesn't exist, and this guy would try to make a real big deal of this and try to make this guy [Carr] look like a dummy, you know. The first day it was okay. The fifth day you start getting sick of the guy. In fact, I didn't even want to listen to him, but I had to. And I think everybody was starting to think like that. That was the biggest highlight. This guy was supposed to be so intelligent and just trying to make a mockery of the court. And the judge would tell him, you do this, and he would just make like a fool out of the judge, and I thought to myself several times, if I was judge I'd slap you in contempt of court I don't know how many times."

I asked Helen Toncoff if she remembered the signaling incident.

"That was very dramatic," she said. "That was just for excitement. And, you know, the others believed it, that this lawyer was sending signals to the witness. Jerry would say, 'Look at the signal!' Mr. Carr knew exactly what to do and when to do it, to fool some of the jurors. But I wasn't fooled all the time—some of the time but not all the time."

What happened after Fenderson was anticlimax. Eckert admitted that the allegations in the memo might have been "in my mind psychologically" when the federal agencies came to have their serious reservations about Piasa's lending practices. Carr, who had him tied in knots by the end of the testimony, accused Eckert in the presence of the jury of "getting together with these lawyers for the *Alton*

Telegraph" and "manufacturing" or "concocting" definitions for real estate lending practice evaluations.

John Hackmann, the Illini Federal official, also appeared for the defense. By now, having participated in the five-week ne exeat trial, he and Carr knew one another's lines thoroughly.

Cox was getting tired. When Green and DeGrand were recalled for a second set of direct examination questions, Cox's cross-examination was faltering. Carr would interrupt to correct details in his questions while the judge looked on benignly. Once, when Cox became irritated at the interruptions, Carr, still full of himself, said: "All right, go ahead and foul it up," and Cox asked him kindly to "let me fumble my way through this."

For the final act—the closing arguments by the attorneys—all the members of the DeGrand family were seated in the front row of the courtroom. Carr began by telling the jurors that the jury system has historically been a bulwark against injustice. "We know you'll bring forward and put in this case the sum of your experiences, and we know that it will be a just result. History has taught us that." He said the function of the jury is to act as the conscience of the community. "You have got to use your own observation and experience in the affairs of life."

If the memo was sent only to report what the newspeople thought was a crime, then, Carr conceded, it was a privileged communication. But if they sent it "for their own purposes, their own wants, their own interests," then he said it was not privileged. He argued that the reporters sent the memo for the purpose of getting a story. "They wanted the Justice Department to do their legwork for them." The key to the entire trial, Carr informed the jury, was—did they have reasonable grounds to believe it was true? "They knew exactly what was going to happen when they sent that memo. They did not bring in a single witness to show the truth of the accusations," he asserted, adding that their identification of their sources was "manufactured out of whole cloth."

"We have seen witnesses here, Mr. Fenderson and Mr. Eckert and Mr. Hackmann, all of whom have been brought in to help the *Alton Telegraph*. Conferences day and night about the best way to defeat this action, and what did they do? They concocted the story, 'Well, we will stand up on this witness stand and swear that we were not influenced by the charges against Jim Green, which as far as we were concerned, were true, these charges that Jim Green is the worst kind of hoodlum.'

"Now, that is their defense, and their defense is one made, I daresay, of chicanery and out-and-out falsehoods.

"What a difference it would have made in this case, in the life of the DeGrand family, the Green family and Wuellner family if they had made it public. It took years of agony of the DeGrands and the Greens not knowing why this happened.

"They destroyed Piasa. They destroyed DeGrand. They destroyed Wuellner, and in a sense they damaged this community. Up until that time, this side of the river was getting multiple buildings. . . . What do we have today? Building after building vacant and boarded up, no sewage plant for the people who live there. A swimming pool that hasn't been used. All because of that memo. . . . The damage was done to this community—no modern theater in Granite City—no Lake of the Seven Fingers for people to live in. None of those things have happened since this happened to Jim Green.

". . . Any kind of investigation would have proven [the memo] false. Call up DeGrand and ask about it. Call up Jim's subcontractors. Call up his schoolteacher. Call up his pastor. Call up any of his business associates."

Carr then chalked up on the blackboard in front of the jury box the separate figures in his damage claim, including the $3,500,000 requested for punitive damages.

Williamson, beginning for the defense, talked of the climate of opinion in the community in 1968 and 1969 and the interest in labor racketeering. He said the reporters received the information from law enforcement sources who had been reliable in the past. "Where do you go? You don't go to Jim Green and say, 'Hey, Jim Green, are you part of the Mafia?' You don't go to Bob DeGrand and say, 'Mr. DeGrand, is there Mafia money in your association?' You don't just go up to somebody and say, 'Hey, are you a hoodlum or not?' And you don't put it in the newspaper. They took the information to the federal government in good faith with reasonable grounds to think it was true. Isn't the memo asking a question rather than making a statement?

He finished by quoting Benjamin Franklin: "If you had to be absolutely certain that whatever you said or printed would not offend anybody, very, very little would be printed."

Cox then took over for the defense. "It has been a long five and a half weeks," he said. "You have been tremendous. I hope you've enjoyed yourself."

He concentrated his remarks on DeGrand's "Song of Lorelei" to Green's "Ulysses." "He [DeGrand] told Green, 'Come on in and bring your friends, I'll make you rich. You give me your business and we will build you up."

"We hope by your verdict you will ensure that reporters have a right to investigate, have a right to attempt to verify, have a duty to verify before they publish a story. That is what the reporters in this case tried to do. And if we are going to have a free press in Madison County, it will have to be because people such as yourselves believe in it and will insist upon it."

The plaintiff's lawyer had the final crack at the jury.

"They malign the unions of this country," Carr said, picking up on Williamson's reference to labor racketeering. "They brand the unions as associates of hoodlums, unions made up of honest, hard working people in this country. All of you know people who are members of those unions that are decent and honorable people.

"What reporter worth his salt isn't capable of going out and doing the legwork necessary to decide whether Jim Green was or was not a hoodlum? It's not just reckless disregard of the truth. It is a horrible, appalling lack of absolute sensitivity to the rights of anybody, including you and including me, because we could be the victims next if this goes on.

"Both the Cousleys approved this kind of action, and that's the reason this punitive verdict is important in this case. You have to teach them that that isn't the American way, the American system of justice.

"He [Cox] says, in effect, that you should believe what [Fenderson and Eckert] say without question and without examination because these men are in high positions. Well, I want to remind you that their role in this took place in 1969, and it was only three years later that we had Watergate. Men in the very highest positions of our government, the very highest position, some of them, the Attorney General, the man over the Justice Department, went to the penitentiary. The very highest men in our government are capable of being corrupt. Corruption is not something that just afflicts you and me. It afflicts the highest as well as the lowest. If you accept Fenderson's testimony without question because he is the president of a $3.8 billion corporation, then the jury system is dead, and properly so."

"You may decide," he told the jury, "that the sin they have committed, as demonstrated in this courtroom for the past five and a half weeks, is so great that it may take $10 million to punish and serve as a deterrent. You decide what you think it's going to take to teach these people that have not learned their lesson what they should do in this case."

He said the "high officials" of the *Telegraph* were guilty as sin for "covering this up until they thought they were free—and you know how it came loose—their greed for another story, that's how it was exposed."

An irresponsible and unregulated press "is as much a horror to our society as the Gestapo or the KGB," Carr said. "Bring in your verdict because you want a free press, because if you don't punish this particular newspaper for their wrongs, then you set an example to the free press, and some other newspaper may say, 'Well, *Alton Telegraph* got away with it. Let's write some stories about somebody we maybe think something bad about.'

"Now, you know there's something I want to tell you and you've got to know it. The DeGrand family is waiting. The Wuellner family is waiting, and the Green family—Mrs. Green has waited here every day that you've been here. She's been waiting silently and she wants vindication. You know the city of Granite City is waiting also. They want to know the truth of what happened. They want to know the truth of this situation. There's also other people waiting. The Federal Home Loan Bank Board is waiting in Chicago, and the

Telegraph is waiting. They're waiting to see if they can get away with it, can they swing it by what they've done here with the testimony of these people, by the signaling of the attorney to the witnesses, by the conferences in the late hours, by making up new definitions, by not bringing in witnesses that have knowledge of the facts. They're waiting to see if they can get away with it, too.

"Ladies and gentlement, this is the only day in court that Jim Green will have, the only opportunity that you'll have or that any jury will have to rule on this set of facts. It's the only time that you'll have the ability or anybody will have the ability to right the wrongs that were done Jim Green.

"We now leave it in your hands to right the wrongs. I've done my job."

On this, the last day, Judge Chapman also delivered his crowning culinary contribution—a steaming vat of delicious bouillabaisse, a highly seasoned fish chowder, for lunch. According to all reports, the gourmet judge outdid himself. His homemade bouillabaisse was stupendous. The jurors lunched in the jury room; the judge, bailiffs, lawyers, and parties to the suit in another room.

All that remained before the case went to the jury was for the judge to instruct the jury on the points of law that must be followed. In any libel trial, because of the complexity of the legal precedents, the instructions are crucial.

Cox and Williamson had maintained that any report to a prosecutor of possible criminal conduct was protected against a defamation suit by an absolute common law privilege, regardless of motives. The judge had, of course, rejected that position before the trial began, and he did so again now.

He chose instead this conditional privilege explanation:

"The communication in question may be conditionally privileged, if the essential elements are present, even though it is not true and even though it charges a crime:

"—good faith by the defendants.

"—an interest or duty to be upheld.

"—a statement limited in its scope to that purpose.

"—a proper occasion.

"—and publication in proper manner and to proper parties only.

"Defendants must have believed in the truth of the communication or had reasonable grounds for believing the communication to be true."

The judge's other instructions advised the jury that damages could be awarded for lost future profits; the newspaper could be held liable even if the FHLBB and/or Piasa had also caused an injury to Green; and "if you believe that justice and the public good require it [you may] award plaintiff an amount which will serve to punish the defendants and to deter others from the commission of like offenses."

At 5:00 P.M. on Tuesday, June 3, the eighty documentary exhibits—which included forty 50-page examination reports—and which could have been inscribed in sanskrit for all they meant to the jurors—were piled on the table. Everyone left the courtroom but the members of the jury. Instead of adjourning to a separate room, the jury used the courtroom for its secret deliberations.

If the newspaper editors and their lawyers had been aware of the number of jurors who brought pocket calculators with them on the last day, they quite possibly would have headed for the nearest Granite City tavern to await the judgment of the jury.

After suggesting a couple of others who begged off, the jurors elected Jerry Pragacz as their foreperson. What to do next? Uncertain, they sent an inquiry to the judge: What do we do now? The bailiff brought back his reponse: you've heard all the facts, you've got all the forms, all the records, all the evidence, now it's up to you to make a decision.

Everyone started talking at once. It soon appeared that everyone wanted Jim Green to get something. But how much? There were vast differences of opinion on that score. Some of the jurors were thinking big—very big. Others were thinking small—relatively small.

Just then, somebody said: "Hell, let's go eat."[7]

Arrangements were made for their one and only free meal outside the courthouse, taken in a private room at a cafeteria three blocks up the street.

Their courtroom was to be used for a meeting of the local city council that evening, so the deliberations resumed in a downstairs traffic courtroom when the jurors returned.

Give Him the Money   145

Now the pocket calculators began humming. The jurors talked awhile, submitted their proposed figures on unsigned sheets of paper, haggled some more, and repeated the process.

"Aren't we supposed to be going over this?" asked Mrs. Toncoff, pointing to the stack of documents on a table.

"Forget it, they're guilty," said the foreperson.

"Don't need it," someone else said. "Give it to him. They did him dirty. Give him the money."

As the discussion continued, two poles of opinion developed.

Pragacz and Mary Alice Gold, the pizza restaurant waitress from Bethalto, settled firmly on $20 million—$10 million in actual damages (which exceeded the $7,045,000 requested) and $10 million in punitive damages. Good round numbers.

Helen Toncoff and the Japanese-American woman, Alice Halbrook, thought that was absurdly high, particularly the punitive damages.

"The punitive damages go to the school district anyhow," somebody piped up.

Helen Toncoff was quite sure that was not true, but there were several on the jury who believed erroneously that the award for punitive damages would be paid not to Green but to some public body.

Where did they get the mistaken idea that the punitive damages would not benefit Green?

"I don't know," Pragacz said later. "With twelve people talking, you come up with some silly ideas. I said I don't care who gets it, the damages were done and I think this figure should be thrown out to the public. When that lady [Mrs. Toncoff] said don't you think that's a lot of money, I said, well, if it's me, I want $10 million."

"My contacts are killing me," complained the man who had explained about the school district and punitive damages. "Let's go home, let's give him the money, let's quit."

Was there any discussion of where all this money would come from? I asked Mrs. Toncoff later.

"Oh, they said, the paper's loaded, they're rich."

Mrs. Gold became irritated at Mrs. Toncoff's intransigence, and the two quarreled.

"Hey, save it for later," demanded the foreperson. "We'll either stay here until we come to [an agreement] or we'll go out there and tell the judge we can't make a decision."

"We're going to have to agree, you know," Mrs. Halbrook whispered to Mrs. Toncoff.

The others were strongly in favor of a figure less than $20 million, but still sizable.

Finally, after four and one-half hours of deliberation, they all agreed to the figures Foreperson Pragacz then wrote on the verdict form:

"We, the jury, find for the plaintiffs and against the defendants. We assess the plaintiffs compensatory damages in the sum of $6,700,000. We assess the damages by way of punishment and deterrence in the sum of $2,500,000."

A total of $9.2 million.

At 10:10 P.M., the judge read the verdict in the open courtroom, then asked each of the jurors individually, by name, "Is this your verdict?"

They all said it was. The trial was over. Judge Chapman thanked the jury for its service in what he said was the longest jury trial in the history of Madison County.

Rex Carr had left after the closing arguments for a vacation in the Caribbean, but many of Green's friends were there to congratulate him.

Green asked the judge if he could shake the hands of the jurors, which he did.

He also shook hands with Steve Cousley, who told him: "This round is yours."

Walt Sharp, the *Telegraph* reporter who covered the long trial for the newspaper, had gone home in the evening.

In a state of semishock at the size of the verdict, Steve pulled out his pencil and notebook and commenced interviewing the jurors for what would, sadly, be a very big story in the next issue of the *Alton Telegraph*.

Jerry Pragacz, for one, did not welcome the questioning from the defendant. "Here's the guy who was the defendant and he's got his pad and he's going to write a story," Pragacz said later. "Well, that just turned me off."

Juror Harold Rhodes said the deliberations had been "more or less like a union negotiation, averaging the figures we'd seen."

"There was no doubt that the man [Green] was completely ruined, no doubt in anyone's mind," commented another juror, Harold Wagner, the retired Shell Oil worker. "The only question was how much to give him. If you saw what he had before, it [the $9.2 million] may not have been enough."

Juror William H. Imel was tired and wanted to go home. He knew he had to get up at 4:45 the next morning to return to his job at McDonnell Douglas. "It was a hard decision to make," he said. "We took several ballots."[8]

Melosi had gone home early. Lhotka called him on the phone with the news. "Well, Joe," he said for starters, "it looks like we're going to be working for Rex Carr the rest of our lives."

Stunned and still not sure he could believe what had happened, Steve Cousley strolled with Cox and Lhotka to a Dunkin Donuts shop up the street from the courthouse. They sipped coffee for two hours while Cox tried to assure the editor that the verdict would be reversed on appeal.

At 5:00 A.M. Melosi woke Lhotka with a phone call inquiring what he had meant by the remark about working for Rex Carr in the rest of their lives.

In Wood River, the marquee on a neighborhood tavern read:

"Congrats, Jim. Screw you, *Alton Telegraph*."

The next day, a reporter for the Granite City paper reached Carr by telephone. Carr said he was thrilled by the verdict more for De-Grand than for Green. "Jim actually was a success but he never lived as a success and this really did not affect his life style as much as it did DeGrand's. After all this happened, for a long period of time, DeGrand could not even get a job. His wife had to go to work [for the Alton public library]. They had to find a way to put their kids through college and he has been fighting this battle for years. . . . I consider this verdict a complete justification of our jury system, if it needs a justification. The jury was tremendous."

He also said he considered Chapman a "tremendously outstanding judge."[9]

Bill Cox told the *National Law Journal* he was shocked by the outcome. "I imagine if you were in my shoes you'd say in relief that you don't have to pay it [the judgment]," he said, "but you sure sweat for your client. I tell you, it's a nightmare. The jury was incensed."[10]

Still in awe of his opponent in the proceedings, Cox described Carr as "a superb performer, articulate, skilled, a fantastically clever lawyer."

Several years later, when I asked Carr about the caliber of the defense in the case, he said: "There is no conceivable way any lawyer could have won their side of the case. These guys could not be hoodlums, either Green or DeGrand. I had two straightforward witnesses. Paul Cousley wouldn't say anything good about anyone. Melosi wouldn't say the same thing twice the same way. There's no question Jim was a flying-high contractor the day before the [FHLBB] exam came down. It was a lay-down case, so to speak. The whole defense came down to a legal issue—that of privilege—which was for the court and not the jury to decide."

At about the same time, I asked Jerry Pragacz for his afterthoughts.

"To me it was a big experience. As a former policeman I had never expected to serve on a jury. But the judge said this was not a criminal case, so it makes no difference. It was kind of a thrill. Then I got kind of scared—am I going to be able to handle this? So then it was a challenge. I enjoyed it. It was five and a half weeks, and it was super.

"To start with, I didn't know nothing about what they were talking about. I had never heard of the *Alton Telegraph* or Piasa Federal, which I guess was good. They said Mr. Green was accused of being hooked up with the Mafia, you know. Well, this kind of interested me, and I got to thinking this must be criminal because the Mafia is criminal. After I started learning more about it, then I saw that it wasn't criminal as far as the case itself was concerned. So, after you get into it you start wondering 'this could happen to me, or somebody I know.'

"What I thought was really important when we got down to the really nitty-gritty stuff is Mr. Green's character being torn apart like it was. To be accused of such a crime—I know the Cousleys, who owned the company, knew what was going on because these reporters worked for them. And then the reporters still didn't have enough, they go to Mr. DeGrand and tell him, 'Hey, we're going to tell you how we closed up this place,' like this is a big deal, you know, nothin' to it. And then they give him the memo, which I thought was stupid on their part. Now I don't know whether there was something in the minds of these two reporters, whether they were just trying to make a name for themselves or get a big story and get a big bundle of money out of this, or they were jealous of Mr. Green or what. But something must have triggered them off—and then there's a lot of money involved. You see a guy who worked all his life, even though he's a young guy, to lose everything, you start to thinking, hey, this could happen to me or somebody else because of this silly stuff. Maybe the reporters didn't think it was silly, I don't know. But nevertheless here's a company that got closed down and Mr. Green got hurt. That's the way, after the whole shootin' match was over, that's the way we evaluated it.

"I can't remember who it was, but somebody said this [case] would be in the lawbooks all over the country. And would probably make history. Because the money came up. It was supposed to be one of the largest awards given for a case like this. I don't remember where it came from, but it was going to be a big deal and would probably appear in law libraries and they'd be citing other cases on this and everything else, you know—that we were kind of lucky to be chosen on that jury . . ."

He said his wife had kept a scrapbook of the news stories so their grandchildren could share the memories.

And what impressions is Helen Toncoff left with?

"It still bothers me how a verdict can be reached from a memorandum that never did appear in the paper. Mr. Carr is not only a top attorney but also a terrific actor. I saw through a lot of the things he was saying, but you couldn't convince the others, except for Mrs. Halbrook. A lot of the jurors had a hard time in life. They just felt like—well, they didn't look at one piece of evidence, one exhibit. Guilty, the *Alton Telegraph* was guilty. They just pushed it [the exhibits] aside.

"Mr. Cox was a very likable person, but he couldn't compare with Mr. Carr, who had a photographic mind. He was a fantastic actor and lawyer. They [the *Telegraph*] should have had a top lawyer. Mrs. Gold didn't like it one bit because Mrs. Halbrook and I held out. But we didn't want to give him $20 million. That's ridiculous. She really got mad. I thought $20 million was entirely too much. I thought $9.2 million was entirely too much. It's just too much money.

"Afterward I felt sorry for the Cousleys. Next time I'll be a lot wiser. I didn't know you could hold out. I just didn't know. I'd never been a juror before, and I didn't know what to expect or what to do. But I was in for a great shock. Every time I see his [Green's] name, my mind goes back to that. There are a lot of things I would have done differently."

Most of the jurors were pleased with themselves after the trial. For almost six weeks they had been the center of attention in what they understood was an extraordinary event. But for occupational and family realities, they would not have minded it going on longer. Except for the friction between Mary Alice Gold and Helen Toncoff, they had enjoyed one another's company. As so often happens after a shared experience of such length, many of them suffered a psychological letdown when it was over.

So they decided to try to sustain the spirit of camaraderie by arranging a party, to which Judge Chapman and Jim Green and the lawyers were invited.[11]

The jurors kicked in five dollars apiece for an outdoor barbecue two weeks later at Mrs. Gold's house in Bethalto. Judge Chapman showed up, and so did Jim Green and his wife. Carr was in the Caribbean on his boat. Cox and Williamson were in no mood for a party. Mrs. Toncoff did not attend, but most of the others brought their spouses and had a fine time. Mrs. Toncoff suspects that Mrs. Gold deliberately chose the one evening of the week when she had been told that Mrs. Toncoff could not make other arrangements for feeding her mother in a nursing home.

It is not unusual for individuals who have been thrown together in such close contact for so long a time to want to meet again as a group, especially if they are of similar social backgrounds and especially if the business in the jury room was easy. It *is* unusual though for the triumphant plaintiff to appear—and even more unusual for the trial judge to participate. But no one ever pretended the judicial system in Madison County was ordinary.

Later in the year, something quite out of the ordinary happened in Madison County. A small group of some of the most powerful personal injury lawyers in Metro East—led by Judge Chapman's former partner Morris Chapman—decided to try to have Judge Mosele and one other sitting judge removed from the bench. A veteran of eight years on the Circuit Court, Judge Mosele had presided at the trial that returned a $3 million verdict for Green and Carr in the ne exeat case against Illini Federal Savings and Loan Association.

Sitting judges in Illinois may run for retention on their record, without an opponent. They must receive the votes of at least 60 percent to remain in office.

In a campaign still known in Madison County as "The Vendetta," Morris Chapman and a few others (Rex Carr not included) contributed funds to organize a Committee for an Improved Judiciary. The purpose of the committee, which was financed entirely by the few lawyers, was to sponsor advertisements urging the rejection of Mosele and Judge John D. DeLaurenti of Bond County. Morris Chapman gave $12,650 to the campaign, which he described to one reporter as "a cost of doing business." Mosele was generally understood to have been the principal target. His friend DeLaurenti was thrown in to make the assault seem less personal against Mosele. The newspaper ads and leaflets distributed door-to-door accused Mosele of being soft on criminals. Many neutral observers agreed with him that the allegations consisted of distortions and half-truths.

"Being fair is not enough," Mosele was quoted as saying. "They want you in their hip pocket. They went after me because I would not play along with them. If you just try to be a judge and decide cases on the law, you get eaten up. They think that a judge should decide for the plaintiff every single time."

"If you're not a pimp," DeLaurenti complained in another story, "they don't want you. They don't want a fair trial. They want everything to go their own way."

Another lawyer who contributed to the campaign, Thomas L. Lakin, accused Mosele of favoring certain law firms, his not included, but presumeably including Mosele's former partner, Paul L. Pratt, who gave $5,000 to Mosele's retention campaign.

The Vendetta succeeded. In the November election, Andreas

Matoesian was elected and Victor Mosele and John DeLaurenti both failed to receive the 60 percent vote of confidence needed to remain on the bench. There would be two vacancies in the circuit to be filled in December by the Illinois Supreme Court.[12]

Several months later, Jerry Pragacz met Helen Toncoff and her husband in a grocery store in Granite City, the first time their paths had crossed since the trial.

"We should have given him more money," he told her.

12

The Struggle to Appeal

Just how big a deal the *Telegraph* case would be, and just what the books in the law libraries would say, would depend on the appellate review process. The jury's money award was, at that time, the largest ever against a daily newspaper in the United States. Media executives and lawyers across the country were most alarmed by the $2.5 million in punitive damages and the tenuous link between what the reporters did while they were searching for a news story and the harm done to Green. Jerry Pragacz's later recounting of what happened in the jury room indicates that the jurors did not understand what punitive damages were, equating punishment with the perceived monetary value of Green's reputation. Nor was it clear that the punitive damages would go into the pockets of Green and his lawyer and not to "the school district."

Typical of the reactions of media law commentators were these observations in the *Washington Journalism Review* by Lyle Denniston, who covers the United States Supreme Court for the *Baltimore Sun:*

> ... There are big issues at stake in the *Alton Telegraph* case, and if the ultimate decision goes against the newspaper on any one of them, the press could lose much. . . .
>
> The case as it now stands is especially maddening to the press because it does not fit the currently popular view that the press frequently misbehaves. There is no hint here of rushing into print, of carelessness in checking a story. There is no refusal to cooperate with authorities by re-

porters concerned about secret sources. The *Telegraph* episode is an exhibit of ethics and good citizenship by the press, and that very conduct is the entire cause of the heavy verdict. . . .

The deepest concern . . . is that the result so far stands as a real, practical threat to some very ordinary and proper news-gathering techniques.

Reporters share tips very often with police, federal agents, and prosecutors, and that usually is a mutually beneficial process. . . .

Beyond the question of sharing tips, there is also in this case the deep and troubling issue of whether the things that reporters say orally or on paper while they are going after a story can be libelous.

The press already has enough trouble with lawyers probing into the news-gathering process for evidence of what reporters and editors had in mind when a story does emerge from the process. It will be something else again if the process itself carries the direct risk of libel whether or not a story results.

A story idea has to originate somewhere, and it has to be pursued somehow. Are discussions about it around the office coffee machine to be evidence of libel? Are reporters going to have to clean up, in a legal sense, their memos to editors? Must a reporter have a story fully in hand before mentioning it to anyone—even the cop at the neighborhood bar?

And, overall, what will the craft and game of reporting be like if reporters can be punished, with millions in extra damages, for their verbal derring-do on the way to getting a story?[1]

Denniston pointed out that courts in three states (Massachusetts, Oregon, Washington) had barred punitive damages in libel cases because of the dangers they pose to free expression. He concluded by remarking that "the thinnest thread tieing the reporter's utterances to [Green's] woe" holds up a punitive damage award fifty times higher than any fine that the state of Illinois allows for any crime.

A similar editorial in the St. Louis *Post-Dispatch* praised the *Telegraph* as "a newspaper with a long history of feisty journalism in the public interest" and one that "does not deserve to be executed by the courts."

That editorial provoked a response from Carr. "The case has about as much to do with 'freedom of the press' as with a judgment against the *Telegraph* based upon injuries suffered by a pedestrian struck by a *Telegraph* delivery truck," he wrote in a letter to the editor. The reporters who sent the "scurrilous memo" were not citizens reporting a crime, he said. "They were hoping to gain a story without working for it. This kind of conduct never has been privileged." Carr also took exception to personal criticism in an article about the case printed by the St. Louis paper. He said, "You have completely ignored the past 30 years that I have spent on the side of the little guy against politicians, against political agencies, against police departments, against courts, against powerful corporations and, finally, against newspapers."[2]

Congressman Paul Findley, a Republican whose district included Alton and a slice of northern Madison County, wrote in his weekly newspaper column: "I've been a newspaperman since my teens [he owned weeklies in west central Illinois] and this case infuriates me. The idea that a newspaper can be sued and possibly driven out of business because of something it didn't print is absurd. The size of the judgment defies all rational explanation."

Back home in Alton, no one hustled to organize a mass demonstration of support for the *Telegraph,* but some prominent citizens were disturbed. Harry Button, the president of the Chamber of Commerce, told a visiting reporter: "It was like killing the child for wetting his pants."

The newspaper in Granite City, the *Press-Record,* confessed editorially to being "pulled in multiple directions" by the issues in the trial, but concluded magnaminously that the *Telegraph* was "providing vitally needed services" and ought to remain in business. The *Telegraph* is worthy of praise for "the probing nature of its approach to newsgathering duties," commented the *Press-Record,* pointing out that "long before it was known who would hear the libel case, the Republican-leaning newspaper was fearful [because] nearly all the circuit judges were Democratic."[3]

Unless Judge Chapman could be persuaded to overturn the jury's verdict—something that seldom happens in Madison County—the Cousleys would have no alternative but to pay for an appeal to a higher court. In Illinois, this meant the Appellate Court in southern Illinois at Mount Vernon. This is the court that had been defying the assertion of federal jurisdiction in the protracted litigation over the control of Green's properties. Carr had an impressive record of successes in that courthouse.

If Mount Vernon rejected the appeal, the next and final step in the Illinois system would be the Illinois Supreme Court in Springfield. The Supreme Court consists of seven justices, who are elected to ten-year terms from districts apportioned according to population. One of them was the previously mentioned Joseph Goldenhersh of St. Clair County, who was serving as chief justice in 1981–82. Four of the others, however, were Democrats from the Chicago metropolitan area. That fact led Cox to recommend to Steve Cousley that the appeal be prepared by a prominent lawyer from Chicago.

An appellate proceeding is unlike a trial court in that there are no witnesses, no testimony, no jury theatrics. All the appellate judges have in front of them is the record of what occurred "below," and the written and oral arguments of the attorneys.

Cousley and the *Telegraph* board, which included other family stockholders, knew that considerably more legal firepower would be needed for the appeal. So, after a trip to Washington to talk the situation over with the guru of all libel law—Tim Hanson—Cousley narrowed his choice to two: Donald Reuben, the state's preeminent libel expert through many years of representing the *Chicago Tribune;* and the huge Chicago firm of Jenner & Block.

Reuben and Albert E. Jenner, the boss man of J & B, were both politically very well connected and very expensive. But the partners of Jenner & Block were just then savoring the anticipation of cutting up their share of a $1.8 billion antitrust action brought by MCI Communications Co. against American Telephone and Telegraph Co.—the biggest judgment ever in any kind of lawsuit—so presumably the J & B people might be in a generous mood.

Before going to Washington to talk strategy at the feet of Tim Hanson, Cox had asked Carr what he and his client would settle the judgment for. The answer was simple enough. According to Cox, Carr said: "We want the newspaper."

From Hanson the Cousleys learned some more unsettling news. The libel insurance would cover up to $200,000 for aggregate legal fees, but the two companies that carried the $1 million coverage—Commercial Union at the time the memo was sent, Zurich-

American at the time Green said he learned of its existence—were fussing over liability. Each said the other deserved to pick up the check.

So Steve Cousley had to be concerned about the less-than-enthusiastic insurance companies, as well as the cost of paying for an appeal at Chicago LaSalle Street corporate law prices, and the baying of the other plaintiffs who smelled blood and were circling in closer to the badly bleeding newspaper. One of them—DeGrand—offered, in the words of his new lawyer, Paul E. Riley, to settle the "situation versus the *Alton Telegraph*" for $566,666.[4]

Steve, Cox, and Williamson flew to Chicago to meet with Jenner & Block's "litigation committee," the senior partners who decide what lawsuits the firm will undertake and at what fees. The visitors from downstate were delighted to learn that the leaders of J & B sympathized with the small newspaper's plight and were willing to take the case at less than their normal hourly rates.

By coincidence, a partner with an unusual job history was unpacking boxes in his office at Jenner & Block that very morning when the delegation arrived from southern Illinois. Philip W. Tone had just given up a lifetime position as a judge on the 7th Circuit United States Court of Appeals, a job most lawyers covet only in their wildest dreams, to reenter the practice of law. Appellate judges spend most of their time reading briefs and writing opinions. Tone missed the trial action. He liked to try cases. So he quit the federal court and went back to his old firm—J & B—just in time to meet Steve Cousley and the two counsellors from Metro East.

Phil Tone's father grew up in a Norwegian farm family in Iowa. His parents moved to the northwest suburbs of Chicago, where his father practiced law and became a justice of the peace. Phil's uncles were all either farmers or lawyers. His law school education at the University of Iowa was interrupted by World War II, in which he participated in the Battle of the Bulge in Belgium as a tank commander. Tone returned home to marry Gretchen Altfillisch, a small-town girl of German and Norwegian parentage who worked as a secretary to put him through the remainder of law school.

He did well enough in law school to land a clerkship with a justice of the United States Supreme Court, Wiley Rutledge. Supreme

Court clerkships confer immediate professional status. A lawyer who has clerked for a Supreme Court justice enters an exclusive club at a crucial point in his career. The contacts with other clerks last all his professional life. One of Phil Tone's sons later clerked for his former colleague on the 7th Circuit—Justice Paul Stevens. His own clerkship gave him an entrée into the prestigious Washington firm of Covington and Burling before he moved on to Chicago with J & B in 1950.

Instead of using judicial patronage to reward active Republicans, Sen. Charles H. Percy of Illinois made a genuine effort to single out the best people for judicial appointments. Some of the judges proposed by him during the presidencies of Richard M. Nixon and Gerald R. Ford were either closet Democrats or of the faintest Republican persuasion. Phil Tone was one of the latter, a moderate Republican distinguished (politically) more by his record with an establishmentarian law firm than by his service to the GOP, though the two are not altogether disconnected. Fifty-seven years old in 1980, Tone was a very proper man with ruddy checks and good manners who worked hard at his profession and liked to read poetry and play golf (an 11 handicap at the Park Ridge Country Club) in his spare time.

Though specializing in commercial law litigation for corporate clients, he was attracted by the issues in the *Telegraph* appeal. He agreed to lead the team that would try to undo what twelve men and women had wrought in Madison County. Neither he nor his adversary Rex Carr were libel experts. They were talented trial lawyers, Carr most often representing workers suing their employers or other powerful interests accused of negligence; Tone speaking for businesses competing in the world of commerce. Their styles were altogether different: Carr was flamboyant, dramatic, shrewdly outrageous on occasion, always at his best performing in front of a jury. Tone, the poet, was a quiet reasoner, at his best marshaling his case with words on paper. If it came to that, oral arguments between these two in the building that houses the Illinois Supreme Court, across from the statue of Lincoln in front of the Statehouse, would be something to see and hear.

Tone and the other lawyers at Jenner & Block worked through

the summer and early autumn preparing a 123-page motion requesting that the judge reverse the verdict, order a new trial, or reduce the damages.

The principal points in Tone's brief were these:

1. The one-year statute of limitations for libel. Green must have had "constructive knowledge" of the existence of the memo more than one year before the suit was filed.

2. Under the state's innocent construction rule, reference to "a possible link" between the Mafia and the savings and loan association was not defamatory as a matter of law.

3. The memo was protected by an absolute common law privilege to report possible criminal conduct to a law enforcement official.

4. The effort to have information verified as part of the news-gathering process was also privileged.

5. Piasa cut off credit to Green without knowing of the existence of the memo. Even if the newspaper was the cause of the FHLBB investigation, it cannot be held responsible for "the discovery of independent and pre–existing circumstances unrelated to the information contained in the memo."

6. No one testified that he thought less of Green because of the memo, or even believed it to be true.

7. And, finally, what the document described as "gross misconduct" by Carr. The lawyer was accused of having "repeatedly insulted, belittled, humiliated, argued with and badgered witnesses. As a result, counsel replaced evidence as the focal point of the trial." The award of enormous punitive damages on five hours of deliberation after a trial of more than five weeks "demonstrates the degree to which counsel's misconduct succeeded in arousing the passion and prejudice of the jury against the defendants," Tone contended.

Tone also pointed out the conflict between Carr's theory of causation in the ne exeat damage case and in the libel trial, although Chapman forbad Cox from using any evidence later than the 1969 audit.

At arguments on November 11 in the same courtroom where the trial had been held, Carr responded in this way:

—Green did not know of the memo until 1976.

—For the memo to have been privileged, the reporters must have believed the information to be true. They wrote the memo "not for the purpose of reporting a crime . . . not for any lofty community purpose, but in order to get it verified so they could print a news story. . . . They knew they would get first shot at this story if the investigation proved there was something to it. That is not the purpose for which the privilege or the immunity exists."

—DeGrand testified that Piasa believed Green was part of the Mafia.

—"I'll admit, Your Honor, that I lost patience on a couple of occasions with Albion Fenderson, but I intended to treat him in the manner that he deserved as a witness in this courtroom."

The post-trial motion made him out to be "some kind of outrageous animal," Carr said. Actually, he suggested to Judge Chapman, Tone was also accusing the Court of misconduct "for not calling me to task" and the defense lawyers of misconduct for "giving these terrible instructions that they tendered to the Court and the Court gave at defendants' request."

Here Carr was making the most of a minefield that Tone was trying to tiptoe through. The new lawyers obviously could not criticize the trial defense. "To suggest that [trial] counsel can sit idly by while I argue . . . that you don't have to make an objection, or at least make an after-argument motion for mistrial because of some outrageous conduct" is not justified, Carr said. "Most of their argument is based upon things that took place during the course of the trial at which their own counsel did not object, but which their new counsel does object. And I submit that is not the way to run a law suit."

"It was interesting to listen to Mr. Tone argue," Carr said, "because not once did he mention the merits of the case, not once did he argue that somehow or other this libel was true, or that somehow or other Jim Green wasn't damaged, or that somehow or other the reporters had no reason to disbelieve the charges, or that they conducted a careful investigation or that they acted in good faith. Not once did counsel argue that the verdict of the jury was improper on the merits of the case."

Given an opportunity to reply, Tone insisted that "if there is an absolute privilege, the motive is utterly immaterial. They [the reporters] did not abuse the privilege. They used the privilege in an effort to have [the information] verified. And when it wasn't verified, they acted properly."

On his last day in office, at the end of November, Judge Chapman entered an order in the Green case denying the motion for reversal, new trial, or reduction of the money award. The $9.2 million verdict would stand.

There is a tradition in Illinois that a judge who has been rejected by the voters is not to be appointed to the bench. Only a few days passed, however, before the Illinois Supreme Court, at the recommendation of Justice Goldenhersh, named Charles W. Chapman to the Circuit Court of Madison County for a second time, this time in the vacancy caused by the removal of Victor J. Mosele. Carr said later that Goldenhersh told him the appointment had been at the request of all the lawyers who practice in Madison County, which Carr said was enough in Goldenhersh's mind to overrule the decision of the voters earlier in the year.

So Chapman unpacked his hardly dusty black robes—and Mosele went back to Paul Pratt's firm.

As *Post-Dispatch* reporter Bill Lambrecht poignantly observed a little over a year later: "The hidden industry takes away and it gives. In one of the first cases he prepared after being dumped, Mosele won a million-dollar verdict for his client."

DeLaurenti ran for his old seat in 1982 and was elected without interference from the Chapman firm.

Judge Chapman, meanwhile, was endorsed again by the party for reelection to a regular term in 1982. He was one of four judicial candidates who balked later in the year at paying the full $10,000 contribution in exchange for the endorsement. Having paid $10,000 once before, only to lose in the primary, Chapman decided $2,500 would be enough this time, a breach of tradition that caused some consternation among party officials. He was nominated and elected, nonetheless, finally becoming a full-fledged member of the judiciary of Madison County.

If John Doe goes to court and sues Joe Bloke, and the court awards a money judgment to Doe, Doe has a legitimate interest in seeing to it that Bloke doesn't dispose of what wealth he has while trying to persuade a higher court to overrule the lower court. For this reason the rules of the Illinois Supreme Court required that the loser in a civil damage suit post a surety bond with the court equal to one and one-half times the amount of the judgment—$13.8 million in the case of the *Telegraph*.

A bond of that size would be no problem for the Columbia Broadcasting System or Time Inc. or the Gannett Company with vast resources to stand behind the bond. But it was a big problem for the *Alton Telegraph*. The newspaper found that it did not have nearly enough property and other assets to qualify for such a huge bond. Its physical assets—the presses and computers and circulation trucks—were worth maybe $3 million, not nearly enough. The real value of a newspaper has little to do with the things it owns. Shortly before the libel trial, according to Henry McAdams, the minority owner, he met with a newspaper broker who offered $18 million for the *Telegraph* in behalf of a newspaper group. That figure was undoubtedly less now, but the market value surely exceeded $13.8 million. Various communications groups—Capital Cities, Hearst, the Thomson newspaper group—were hovering over the wounded company, available to buy at bargain basement prices. In any event, the price that a newspaper might bring is no security for an appeal bond.

No one—not the libel insurance companies, the American Newspaper Publishers Association, the Society of Professional Journalists/Sigma Delta Chi, the Reporters Committee for Freedom of the Press, the American Civil Liberties Union, or anyone else—rang up the Cousleys to offer help on the bond. "Anyone like to help with a bond?" Cousley joked later. "Your friends narrow down quickly." Phil Tone, ironically, had been chairman of the Supreme Court rules committee that, many years before, had written this and the other rules of civil practice in Illinois.

Without the "supersedeas" bond, one that suspends the proceedings in a law suit, it was conceivable that the sheriff could show up one morning and padlock the newspaper to make sure Jim Green got what was coming to him—the pending appeal notwithstanding.

Tone and another J & B attorney, David Sanders, then asked the Circuit Court to allow the newspaper to pledge all its fixed assets—

the newspaper, in effect—as security in lieu of a bond while the appeal was being pursued. "Unless enforcement of the judgment is stayed pending appeal, plaintiff will be able to execute upon the judgment [another way of saying collect the damages] during the pendency of the appeal and thereby deprive defendants of all their assets," the motion explained. "This would not only make it impossible for the defendants to pay the expenses of an appeal, but would in any event effectively deprive them of their right of appeal, for when they ultimately prevailed on appeal, their assets would have been long since sold and the proceeds dissipated. Something would be grossly wrong with a legal system that would not prevent such a result, especially in a case involving constitutional and legal questions of great importance to our society."

Carr argued back that the rule was mandatory. Merely putting up the fixed assets of the newspaper as security would amount to "no bond whatsoever," Carr contended, the effect of which would be asking Green to finance the *Telegraph*'s appeal. "The *Alton Telegraph* is no better or worse than any other judgment debtor," he said.

Where is the justice in a system in which the newspaper is in danger of being seized before any higher court has had a look at its appeal? inquired the Chicago lawyers. Nonsense, retorted Carr, let the Cousleys and the McAdamses put some of their personal wealth behind the bond.

In rapid succession, the Circuit Court, the Appellate Court in Mount Vernon, and the Illinois Supreme Court all ruled for Carr and against an exception being made for the newspaper on the appeal bond rule.

What now? While the owners of the *Telegraph* were scratching for a surety bond, the lawyers were discussing possible settlement terms. Carr suggested the $1 million insurance money plus $75,000 a year for fifteen years or a little over $2 million in all. All this time the legal fees were ticking away. In the year 1980 alone, the newspaper's legal fees totaled $311,982—$50,188 to Bill Cox, $42,616 to Charlie Williamson, and $219,178 to Jenner & Block. The J & B toll included fifteen minutes of Albert E. Jenner's time at $275 per hour, or $68.75. However Phil Tone's hourly rate of $150 was far below his customary fee.

On April 13, 1981, Carr turned up the pressure by asking the

Circuit Court to require that former reporter Melosi list his assets with the court, the first step in collecting on a judgment.

For some reason, the Jenner & Block lawyers did not seriously consider going to the federal courts with a *Henry* case argument. In 1976, a state judge in Mississippi had awarded $1.25 million in damages to a group of merchants in Claiborne County who had been the target of a boycott organized by the NAACP to protest racial discrimination. Mississippi had an appeal bond law similar to the one in Illinois, requiring a bond of $1.56 million. Unable to post a bond of such size, the NAACP asked the federal courts for relief, supported by the United States Department of Justice. The United States Court of Appeals for the Fifth Circuit upheld an injunction against the bond requirement, ruling that a state could not use it to effectively deny the right of appeal to certain parties. Eventually, in *Henry* v. *First National Bank of Clarksdale,* the United States Supreme Court decided in favor of the NAACP.

Later, in 1986, when the same appeal bond issue arose in multi-billion-dollar litigation involving Texaco Inc. and the Pennzoil Co., I inquired of Tone why Ackerman or some other federal judge had not been requested to remove the state court barrier preventing an appeal. Tone's partner David P. Sanders replied: "[We] looked at various options which would permit the owners of the *Alton Telegraph* to continue to own and operate the newspaper while we pursued the appeal from the adverse trial court judgment. Our recollection is that we did not seriously consider pursuing relief based on a *Henry* argument. Our ultimate goal was to obtain a reversal on the merits, and there would have been some reluctance to pursue a course that might be viewed by judges in the state court system as an effort to have the federal courts dictate to the state courts on an interlocutory procedural matter, albeit a vital one."[5]

The safest choice, as far as the lawyers were concerned, was one that Cox had first suggested some months before. On April 14, the Telegraph Co. filed in the United States District Court in East St. Louis for corporate reorganization under the federal bankruptcy law. This is precisely what Carr had done back in October of 1979 for Granite Investment Co. on the day before the mortgage foreclosure trial was to proceed in federal court. Lawyers refer to it as "preemptive bankruptcy." In both instances the purpose was to freeze the regular progress of litigation—in the case of Granite, the foreclosure of the mortgages after the federal courts had asserted their jurisdiction in the fight for control of Green's properties; in the case of the *Telegraph,* the carrying out of the judgment at a time when the newspaper could not arrange for an appeal bond. "We believed that the safest course was to pursue the Chapter 11 bankruptcy proceedings to stay the enforcement of the judgment while we prosecuted the appeal," Sanders explained in his later statement. "Admittedly, our judgment was the result of an effort to balance imponderables, but we followed our best judgment under the unusual circumstances."

Until 1978, federal bankruptcy referees, as they were then called, had limited powers to sort out the tedious details of individuals and businesses in over their heads in debt. In effect, the referees were clerical patronage for the United States district judges, who stepped in themselves whenever complicated legal issues arose. Congress changed that in 1978 by creating a system of bankruptcy courts with judges who would have authority to decide all legal questions that came up in a bankruptcy case.

More and more often in recent years, the bankruptcy escape hatch was being used by big corporations to put a halt to mass product liability claims.[6] In 1982, for example, the world's leading asbestos maker, the Manville Corp., went into bankruptcy court to protect itself against a flood of damage suit judgments. Technically, the bankruptcy judge assumed jurisdiction over not just the financial condition of the company but all the lawsuits as well. (Also in 1982, the United States Supreme Court would hold that the powers given the bankruptcy judges were excessive without also upgrading their status by giving them the same lifetime tenure as other federal judges.)

But in 1981 one of the appointed federal bankruptcy judges—James D. Trabue of East St. Louis, the same judge in whose lap the Granite Investment bankruptcy matter had been dropped—suddenly found himself in the middle of a big libel case.

Confronted as they are with financial disorder of formidable proportions, bankruptcy judges are more appropriately clerks than judicial scholars. Trabue is a short man with a thick, black whiskbroom of a moustache. The son of a school administrator in St. Clair County, he collects antiques and is an officer of the county historical society. At the time of his appointment as a bankruptcy referee, he was a staunch Republican chosen for the job by a federal district judge who had been sponsored by Senator Dirksen during the Eisenhower presidency. Consequently, Trabue has used his power to designate trustees in bankruptcy to reward Republican-connected lawyers, something of a minority group in Metro East.

Though the bankruptcy action was a desperate move, Steve Cousley said it was the only way to keep the newspaper operating and out of Green's grasp while the case was being appealed. In his public comments about his predicament, Cousley characterized the entire affair as "an attempt by the local political machine to put us out of business. We've done a pretty hard-nosed job of reporting on officialdom in the county, digging into things over the years that need digging into. Over the years we've made lots of enemies." In another comment, he said: "We're fighting for our life down here. We don't like [this], but we don't have any choice. In effect, we're being held hostage here."[7]

Tone's advice at this stage had been not to consider settling for more than the insurance ($1 million), but even at that the settlement package had to take into account the claims of the other plaintiffs. The function of a bankruptcy court ordinarily is to preside over the reorganization of the business and the settlement of the outstanding debts. Here it was highly uncertain what would happen. The bankruptcy court could sit on the reorganization case while the appeal was being successfully completed, the best outcome as far as the *Telegraph* was concerned.

Never one to stand idly by, Carr struck back. He told Green to call Melosi and urge the two reporters to sign their interests in the libel insurance over to him and hence be relieved of any further liability. This would have been an act of betrayal of the Cousleys, who had paid for the reporters' legal defense. After talking to a lawyer of their own, Melosi and Lhotka rejected the suggestion, whereupon Carr went ahead with the collection process against Melosi. (Because Lhotka was a resident of Missouri, the collection from him would be more complicated.) Carr also challenged the *Telegraph*'s motives for declaring bankruptcy, alleging that it was a subterfuge "to defeat the orders and jurisdiction of the state courts."

Although the federal bankruptcy statute says nothing about good faith, a growing body of cases had developed establishing such a requirement. So, in his disposition of Carr's motion, Trabue addressed what was obvious to all: that the newspaper was in bankruptcy court to obtain the benefits of a supersedeas bond without paying for it. The judge said he recognized the possibility that some litigants would use his court "to circumvent jurisdictional restrictions . . . absent any economic reality." But, he said, the *Telegraph* clearly was "not in sound financial shape at the present time." Nor did the newspaper pretend that it was in anything but a bad fix economically because of the libel judgment, forcing it into the action "in order to preserve its status as an ongoing concern while the claims against it are being litigated."

On what everyone knew was the most vital issue raised by Carr, Trabue said the filing of the reorganization petition "does not affect the state court's ability to hear the appeal, and, in fact, facilitates the state court's jurisdiction rather than defeats it." By that statement, the bankruptcy judge brushed aside any possible interest that he might have had in taking over the libel appeal.

In the meantime, the *Telegraph*'s lawyers filed an application with Trabue for the "removal" of the Green libel case "to this court . . . because the suit involves the debtor [the *Telegraph*] and affects the property of its estate." As the defendants were scurrying around trying to repel Carr's sorties against them, the federal judge was being drawn deeper and deeper into *Green* v. *Alton Telegraph*. The proceedings were following an astonishingly similar path paralleling the contest for control of Green's properties—Carr utilizing the state courts of southern Illinois and his opponents resorting to the federal courts.

Crucial to the *Telegraph*'s position was the understanding that the "removal" to the federal court involved only the "supplemental proceedings"—namely the attempt to collect from Melosi and the other defendants—and not the appeal itself in the state courts. For how could the court in Mount Vernon consider an appeal that had been taken out of its hands?

In his order of October 16 making the restraining order against the state courts permanent, Trabue used some unsettling language. "The Court does not make any ruling on the question of whether the case should be remanded [sent back] in its entirety," he said. "Under the facts of the present case . . . it is clear that the state court proceeding could have an effect upon the estate of the *Telegraph,* and, as such the entire case should be removed." Stunned by those words, and very much aware of their implications, the men and women of Jenner & Block asked immediately for a clarification. Three days later, on October 19, Trabue said he wanted no misunderstanding about the authority of the state courts to proceed with the libel appeal.

Twice, first in his dismissal of Carr's challenge to the bankruptcy petition, and now on October 19, the judge had said the state appellate court was free to proceed with the libel appeal, although, inexplicably, on October 16 he said just the opposite.

Leaping at the opportunity created by this contradiction, Carr asked the state Appellate Court in Mount Vernon on October 28 to dismiss the *Telegraph* appeal for lack of state court jurisdiction. At the beginning of August, Carr had been granted a three-month extension of the due date for his appellate brief, and now the court postponed the deadline indefinitely.

The Jenner & Block team filed 143 pages of printed argument in the newspaper's behalf with the appellate court in July. The principal authors of the brief were David P. Sanders and Dorothy B. Zimbrakos, though Tone spent considerable time polishing the opus, beginning the argument section with these words:

> That a citizen could be held liable for millions of dollars in damages for reporting information about possible organized crime activities to the Organized Crime Section of the United States Department of Justice is almost inconceivable. Yet, that is precisely what happened in this case.
>
> The law provides an absolute privilege to prevent just such perversions of justice. The reporters' communication to a prosecuting attorney

about possible criminal activities was protected by that absolute privilege. The trial court's refusal to recognize that privilege resulted in the outrageous spectacle now to be reviewed by this Court.

Among the other arguments raised in the brief were these:
1. The plaintiff failed to prove that his injury was "proximately caused" by the alleged defamatory statement.
2. The reporters cannot be held responsible for the results of the several "republications" of their confidential memo.
3. There is no evidence from which the jury could properly have found that the FHLBB's conduct was influenced by statements deriving from the reporters' memo, rather than by the serious deficiencies it discovered in Piasa's lending practices.
4. In his instruction to the jury on what had to be proven to establish "proximate cause," the judge "erred in treating this multimillion dollar libel case like a simple accident case."
5. Green was improperly compensated for damage sustained, if at all, by his corporations, which were not parties to the suit.
6. There was insufficient evidence to support $6.7 million in compensatory damages.
7. "The jury's staggering verdict of $9.2 million was the result of passion and prejudice kindled by the pervasive gross misconduct of plaintiff's counsel, which made a fair trial impossible."
8. The defendants were denied a fair trial by the judge's preliminary rulings.
9. The $2.5 million award of punitive damages was unconstitutional, against the manifest weight of the evidence, grossly excessive, and contrary to law and public policy.
10. The case, filed nearly eight years after the delivery of the memo to the Justice Department, is barred by the Statute of Limitations.
11. The First Amendment precludes liability from being imposed on newspaper reporters for defamatory statements made in the course of newsgathering.

Several of the professional organizations that had been nowhere to be seen when the *Telegraph* was trying to put up an appeal bond submitted *amici curiae* (friend of the court) briefs to the court in Mount Vernon. These included the American Society of Newspaper Editors, the Society of Professional Journalists/Sigma Delta Chi, the *New York Times,* the Chicago *Sun-Times,* the *Chicago Tribune,* Copley Press, Inc., the *Danville* (Ill.) *Commercial-News,* the *Peoria Journal Star,* the *Waukegan News-Sun,* and the Reporters Committee for Freedom of the Press. Not needing or wanting any newspaper "friends" offering advice, apparently, the court bundled up the *amici* briefs and sent them back, refusing without explanation to permit them to be filed.

Don Reuben, for the *Tribune* and Copley Press, began his would-be *amici* brief by quoting Oliver Wendell Holmes' statement that an appellate judge "will know the judgment must be reversed when, after reading the trial record, he feels the urge to retch."

The brief for the *Sun-Times,* recalling the legal doctrine that punitive damages be limited to the amount that could be imposed as a fine in a criminal prosecution for the same act, noted that the penalty for criminal libel in Illinois is a fine of not more than $1,000.

Earlier in 1981, Hope Apple, Paulie Cousley's daughter, mailed a newspaper clipping of a story about the case to the producers of "60 Minutes," the Columbia Broadcasting System's Sunday evening television investigative program. In June, correspondent Morley Safer and producer Joseph Wershba arrived in Madison County with two cameramen and a lighting technician. They shot two miles of videotape that were then edited down to a fifteen-minute segment that was not aired until October.

Television lives by simple themes. The simple theme of Safer's segment on "60 Minutes" was that the *Telegraph* had been guilty of "sloppy" journalism and the case "should teach us to be careful." Unlike the stories that were published in newspapers around the country highlighting the threat to the survival of the *Telegraph,* the network's fleeting treatment was highly favorable to Green's cause. The builder was pictured walking around some of his boarded up apartment buildings. Had it not been for the memo, Green said he probably would "be worth $25 million or $30 million." No mention was made of Piasa's overfinancing of his projects, the straw-party loans, or his mortgage delinquencies. In a *Telegraph* newsroom scene, Steve Cousley suggested that contacts with law enforcement officials are standard practice in journalism. But the correspondent for a program that has itself been accused of unethical practices—including distorted editing of interviews and the so-called "ambush interview" of uncooperative characters in the story—said his associates confined themselves to "picking the brains" of authorities. The key interview in the segment occurred with DeGrand in the living room of his home. The intensity of his indignation came through impressively. He said it had been an agonizing 12 years, "but if I have to face another 12 years [to clear my name], I will." Speaking movingly of his five sons who would carry the DeGrand name into the future, he said he wanted them to be able to hold their heads high and not be ashamed of their father. It was superb television. Later, when Safer was asked about the program, he said the *Telegraph* case had been "a comedy of errors . . . bad editing and questionable reporting. I believe in strong libel laws. I think the laws of libel should be very strong so that when you go out on a story it's got to be brassbound or you're in trouble."[8] His was probably the only media portrayal of the case that took Green's side—and it was primarily due to the force of DeGrand's emotional sincerity.

All through the years of litigation, it was his anger and his persistence that propelled the matter onward. He discovered the existence of the memo. He and his lawyer closed some of the links between the memo and what happened later in Madison County. He filed the first libel suit and encouraged the other plaintiffs to do the same. He was, as jury foreperson Pragacz tells us, a key witness in the Green libel trial—more so probably than Green himself. And yet, because of the death of his lawyer just before the libel suit was to go to trial, DeGrand's case was not heard and Green's was.

On July 16, 1981—after the CBS segment had been taped but before it was telecast—DeGrand awoke in the night and called to one of his children, saying he was not feeling well, and asking for a glass of water. Before the youngster could return, Bob DeGrand suffered a massive heart attack and lost consciousness. He died a short time later in Alton's St. Joseph Hospital. He was fifty-seven years old. The last twelve years of his life had been wracked by an unwavering mission to avenge what he believed had been an act of injustice against him. In the end, Bob DeGrand went to his grave without seeing a penny of the *Telegraph*'s (or the Federal Home Loan Bank Board's) money.

By placing itself under the protective wing of the federal bankruptcy court, the *Telegraph*'s strategy was to move ahead with the appeal to Mount Vernon and, most likely, then to Springfield, while neutralizing Carr in the Madison County Circuit Court, and, of course, putting out the newspaper every afternoon. There were, however, certain handicaps. Employee paychecks came from "Alton Telegraph Printing Co., Debtor in Possession." No dividends could be disbursed to the owners. Any creditor could propose at any time the appointment of a trustee to oversee the newspaper. Eventually, under normal procedure, there would have to be a resolution of various plans for reorganizing the company and its debts. Beside which, Carr was now maintaining, Mount Vernon could not hear the appeal even if it wanted to.

So, for the third time, and somewhat more emphatically, Judge Trabue issued another order in January of 1982 declaring the libel case belonged where he said it was: in the state Appellate Court in Mount Vernon. All that had been removed to his court, he explained again, were the "supplementary proceedings that were pending" in the Circuit Court—namely the effort to begin collecting from the defendants—but which he said had no effect on the appeal in the libel case.[9] Green's lawyers had ignored the bankruptcy judge's restraining order by instituting collection procedures against Steve Cousley and in Missouri against Lhotka, too. A document demanding the list of assets was served by a deputy sheriff at Cousley's home to his fifteen-year-old daughter, who was alone at the time.

"The timely resolution of the appeal is important to the ultimate disposition of this [bankruptcy] case," the judge said, adding that the federal law "was not meant to give a bankruptcy court jurisdiction over a state court appeal." Then, to eliminate any possible ambiguity, he expressed his hope that "the appeal proceed in the state court system as expeditiously as possible."

Carr served notice of his intention to appeal Judge Trabue's clarifying order to the United States District Court for the Southern District of Illinois. And, on February 10, he filed in Bankruptcy

Court a "joint plan" for the reorganization of the *Telegraph* along with the attorney for DeGrand's widow, Nancy DeGrand.

Under the Green-DeGrand plan:

—Green would get the $1 million insurance money, out of which would be paid: $275,000 to Mrs. DeGrand, $50,000 to Bert Simpson, $30,065.50 to John Sobol, $6,065.50 to Ray Kozielek, $12,000 to Stanley Kowalski, and $1 to the Green Construction Company.

—Green would receive all the common stock of the *Telegraph* Co.—equity valued at about $2,350,000.

—The new board would consist of Green, Green's wife, Carr, two of Carr's law partners, two of Green's company employees, and a bank president in East St. Louis.

—All of the *Telegraph* employees would be retained, except Paul and Steve Cousley.

—The new owners would retain the right to liquidate the business if it became unprofitable.

The *Telegraph* had filed its own plan earlier, providing for no change in the management of the paper until all legal appeals had been exhausted.

A date was set in April for a Bankruptcy Court hearing on the two plans. Paulie Cousley wrote a letter to the employees reminding them that they would have a chance to vote on the plans, which he said "differ dramatically as to who will own the *Telegraph*." Green would "take control and ownership of the paper" under his plan and, Cousley said, would "run the paper as he saw fit. Because of his total lack of newspaper experience, it is utterly impossible to predict how he would run the paper. On the other hand, you know the Cousley family and the McAdams family, who have run the paper as a family enterprise for several generations."

All this time the newspaper's lawyers were chasing around trying to repel Carr's commandolike landings in the state Appellate Court, the Bankruptcy Court, and the federal District Court. They filed a motion in Mount Vernon demanding that Carr submit his appellate brief "forthwith." He has already had more than six months, argued J & B lawyer David Sanders, and the bankruptcy judge has "removed any conceivable basis for questioning this

Court's jurisdiction over the appeal." "The unusual circumstances of this case, in which the appellant newspaper has been forced into the bankruptcy court in order to effectively preserve its right to appeal, cry for an expeditious determination of this appeal," Sanders told the state justices. Another J & B lawyer, Donald Cassling, filed a brief with the United States District Court describing Carr's appeal of Trabue's order as "patently frivolous." If Green were to be given control of the newspaper before the libel case appeal received a hearing, "he [Green] would be extravagantly rewarded for a claim which is quite possibly worthless," Cassling contended. "Green obviously felt that delay or dismissal of the state libel appeal was crucial to his plans to take over the *Telegraph*," the brief continued. "Green's interminable dilatory tactics, including the taking of his indefensible appeal, *have* had a deleterious effect on both the state court appeal and the bankruptcy proceedings."

And in Bankruptcy Court, the Jenner & Block lawyers argued that a resolution of the reorganization plans would deprive the debtor of its right of judicial review of the libel judgment. "This unjust scheme [would be carried out] by providing for the transfer of ownership [to Green], prior to a ruling from the Appellate Court in the Green case. As one of his first official acts, Green would dismiss Debtor's appeals of his judgment, and pay outrageous sums to settle the claims of the other opponents of the Joint Plan. Since dismissal of all pending appeals and law suits would be final and irreversible, confirmation of the Joint Plan would be the equivalent of an economic death sentence for the Debtor and its current shareholders." The motion also referred to "an undisclosed fee arrangement [between Green and Carr] which would award an undisclosed amount of attorneys' fees upon confirmation of the Joint Plan."

The other shoe dropped in Mount Vernon a few days before the scheduled hearing in the Bankruptcy Court. On April 7, a panel of three judges dismissed the *Telegraph*'s appeal in the 5th District Illinois Appellate Court. Justice Jones wrote the opinion holding that "the entire case, including the appeal, was removed to the Bankruptcy Court" and that all of Judge Trabue's words and orders were "insufficient to revest this Court with jurisdiction of the case."

Try as he might, the bankruptcy judge cannot take over some of the case and not all of it, proclaimed Justice Jones. "By virtue of *Alton Telegraph*'s application as petitioner in bankruptcy, the entire action, and not just the portion directed toward an individual defendant, was removed to Bankruptcy Court. . . . [To rule otherwise] would allow [the *Telegraph*] to subvert the procedural rules governing the enforcement of judgments pending appeal in Illinois, as *Alton Telegraph* bluntly admits it has endeavored to do. . . . Defendants have sought the protection of the Bankruptcy Court by removing their action to that Court and have accepted the benefits of removal. By doing so they have given up their right to continue with the appeal in this Court. Because the administration of *Alton Telegraph*'s estate in Bankruptcy Court is dependent upon whether the libel judgment obtained by Green is allowed to stand, it is evident that the ultimate determination of the matter will have to be made by the Bankruptcy Court rather than by this Court."

For want of a bond required by the Illinois courts before a jury award in a civil suit can be reviewed by a higher court, the *Alton Telegraph* looked to the federal bankruptcy law for temporary protection. Thrice the bankruptcy judge said: I will stop the plaintiff from pestering the reporters and collecting the judgment before the appeal can be heard by a higher state court, but I have no business getting involved in the libel appeal, and what's more I won't. Too bad, said the state Appellate Court. If you're going to put a stop to the carrying out of the judgment, you're also preventing us from considering the appeal. Sorry.

The other two on the panel who joined in Justice Jones' opinion were Justice George W. Kasserman, Jr., of Newton, another small town in southeastern Illinois, and Ralph S. Pearman, a Circuit Court judge from Danville in the east central part of the state.

Now the *Telegraph* found itself in a real box. The state courts wouldn't hear the appeal. The bankruptcy judge wouldn't hear the appeal. Almost two years had passed since the trial, and the winner was pushing for a reorganization of the company that would give him and his lawyer control of the newspaper. In point of fact, the *Telegraph* was far from bankrupt. Its undistributed profits in 1981 were a mere $207,500. But if Green and Carr were to capture the newspaper, they could sell it to a group at considerably more than the amount of the libel judgment. The newspaper's ordeal was made no easier by the constant bickering between the Cousleys and the McAdamses over what to do next. Neither family had been willing to gamble personal wealth on the appeal bond. And now the bankruptcy ploy had failed. Without even having to prepare an appellate brief, Rex Carr had frustrated the big-city barristers once again.

There were only two options left. If the bankruptcy judge held off a while longer, an appeal to the Illinois Supreme Court conceivably could compel the court in Mount Vernon to hear the case. But how long would it take? And at what price? More time would be needed for the actual appeal—and then the appeal of the appeal to Springfield.

"We could see," said Steve Cousley, "that we were about to be eaten alive"—either by Green and Carr or by the legal fees. The only other option was to settle the case on Carr's terms.

13

The Settlement

With much less public notice, the central struggle for control of Jim Green's buildings went on. On September 12, 1980—three months after the Green libel trial—Judge Bauer wrote for the federal Appeals Court that "the circumstances in this case fully warranted injunctive relief" and the District Court in Springfield "properly invoked its injunctive powers to protect its jurisdiction from further interference by the Illinois state courts."[1] A little over a year after that, Justice Howard C. Ryan held for a unanimous Illinois Supreme Court that the state Appellate Court had acted improperly in directing the FSLIC not to proceed with the foreclosure action in federal court.[2] The butting of heads on the jurisdictional issue had ended. The state courts backed off.

"There must be an end to litigation" lectured Justice Ryan, a small-town Republican from northern Illinois. "This case appears to be interminable and will certainly prove to be so if the various courts through which it passes consider and reconsider each question several times."

Were it not for Granite Investment's bankruptcy petition, the foreclosure of the mortgages presumably could proceed. The lawyers had quibbled over such questions as whether the laundry receipts at Spencer Gardens had been properly applied by the receiver. But the primary issue—who would get Green's buildings—still had not been decided by any court anywhere. The advantage, though, seemed to lie with the FSLIC. If the *Telegraph* could be pressured to resolve its bankruptcy reorganization, why not Granite

Investment, too? If the bankruptcy judge could give the go-ahead to the trial of Carr's suit in St. Clair County, why not the foreclosure suit in the federal court?

All the parties were aware, however, of the flogging administered to Albion Fenderson by counselor Carr for nine days of the libel trial. They were aware that the *Telegraph* had lost the libel case, in part because of its inability to convince the jury that the FHLBB's actions against Piasa were justified regardless of the reporters' memo.

So after almost ten years of wearisome legal gamesmanship, the feds were in a mood to talk peace. Late in 1981, Patterson and Carr agreed to the terms of a "Memorandum of Mortgage Modification and Settlement."[3]

The settlement provided that ownership of the properties would be returned to Granite Investment Co. and the mortgage delinquencies forgiven, with the understanding that the FSLIC would be paid $14,867,143 on the mortgage debt, which the FSLIC calculated to be close to the current market value of the properties. All the pending lawsuits, the $3 million ne exeat claim against Illini Federal, and Granite's bankruptcy petition were wiped out.

Technically, title to the properties was conveyed to a land trust, and the beneficiary of the trust, Granite, assigned its interest in the trust to the FSLIC as further security for the debt. The FSLIC considered itself fortunate to have come out of the deal with a substantial part of the debt intact and without having to pay Green any money. "We settled because we wanted to get out," Hackmann said later. "It was cheaper to settle than to continue."

What happened next is complicated. Granite Investment sold the rental apartment projects to a West Coast banking company and real estate syndicator—Security Pacific Corp.—which was in the business of putting together tax shelter packages.[4] Investors would buy into the syndicate, which now owned the apartments, for tax loss purposes. "In effect," explained one FSLIC official, "he [Green] got Uncle Sam to pay off our mortgage."

Any cash flow from the rents goes toward the FSLIC debt. By 1990, at the latest, the FSLIC debt will have been paid off in full by Security Pacific. Under the terms of the financing arrangement, Security Pacific has the option then of "walking away" from the properties after fifteen years, at which time—the tax shelter purposes having been used up—ownership would revert to Green's and Carr's company. If inflation resumes, real estate values have gone up, and Metro East is thriving economically, Security would be expected to keep the property (if, that is, the properties are worth more than the cost of paying off the last half of *its* mortgage).

If the latter happens, Granite would wind up with Security's full purchase price of $17,705,334 at the end of fifteen years. If the former happens, the difference between the purchase price and the cost to Granite would be between $9 million and $10 million—in effect, Granite's "profit" in the deal.

"The worst that could happen," explained Carr, as a one-third owner of Granite, "is I'll have one-third of property worth $9 million—or $3 million—a decent fee."

"When I first represented Jim Green, he had not a dime," Carr said. "In matter of fact, I had to lend him money. It was on that basis that my firm has one-third interest. If I had known all the work that was going to be involved, I probably would have made it a 50 percent contract. At one time, I had $50,000 in costs alone—accountants, appraisers, and so forth."

"I make a lot of money. But I determined when I first started practice that I wanted to be a good lawyer and the money would take care of itself—and it's been true."

So, all the parties came out of the litigatory hodgepodge in reasonably good shape. The FSLIC is out from under some $14.9 million in delinquent mortgages. Illini Federal need worry no longer about the $3 million ne exeat verdict. For better or worse, Jim Green is back in the building business. And as compensation for his years of legal service, Rex Carr will be worth between $3 million and $6 million more, not counting the losses he was able to report on his own taxes while Granite Investment was in a state of limbo.

When all the debris was swept aside, the FSLIC's Green case legal fees were estimated by one knowledgeable source to have been in excess of $3 million.

There were many human casualties on both sides of this war, but the lawyers were not among them. In February of 1983, Patterson and Carr exchanged letters withdrawing their pending complaints of unethical conduct. Carr is, Patterson told me, now "a good friend." The litigators fold their tents, stow away their weapons, and move on to other litigation, and other fees.

And what of the *Alton Telegraph*?

The owners of the *Telegraph* had spent well over a quarter of a million dollars to hire a top-flight Chicago law firm to prepare an appeal of the local jury's libel award, only to find that:

1. They could not afford the bond required to guarantee that the newspaper could not be disposed of during the appeal.

2. It was necessary to go to the federal Bankruptcy Court to prevent Jim Green from taking the newspaper in payment of the judgment.

3. The bankruptcy judge consented three different times to the state Appellate Court's consideration of the libel appeal because the newspaper's financial uncertainty could not be cleared up until the libel debt, if any, was finally determined.

4. Without requiring that Green's lawyer submit a brief in support of what had happened in the trial court, the state Appellate Court ignored the pleas of the bankruptcy judge and dismissed the libel appeal. Let the Bankruptcy Court hear the libel appeal, said the Appellate Court, knowing full well that the bankruptcy judge had said repeatedly he would *not* hear the libel appeal.

5. Green was clamoring for a decision by the Bankruptcy Court that would reorganize the *Telegraph* into his control.

Paulie Cousley had aged visibly through the long ordeal. He withdrew from the daily decisions concerning the libel suits, delegating responsibility to Steve. The younger man maintained his composure. Even at board meetings, he refused to lose control of his emotions. Relations with the McAdamses deteriorated as the company's problems multiplied. The McAdamses took the position now that the suits should have been settled when they were first filed, but weren't because of Steve's "stupidity and egotism," words used later by Peter McAdams.[5]

Probably the most galling of Steve's many disappointments was the willingness of the Mount Vernon court to excuse Carr from the time-consuming obligation of submitting a brief in support of the trial court decision. The thick brief prepared by Jenner & Block was a legal masterwork, setting out all the precedents and arguments in support of the *Telegraph*'s position in easily understandable language. But the effect of that quarter-million dollar document turned out to be exactly nothing; because of the court's dismissal of the case, on the grounds that it belonged in the Bankruptcy Court, neither Carr nor the court had to respond to the *Telegraph* brief in any way.

Following the Appellate Court's dismissal of the appeal, the newspaper's attorneys were backed into a corner. The debt reorganization hearing was fast approaching, and a June 14 trial date had been set in Madison County Circuit Court for Elvin (Bert) Simpson's $12.4 million libel suit. There was no way out. The *Telegraph* would have to try to settle.

The last previous settlement offer by Carr had been made the month before: $950,000 of insurance money to Green and $100,000 to Carr's firm in each of the next fifteen years, a fee of $1.5 million, and a total of $2,450,000.

After three days of new negotiations between Carr and Jenner & Block attorney Ronald Peterson, the two sides agreed on a figure of $1.4 million, plus a token payment of $1 to the James Green Construction Co. Over the next six weeks, Simpson settled for $20,000; John Sobol for $30,065.50; Raymond Kozielek for $6,065.50. All that remained were Stanley Kowalski and possibly Nancy DeGrand. Under Illinois law, a libel suit dies with the death of the plaintiff. The DeGrand suit had been dismissed by Judge Trabue, but Mrs. DeGrand's lawyer appealed the decision to the United States District Court and a recently installed federal judge—William Beatty—the same judge who had ruled against the *Telegraph* in the state court on the original statute of limitations and privilege questions, and who had since been named to the federal bench by the Carter administration. The newspaper was willing to settle her claim for $42,000, but her lawyer demanded $50,000, and the negotiations were continuing.

Steve Cousley described the Green settlement as "not a clear-cut win or loss" for the paper. But he said it would "preserve the newspaper and its ability to do its job. A newspaper that is solvent has the freedom to do its job. A newspaper where the doors are closed can't print the news or do its job. It's a war of attrition. A newspaper has to be economically sound. The tremendous cost of defense was eating us alive. We might have wound up losing the whole shooting match. We've got to keep this newspaper running. We'd rather be paying off a loan to the bank than to Rex Carr and Jim Green."

"When you get a bird in hand, it's worth several in the bush," commented Carr, whose share of Green's check would be one-third—$466,667.

Kowalski, alleged in the memo to have been a "bagman and vicious hood," apparently missed a Bankruptcy Court claim filing deadline somewhere along the line, so he got nothing.

However, the *Telegraph* did eventually agree to Mrs. DeGrand's claim of $50,000, thus closing the cases, with Bob DeGrand's survivors the last to collect.

Whichever libel insurance company got stuck with the bill would pay $1 million of the total settlement—$1,506,132.[6]

To pay the remainder, the company borrowed $400,000 more from an Alton bank.

At the final hearing terminating the *Telegraph*'s fourteen months under the jurisdiction of the Bankruptcy Court, Judge Trabue's last major question was: "Is everything set up so the attorneys can get paid?"

When it was over, the *Telegraph* calculated its overall legal bills at $612,795—of which $322,198 went to Jenner & Block—not all that much for a *New York Times,* but an enormous sum for a newspaper operating with the *Telegraph*'s profit margin. The primary insurance carrier reimbursed the newspaper for $200,000 of that amount.

"I was very happy with the settlement," remarked Henry McAdams a few days later. "We were hooked. The huge legal fees were adding up. He [Green] had a very smart lawyer. We had two dumb [trial] lawyers. All the good lawyers are plaintiffs' lawyers here. Madison County lawyers are probably the smartest lawyers in the state of Illinois."

One of the terms of the settlement was the "vacation" of the trial court judgment in *Green* v. *Telegraph*. The case is wiped off the records. Jerry Pragacz, the jury foreperson, will have to content himself with the knowledge that, as far as "the law books" are concerned, none of it ever happened.

The trade periodical for the newspaper business, *Editor & Publisher,* took note of the settlements in this editorial:

> An itemized progress report on the libel suit against the *Alton Telegraph* reads like a mystery story on how to murder a newspaper legally. Agatha Christie couldn't have done any better.
>
> This case has newspaper editors and libel lawyers shaking their heads in wonderment as to how and why it happened and in fear as to when it might be repeated against another newspaper elsewhere. It contains all those developments that never should have taken place, but did, and all those adverse decisions that never had been made before. . . .
>
> It is an outrageous scenario that we fear will be repeated.[7]

Thirteen years had elapsed between the communication from the news reporter to news source and the payment of money to some of the names in the memo. The *Telegraph*'s long ordeal provoked a compassionate response from journalists much bigger and more powerful than the Cousleys of Alton, but especially from small-town editors. "What happened to the *Alton Telegraph* is one of the most tragic episodes in the history of American journalism and the American system of justice," wrote publisher David E. Toney from tiny West Columbia, Texas.[8]

"I'm horrified," said Martin A. Dykeman, chief editorial writer at the *St. Petersburg Times*. "Here were two reporters diligently trying to determine if something was true, and they nearly lost the newspaper. This isn't merely chilling. It's frigid."[9]

The University of Arizona bestowed upon Paulie Cousley and the *Telegraph* its annual John Peter Zenger Award for Freedom of the Press and the People's Right to Know. Zenger is enshrined in journalism history as the German immigrant who was imprisoned ten months before being brought to trial in 1735, and freed by a jury, on a charge of libel for criticizing the government of New York Colony.

In his routine fashion, the Rev. Mr. Burroughs mentioned the award in his regular announcements at the Sunday morning worship in the First Presbyterian Church. He extended the congratulations of the congregation to Mr. Cousley. The Cousleys were seated, as is their custom, close to the front on the left side. Dr. Pfeiffenberger was not in church that morning, but his wife Marthaine, Marty for short, was in her customary seat up front on the right side. She rose from her seat, bolted up the middle aisle and through the door at the rear, slamming it on the way out.

The Pfeiffenbergers were incensed at the idea that the Cousleys would be honored for what had happened in Madison County. While the merger of Piasa faded from memories of others, the doctor felt that he had been personally victimized by the affair. He brooded over the death of an institution that his grandfather had founded. The disintegration of a family friendship that had begun with Paulie and Mather's grandfathers—the architect Lucas Pfeiffenberger and the former printer's devil John Cousley—was one of the more poignant of the many side effects of the Green affair.

When I talked with Dr. Pfeiffenberger later in his surgeon's office above the old office of Piasa in downtown Alton, his hatred would have sliced through flesh.

"I don't think the people at the *Telegraph* are very admirable people," he said. "I've known Paul almost all of his life, known his dad and his mother, operated on his father, operated on Steve's father and mother, sat in the same pew in church for umpteen years, my sisters were best friends with Paul's sisters, my uncle was the architect that built the *Telegraph* building. The connections have been very close for many, many years, and I feel absolutely betrayed.

"They talked about freedom of the press and the right to question police officials, but this was pure and simple McCarthyism. You just don't make serious charges against the leading financial institution in your community, one that had been doing business for eighty-some years and had an excellent reputation. You just don't do that. Particularly you don't do it in a small community where you know intimately all the people associated with it. They never said one word [of remorse], publicly or privately. I'd have put it right on the front page: 'We made a mistake.'

"My beef with the *Telegraph* is, they knew intimately, on a first-name basis, all the directors of Piasa and Bob DeGrand. Not one word was ever said. They didn't openly accuse. They secretly accused.

"They talk about freedom of the press and the people's right to know. The bottom line is, they're interested in money, and this is the only way to get their attention. If you hurt 'em a little bit financially, maybe they'll wake up."

14

The Chilling Effect

Paulie Cousley retired as publisher and president of the company in the middle of 1983 at the age of seventy-five. People in Alton tried to express their regrets over what had happened to him and to his newspaper in various unusual ways. The East End Improvement Association, for example, invited him to be the grand marshal of the Halloween parade, an honor he declined because he was not feeling well. A short time later, he entered a hospital for treatment of cancer of the prostate. His health continued to decline and in 1986 Paul Sparks Cousley died.

By then the relations between the remaining Cousleys and the McAdamses were beyond repair. Just as a marriage will sometimes be unable to survive a severe family tragedy, the years of tension over the libel suits had magnified enormously the basic journalistic philosophical differences between the businessmen McAdamses on the counting house floor of the *Telegraph* building and the newsmen Cousleys on the newsroom floor. Steve Cousley, the new president and publisher, opened *Editor & Publisher* one day to discover a classified ad announcing that the McAdams interest in the newspaper was for sale. Prospective buyers were conducted by the McAdamses on tours of the plant without even being introduced to the majority share-holding Cousleys on the premises. One prospective buyer who found the McAdamses' price attractive began contacting relatives of Steve's and Paulie's to test whether it would be possible to pick up enough additional stock to convert the minority into a controlling majority. This had to be a real concern—the possibility of living through all the sniping from the McAdamses throughout the years of agony in the courts only to lose control of the newspaper because one of Paulie's second cousins broke ranks. In fact, the Cousley who appeared most receptive to cashing in his interest in the newspaper was Steve's own younger brother, David R. Cousley, the advertising manager of the *Telegraph*. But David resisted the temptation and stuck with the rest of the family.

At last, in January of 1985, the McAdamses completed the sale of their 49 percent interest to a new buyer, a subsidiary of Ingersoll Publications Co.[1] The chairman of that privately held newspaper chain is Ralph M. Ingersoll II, whose reputation is as an "up and coming media magnate, a tireless pursuer of potentially profitable papers, and a ruthless cost-cutter."[2] His father founded the experimental New York liberal newspaper *PM* in 1940. The elder Ingersoll was a quixotic upper-class radical who refused to accept advertising in *PM*. His newspaper folded, of course, but in the mid-1950s, he and two sons acquired a chain of small- and medium-sized papers in the Northeast—papers that were, according to one observer, "the very model of mediocrity that *PM* was supposed to shame."[3] The father and son Ralph Ingersolls had a falling out over the son's preoccupation with profits. "[My father] came to believe I had sold out because he thought I was devoting myself mindlessly to the making of money," Ralph II said later. In that same interview, the son said: "My conception of a well-managed newspaper is the difference between a 10 percent profit margin and a 30 percent profit margin."[4] In 1981 Ralph II forced his father out of the business, eliminating the senior Ingersoll's $1 million-a-year share of partnership profits, and the two men never spoke again after that. In 1985, the year the father died, the newspaper group managed by the son consisted of twenty-six dailies and sixty weeklies in fourteen states. A sizable portion of the group's $207 million in annual advertising revenue—about $70 million—came from recent acquisitions in the St. Louis area. Among these were bi-weeklies in Granite City and Collinsville to go along with a highly profitable string of thirty-three free-circulation suburban "shoppers" purchased in 1984.

The characters in the drama could not avoid living with their memories. Steve Cousley remained adamant. "I still don't believe they [the reporters] did anything wrong in sending that memo," he says. "How could they [Piasa] have made all those bad loans and not know it was going to blow apart some day?"

Joe Melosi sits in the kitchen of his home in Collinsville drinking cup after cup of coffee. His face is lined far beyond his years. "I wanted to get away from all this garbage . . . the newspaper business," he says. "Now I'm poison. I can't find a job. It's as though I had shot somebody. I wouldn't want to go to work for a newspaper. They don't know what their job is anymore. I know the *Telegraph* holds it against me, but I don't know why. I didn't make a dime out of it. It was very gutsy of them, though . . . they stuck behind me all the way.

"I sometimes wonder why I got in the business in the first place. It's been nothing but misery. Newspapers don't do their job anymore. It's all a game, everything is. Play it safe. These mobsters and politicians have got the press just where they want them. It's a way of controlling the press. The *Telegraph* did a lot of hard stories about politicians. I covered the courthouse for eight years. You keep banging away. You make a lot of people mad. A reporter's job is to find out what is really happening."

Rex Carr insists that the *Telegraph* case had nothing to do with freedom of the press. "You mention libel to a newspaper, they go berserk," he says. "They can't think rationally when they see that word." The damage to Green was exactly the same as if a newspaper delivery truck had run him down and crippled him, Carr is fond of declaring. The case, he suggests, was "about lazy reporters and uncaring editors who, but for [Melosi's] ongoing stupidity, would not have been caught up in the mess."

Phil Tone in Chicago thought it "most unjust that the newspaper or its insurers had to pay anything, but it enabled the newspaper to survive." "Lawyers," he said, "are in the business of representing people in contests, and we don't always agree with the arguments we advance in their behalf. But this was one brief I personally believed in very strongly."

The dispute over which the insurance companies would get caught with the $1 million check was settled when the Circuit Court of Madison County held that the policy in effect when the memo was written should apply rather than when Green said he learned of its existence. So Zurich got its $500,000 back from the unlucky company, Commercial Union.

Bill Cox said he thought at the time of the trial that he had been "snookered, abused" by Judge Chapman. "But as I look back," he said, "it wasn't his intent. There were his natural tendencies and biases. The judge was psychologically David fighting a newspaper. If he had a psychological prejudice or bias, it was because his firm had been a plaintiff's firm."

Reflecting on the case, Cox believes "the *Telegraph* paid for the federal government's mistakes. I think I did everything possible [in the trial] from the standpoint of points made."

Cox has nothing but admiration for Steve Cousley's "courage and idealism." "He put it all on the line," meaning the newspaper, "but the people don't see a need for a free press. They think the press is heartless."

Ed Eckert is aware of no mistakes by the federal agencies. "We made the proper decisions," he said. "My only regret—and it's a real tragedy—is that the [FHLBB] couldn't protect our supervisory function."

After first agreeing by telephone to meet with me and discuss the case, Jim Green changed his mind and declined. In my only conversation with him, one that he tried to avoid, of about five minutes in his office in Pontoon Beach in 1984 with his desk top littered with notes to himself about the new building projects he was involved in, Green described himself as "full of piss and vinegar."

I asked him if he had recovered from the years of struggle. "I guess I recovered. But that don't mean it didn't happen. It was so difficult. It was twelve years. That's a long time to battle a $7 billion organization, which is the FSLIC. They've got unlimited funds. And for you to stand up and challenge them and tell them, in effect, that you're going to battle them all the way to the wire . . .

"Can you appreciate my position? I'm saying I don't want to [talk to you]. I've had four or five magazines call me. And I just don't want it. I've drug my family through hell. I lost a son [in an automobile accident] a year and a half ago, just after I won the case. I'm not in the mood to go makin' some wild statement that goes out and somebody writes something about me. I've had enough about me . . ."

The lives of others were changed by the aftershocks of the Green affair. John Sobol put his real estate company "in mothballs" and took a job across the river in Missouri, the victim, he says, of "animosity in the business community" attributable to the memo.

The *Telegraph,* meanwhile, obtained a new libel insurance policy—for $10 million coverage. How the reporters and editors go about their jobs changed in many ways. A reporter who talked to many of them in 1983 concluded that "the *Telegraph*'s crusading spirit [had] all but died."[5] The paper is more cautious. It's like "a tight end who hears footsteps," is Steve Cousley's football analogy. "We're doing less hip-shooting than we did 10 years ago."[6]

No longer did the *Telegraph* have any stomach for investigative stories. "Let someone else stick their neck out this time," Steve told a reporter who had received a tip about possible misconduct in the sheriff's office.

"All the ideals and principles in the world don't mean a damn when it comes down to hard economics," Cousley asserted. "I like aggressive journalism. Newspapers have to keep doing their job—it's their constitutional responsibility. But when the trail of the story leads into the counting house and threatens the economic existence of the newspaper, watch out."

More of the business of the newsroom was being conducted conversationally. Reporters and editors didn't write many memos, even to each other. Reporters were told to destroy their notes after a story is published. "We don't want someone coming in here asking about our state of mind," Steve told the *Wall Street Journal* reporter, John Curley.

Asked how he thought the paper had changed, Dr. Pfeiffenberger said he didn't think the *Telegraph* was "quite so high and mighty" as before the Green affair. "They're not taking after people quite so much. They're trying to curry favor. There isn't so much of their damn sick attitude that everybody successful is on the make. It will take more than a generation of good responsible action on their part to get any confidence back."

No one thought that Ingersoll's executives would be content with a minority interest in the Alton newspaper—and they weren't. No sooner had the new partners taken their seats on the board of directors than Ingersoll and his associates began negotiations with Steve Cousley for the sale of the rest of the stock. At a meeting with *Telegraph* employees, the representatives of the Ingersoll regional subsidiary—which was called Sunrise Industries, Inc.—spoke enticingly of a future with a new offset press, a Sunday edition, and improved health insurance for the staff.

On May 21, 1985—150 years after the founding of the *Telegraph* and 5 years after the trial of the libel suit—Steve Cousley announced the sale of the Cousley family stock to Ingersoll's company.[7] He indicated later that it had been impossible to hold the family together in the face of Ingersoll's offer to buy. The price that the new owners paid to acquire the *Telegraph* has never been officially disclosed, but reports filed with the federal Securities and Exchange Commission suggest that it was in the neighborhood of $12 million—slightly more than half of which presumably went to the Cousleys and slightly less than half of which went to the McAdamses.

"While Sunrise is well-positioned to contribute to the *Telegraph*'s continued development," Ingersoll said in a prepared statment, "we are committed to Stephen Cousley's judgment and leadership. I view the new business arrangement with the Cousley family as the joining of a new partnership which will ensure the editorial independence and prosperity of the *Telegraph* into the next century."

Ingersoll said Steve would continue as president, editor, and publisher. In his statement, Steve said the merger of the daily newspaper and the suburban shoppers with which it had been competing for advertising "signals a new day for the *Telegraph*."

Almost overnight, modern management techniques were introduced at the *Telegraph*. The newspaper was wired into Sunrise's regional classified advertising computer, which enables customers to buy combinations of exposure for their ads and receive a single bill. The new offset press that the new owners had promised was installed, with full-color printing capability. Through Sunrise's volume purchasing of newsprint, the *Telegraph* began paying $375 a ton for paper that had been costing $500 a ton. Most of the department heads were put on incentive plans. Employees were made aware of the profit enhancement goals. David Cousley soon resigned to enroll in Washington University's Graduate School of Architecture. Then three advertising salesmen—half the staff—reacted to the announcement that they would henceforth be paid entirely on commission by quitting and starting their own community shopper. In the most radical development of all, the *Alton Telegraph* entered 1986 with something it had never had before in its century and a half of existence—an operating budget!

Ingersoll's commitment to Stephen Cousley's judgment and leadership did not last long. Steve named Executive Editor D. G. Schumacher to also be general manager, but that decision was overruled. The corporate policymakers sent in a new general manager from one of Ingersoll's California properties. The new GM—Robert L. Carl—suggested the early retirement of Managing Editor John Focht and involved himself in minor editorial decisions, ordering, for example, a smaller type size for the headlines on obituaries, a serious enough change to cause a number of elderly readers to cancel their subscriptions.

By solidifying his position on the outer rim of the metro area, Ingersoll was priming his combination of paid dailies and free weeklies for a "showdown with Pulitzer"—meaning the *Post-Dispatch*. He said he was confident that his saturation distribution coupled with low-cost nonunion production would leave the *Post-Dispatch* as "sort of a boutique operation that will serve the market's understandable need for a local [St. Louis] daily."[8]

Ingersoll said he wants his suburban papers to become more parochial and to devote themselves to local "hard news of record"—but not "lengthy pieces on county government, which people find very tedious."[9] In the case of the *Telegraph*, Carl directed Cousley to print more and shorter stories on the front page.

In another analysis, Ingersoll said he was impressed by the *Telegraph*'s high penetration of its local market but worried by its "inability to grow with the expanding Madison County market." "Unaddressed, over less than a generation this problem would seriously erode the *Telegraph*'s penetration of the advertisers' defined market," he explained. "With declining net readership, the *Telegraph* would decline economically." To deal with this problem, he mentioned plans to start a Sunday edition, improve sports coverage, promote the newspaper to new arrivals in the community (through price, prizes, charity appeals, etc.), and, most significantly, establish a special edition for the Granite City area.[10] "He doesn't understand," Steve Cousley had told me earlier, "that we don't like Granite City."

Thus, the *Alton Telegraph* has become one of Ingersoll's divisions to be deployed in the battle against Joseph Pulitzer's once distinguished old central city daily for domination of supermarket and other retail advertising in the St. Louis area. To understand what is at stake here, it is helpful to consider Schnuck Markets, a local supermarket chain that spends in excess of $2 million a year for print advertising.[11] The suburban weeklies now owned by Ingersoll, which are delivered free to 827,000 suburban households, wrested Schnuck's advertising from the *Post-Dispatch* only to themselves lose the account to a direct mail firm that delivers Schnuck's ads on a more timely day of the week. The *Post-Dispatch* then fought back by founding a new weekly supplement of its own, entitled *You,* into which the grocers were urged to insert their advertising. The name of the new section reflects a secret of modern newspapering that the original Pulitzer and surely O. K. Bovard would never have understood: in the video age, newspapers must do a better job of giving the reader personally useful features about trimming one's thighs and using the right eyeliner.

On September 1, 1986, the last of the Cousleys at the *Alton Telegraph*—Stephen A. Cousley—announced his resignation. He said he would no longer be involved in the daily operations of the newspaper.

In its new life the *Telegraph* is unquestionably a better managed business. The fiscal accounting system is vastly improved, the press bigger, the computers more versatile, the libel insurance more comprehensive. It is undoubtedly more profitable. Advertising rates have been raised twice since the sale. Dr. Pfeiffenberger also has less cause to fret these days. The newspaper is less inclined to stumble around raising hell, as it did in the past, or even to do tedious pieces about county government. The libel suit nightmare is one of the reasons for that. And Ingersoll's brand of corporate journalism is another. Hell raising, after all, is not likely to help Schnuck's sell groceries.

The most meaningful change of all may be symbolic. When the new offset press was installed, the old Mergenthaler linotype had to be moved from its place at the front of the building to the rear of the museum building next door. There it remains near all the other dusty relics of Alton's past. The Ingersoll organization is interested in dollars, not quaint symbols.

15

The Price We Pay

A professor of psychiatry in New Jersey wrote a letter to the editor of the *Wall Street Journal* after reading that newspaper's account of the effects of the libel suits on the *Telegraph*. In his letter, he said the case "illustrated excruciatingly [how] the unfettered legal power structure in the United States has led to the establishment of a 'legocracy' which is not subject to any system of checks and balances."[1]

The juridical whirlpool into which the *Telegraph* was drawn may be a case book example of the wastefulness—in money and human talent—that Harvard University President Derek Bok has criticized in the American legal system. Bok, in his 1982 report to Harvard's Board of Overseers, focused on the "massive diversion of exceptional talent into pursuits that often add little to the growth of the economy, the pursuit of culture, or the enhancement of the human spirit."[2]

The incredible convolutions of this story occupied the time and attention of many talented individuals for many years before winding their way to a conclusion reasonably satisfactory to almost everyone, except, of course, the newspaper. When it was over, John Hackmann, the mild-mannered Illini Federal executive who had been in on the first legal action against Green, noted that the controversy had been settled "eleven years, I don't know how many millions of dollars in legal fees, and I don't know how many years off my life later."

Sadly, one must assume that the many grotesque vagaries of the "legocracy" in southern Illinois—complete with the institutionalized redistribution of wealth in Metro East—exist with the consent of the governed. The voters of Illinois had an opportunity in 1970 to get rid of the partisan nomination and election of judges. They decided to stick with something close to what they had, but worse— party organizations still use judgeships as patronage, but the retention feature makes it more difficult to jettison bad judges. Every two years since then, the people's representatives in the General Assembly of Illinois have considered and rejected various proposals for "judicial reform."

In this book I have endeavored to trace some of the historical roots that help explain the public attitudes toward the Metro East "legocracy"—and toward the newspaper in Alton. That the citizens of Madison County did not rise up in mass indignation when the best and most courageous newspaper in all of southern Illinois was assessed the biggest damage award for libel in United States newspaper history for something it hadn't printed—and then when that newspaper was denied the opportunity for appellate review of that decision by the jury—and then when it appeared that the newspaper might actually be given over to the plaintiffs without any court having condescended to look at the appeal is, well, it's curious, to say the very least. After the trial, the tavern owner in Wood River exercised his First Amendment rights by putting up a sign saying, "Congrats, Jim—Screw you, *Alton Telegraph*." But none of the people of Alton organized a demonstration to protest what had been done to their newspaper and to *their* First Amendment rights.

For counselor Carr misses the point when he maintains that the case had nothing to do with the freedom of the press. To the extent that the *Telegraph* had been "chilled" in its pursuit of the news when Steve Cousley said let someone else stick their necks out this time, it is the readers, the citizens of the community, who are the victims— who are, indeed, less free.

"The public doesn't like newspapers, period," says Tim Hanson, the lawyer for the publishers. "The sooner we learn that, the happier we're going to be."[3]

"We had 20 good years," adds Eugene C. Patterson of the *St.*

Petersburg Times, "and now the courts are beginning to pull in the corners of the net. We're getting trouble, especially when cases go to a jury. Juries are the American public, and they don't like us. They picture the American press as a big fat corporate body, and it's difficult to explain to juries the problems of the journalist trying to do his or her job, and get to the truth."[4]

Some of today's overt hostility is undoubtedly explained by the smug, depersonalized corporate journalism, though the *Telegraph* experience suggests that the causes are more deep-seated. The origins of those causes can be found in an earlier era when the newspaper voices were harshly partisan, but also more numerous, and newspaper readers were more reticent about talking back to their local newspapers.

If the "legocracy" is unfettered, so too is the only newspaper in town. The opportunity to talk back to that newspaper is more important now than when there were several competing organs. When Melosi promised DeGrand a chance to have his turn at bat in the pages of the *Telegraph,* DeGrand should have been given that opportunity. When the initial story of DeGrand's resignation from Piasa broke, he should have been asked for his side immediately.

Most would agree that the subject of the *Telegraph*'s inquiry—a possible connection between the region's leading savings and loan association and organized crime—was of the utmost public importance and worthy therefore of its journalistic attention. But did the newspaper act responsibly? The two reporters were trying to establish the truthfulness of what they had been told, in the only way they thought they could, by cooperating with law enforcement authorities. The newspaper insists that it could not have foreseen that Piasa would stop making loans to Green; that the Federal Home Loan Bank Board would force Piasa's merger with another institution; or that the other institution—Illini Federal—would become embroiled in a controversy over its handling of some of the earnings from what had been Green's properties. But, one might ask, should not the reporters and editors have been more sensitive to personal and institutional reputations?

Here we wander into the thorniest of concepts: What exactly is "press responsibility"?

Alan Barth, until his death in 1979 a very wise editorial writer for the *Washington Post,* once wrote this:

> If you want a watch dog to warn you of intruders, you must put up with a certain amount of mistaken barking. Now and then he will sound off because he sees a cat or a squirrel or is outraged by a postman. And that kind of barking can, of course, be a nuisance. But if you muzzle him and leash him and teach him to be decorous, you will find that he doesn't do the job for which you got him in the first place. Some extraneous barking is the price you must pay for service as a watchdog. A free press is the watchdog of society.[5]

Though every editor should strive to be as truthful, fair, and responsible as he can, Barth also observed that the imposition of standards of responsibility by some board of "chosen judges or sages" is fraught with the gravest peril to freedom of the press.

"The imposition of standards means the extirpation of eccentricity," Barth said. It operates to eliminate the rebel. And in the search for truth, rebels and eccentrics are indispensable.

"Moreover, responsibility would become, almost inescapably, synonymous with conformity. Responsible conduct would be conduct considered becoming by the majority—and, more than that, by people in power—what is commonly called 'the establishment.'"

Dr. Pfeiffenberger symbolized "the establishment" in Alton. He became very angry with Melosi and Elmer Broz, and eventually the Cousleys, because they did not display the proper deference toward the sources of power in the community, beginning, of course, with the savings and loan association that Dr. Pfeiffenberger's grandfather had founded. Melosi and Broz were too untamed, too eccentric to fit into today's big business journalism of conformity and caution. In this instance, their groping for the truth went seriously awry, which does not lessen the value of people like them in journalism's highly unscientific, often irregular truth-seeking process.

No one should doubt, Alan Barth said in his essay, that if the press is granted full freedom, it will sometimes abuse it. "It will sometimes pry into the privacy of individuals and publish stories that inflict wanton injury." The injuries in Madison County were beyond the control of the newspaper, which acted "responsibly" by trying to determine the facts before publishing them. But that will not always be the case. Some newspapers will be irresponsible sometimes. Barth concluded that "only a wholly independent, somewhat obstreperous and slightly irresponsible press can serve as a sentinel of freedom." If the American people want what O. K. Bovard called "true newspapers" exercising true freedom of the press, they must be willing to put up with some mistaken barking.

Group journalism already is producing a softer, safer, less outspoken, more conformist American newspaper. "We are in an era of 'happy journalism,'" *Chicago Sun-Times* lawyer Dan Feldman said not long ago. "Editors are beginning to think like lawyers," agreed the Washington bureau chief of the Gannett News Service, John Hanachette. "They are losing their zeal for [investigative] stories."[6]

What happened to the *Alton Telegraph* in the end—its acquisition by a mass merchandising group and the removal of that old linotype from the sidewalk out front—might have occurred anyway, without the Melosi-Lhotka memo and all that transpired afterwards. Maybe the courageous home-owned watchdog/newspaper that digs into government news because the people need to know is or soon will be extinct.

There is, however, that last, most crucial question of all: Could what happened to the *Alton Telegraph* in this case happen elsewhere? Could a newspaper in a small- to medium-sized city, regardless of style of ownership, be struck with a libel verdict so large, so far beyond the civil "crime," that it could be wiped out? The answer is yes—in a jurisdiction in which the political and judicial systems permit it to happen. Regardless of how the judges are chosen, and regardless of how the juries are chosen, the courts will continue to be political institutions. It will be ever thus. The words of the First Amendment will mean what the American people want them to mean.

Summary of Key Cases
References
Notes
Index

Summary of Key Cases

The Green Libel Suit

James C. Green v. Alton Telegraph Printing Co., Joseph Melosi and William Lhotka. No. 77-L-66, Filed February 13, 1975, in Madison County Circuit Court, seeking $10,545,000 in libel damages. Trial began April 28, 1980, and ended June 3, 1980. The jury awarded $6,700,000 in compensatory damages and $2,500,000 in punitive damages. A motion for a new trial was denied November 26, 1980.

In re Alton Telegraph Printing Co. The newspaper petitioned April 10, 1981, for reorganization under Chapter 11 of the Bankruptcy Code. Number 81 BK 50082 in the United States District Court for the Southern District of Illinois.

The Appellate Court of Illinois for the Fifth District dismissed the appeal of the trial court judgment in an order issued April 7, 1982. Number 80-602.

The case was settled by the parties June 10, 1982, for $1,400,001.

The Ne Exeat Case

James C. Green v. Illini Federal Savings and Loan Association, PSL Realty Co., and R. W. McGovern, No. 74-L-228 in the Madison County Circuit Court, a wrongful imprisonment suit seeking $6,000,000 damages for the overnight jailing of Green on a writ of ne exeat republica issued April 11, 1972. Following a five-week trial, the jury returned a verdict of $3,000,000 in damages June 7, 1979.

The judgment was released in the settlement agreement of October 22, 1981 (described below).

For Control of Green's Properties

In the State Courts

PSL Realty Co. v. Granite Investment Co., March 27, 1972, Madison County Circuit Court No. 72-E-77, demanding the books and records of Granite and seeking to enjoin Granite from interfering with rent collections. Injunction issued and FSLIC appointed receiver by Judge Joseph J. Barr.

Granite Investment Co. v. PSL Realty Co. and Illini Federal Savings and Loan Association, May 11, 1973, St. Clair County Circuit Court No. 73-L-1677, alleging a civil conspiracy to breach the Base Agreement and forfeit the contracts for deed. Seeking $25,000,000 in damages.

Interlocutory appeal to the Illinois Appellate Court for the Fifth District (Number 77-125) by Green and Granite seeking to overturn the Madison County Circuit Court's issuance of the injunction and its appointment of the receiver.

Opinion by Fifth District Appellate Court dissolving the temporary injunction and the receivership, July 23, 1976, 42 Ill. 3d 697, 703.

Opinion by Fifth District Appellate Court, September 13, 1979, directing FSLIC to return mortgages to Illini Federal and enjoining FSLIC from proceeding with mortgage foreclosure action in federal courts, September 26, 1979, 76 Ill. App. 3d 978.

Illinois Supreme Court opinion September 30, 1981, in *PSL Realty Co. and Illini Federal Savings and Loan Association* v. *Granite Investment Co., James C. Green, Darryl Layman, and First National Bank in Madison; and Granite Investment Co. and James C. Green* v. *FSLIC*. Number 52598. Citation: 86 Ill. 2d 291. The decision ruled against Granite Investment.

In the Federal Courts

FSLIC v. PSL Realty Co., Granite Investment Co., James C. Green, Shirley J. Green, Capitol Indemnity Corp., Howard Steele Construction Co. A mortgage foreclosure suit, Number A-Civ-76-0079, filed August 26, 1976, in the United States District Court for the Southern District of Illinois.

In re Granite Investment Co., Debtor. A petition for reorganization under Chapter 11 of the Bankruptcy Code, October 9, 1979, Number BK 79-04387. United States District Court for the Southern District of Illinois.

Opinion by the Seventh Circuit United States Court of Appeals, September 12, 1980, in *FSLIC* v. *PSL Realty Co., Granite Investment Co., James C. Green, Capitol Indemnity Corp., Howard Steele Construction Co., the Hon.*

Charles E. Jones, the Hon. John M. Karnes, the Hon. George W. Kasserman, Jr., and all other Justices of the Illinois Appellate Court for the Fifth District, the Hon. Victor J. Mosele, and all Judges of the Third Judicial Circuit of Illinois. Case numbers 79-2134, 79-2211, 79-2212, 79-2302. Citation: 630 F. 2d 515. The court held for FSLIC.

The parties agreed to a settlement filed with the Recorder of Deeds in Madison County October 22, 1981, that the disputed properties would be returned to Green and Granite Investment with the assumption of a debt owed to FSLIC.

References

Books

Barrett, James W. *Joseph Pulitzer and his World*. New York: Vanguard, 1941.
Beecher, Edward, *Narrative of Riots at Alton*. New York: E. P. Dutton, 1965.
Behrens, John C. *The Typewriter Guerrillas*. Chicago: Nelson-Hall, 1947.
Bogart, Leo. *Press and Public*. Hillsdale, N.J.: Erlbaum, 1981.
Eastman, Susan H. *River Bend: An Area That Knows No Panics*. Research Report 17. Coordinator of Area Development for Riverbend Civic Progress, Southern Illinois Univ. at Edwardsville, Sept. 1981.
Ernst, Morris E., and Alexander Lindey. *Hold Your Tongue*. New York: Abelard Press, 1950.
Filler, Louis. *The Muckrakers*. University Park: Pennsylvania State Univ. Press, 1976.
Gavin, Clark. *Foul, False and Infamous*. New York: Abelard Press, 1950.
Hanson, Arthur B. *Libel and Related Torts*. Vol. 1. New York: ANPA Foundation, 1969.
Harrison, John M., and Harry E. Stein, eds. *Muckraking: Past, Present and Future*. University Park: Pennsylvania State Univ. Press, 1976.
The Kefauver Committee Report on Organized Crime. New York: Didier, 1951.
Kimball, Stanley B. *East Europeans in Southwestern Illinois: The Ethnic Experience in Historical Perspective*. Research Rept. 14. Coordinator of Area Development for Riverbend Civic Progress, Southern Illinois Univ. at Edwardsville, May 1981.
Lincoln, William S. *Alton Trials of Winthrop S. Gilman*. New York: John F. Trow, 1838.
Markham, James W. *Bovard of the "Post-Dispatch."* Baton Rouge: Louisiana State Univ. Press, 1954.

Norton, Wilbur T., ed. *The Centennial History of Madison County, Illinois, and its People, 1812–1912.* 2 vols. Chicago: Lewis Publishing Co., 1912.

Phelan, James. *Scandals, Scamps and Scoundrels: The Casebook of an Investigative Reporter.* New York: Random House, 1982.

Robinson, Charles Mulford. *The Advancement of Alton: A General City Plan for the Board of Trade.* Alton: Melling and Gaskins, 1914.

Simon, Paul. *Lovejoy: Martyr to Freedom.* St. Louis: Concordia, 1964.

Stevens, John D. *Shaping the First Amendment: The Development of Free Expression.* Beverly Hills, Calif.: Sage Publications, 1982.

Unpublished Dissertation

Fairbanks, Merwin G. "A History of Newspaper Journalism in Alton, Illinois, from 1836 to 1962, as represented by the *Alton Evening Telegraph* and its Predecessors." Ph.D. diss., Southern Illinois Univ. at Carbondale, Sept. 1973.

Newspapers and Periodicals

Alton Evening Telegraph. "Ye Editorial Staff Takes its Stand." Jan. 20, 1912.

Alton Telegraph. Editorial: "Faith Must be Restored." Mar. 15, 1971, p. 8.

———. "McAdams Family Sells its *Telegraph* Minority Share." Jan. 28, 1985, p. A1.

Bailey, Greg. "Million-dollar Master: Rex Carr Builds Awards From an Unlikely Base." *National Law Journal,* July 14, 1980, pp. 1, 24.

Barbash, Fred. "*Alton Telegraph* Libel Judgment Sends Fearful Message to Press." *Washington Post,* Aug. 25, 1981, p. A3.

Barth, Alan. "A Plea for a 'Slightly Irresponsible Press.'" *ASNE Bulletin,* American Society of Newspaper Editors, Apr. 1984, p. 16.

Berman, Phyllis. "A Quixotic Father's Acquisitive Son." *Forbes* magazine, Oct. 20, 1986, pp. 105–8.

Bok, Derek. "A Flawed System." *Harvard Magazine,* May–June 1983, pp. 38–45, 70–71.

Broadway, Jim, and Jim Orso. "3 Lawyers Gave Big to Judicial Campaigns." St. Louis *Globe-Democrat,* Dec. 15, 1981, p. 9A.

Curley, John. "How Libel Suit Sapped the Crusading Spirit of a Small Newspaper." *Wall Street Journal,* Sept. 29, 1983, pp. 1, 25.

Denniston, Lyle. "A Punishing Verdict in Illinois." *Washington Journalism Review,* Mar. 1982, p. 52.

Dunlap, William H. "How Lost Confidence Forced Merger of Piasa S & L." St. Louis *Post-Dispatch,* Apr. 25, 1971, p. 7C.
———. "Illini S & L Fortunes." St. Louis *Post-Dispatch,* Apr. 26, 1971, p. 13A.
———. "Piasa Merger Meant Federal Policy Shifts." St. Louis *Post-Dispatch,* Apr. 27, 1971, p. 5B.
Editor & Publisher. Editorial: "Legalized Execution." Apr. 24, 1982, p. 4.
———. "Is Investigative Reporting Dead?" Aug. 25, 1984, p. 14.
———. "Dealing with Libel Suits." May 11, 1985, p. 16.
———. "Ingersoll Acquires *Alton* (Ill.) *Telegraph.*" June 1, 1985, p. 18.
Edwardsville Intelligencer. "Circuit Judge Chapman Suggests Quicker Handling of Court Cases." Jan. 31, 1980, p. 3.
Fiske, Edward B. "President of Harvard Brands Legal System Costly and Complex." *New York Times,* Apr. 22, 1983, p. 1.
Goldstein, Tom. "Odd Couple: Prosecutors and the Press." *Columbia Journalism Review,* Jan./Feb. 1984, pp. 23–29.
Jenkins, John A. "Betting on the Verdict." *New York Times Magazine,* Nov. 25, 1984, pp. 88–96.
Jensen, Mrs. Dana O., ed. "Lucas Pfeiffenberger, Architect." *St. Louis Bulletin,* Missouri Historical Society, vol. 24, 1967, pp. 47–49.
Knorr, Bryce. "Rex Carr: From Civil Rights Suits to Malpractice Suits, He Retains Notoriety." *Belleville News-Democrat,* Jan. 1, 1978, pp. 1B, 2B.
Lambrecht, Bill. "Land of Multimillion-Dollar Judgments." St. Louis *Post-Dispatch,* Feb. 7, 1982, pp. 1, 14.
———. "Trial Lawyers' Million-Dollar Club." St. Louis *Post-Dispatch,* Feb. 9, 1982, p. 9A.
———. "Elected Judges Take Lawyers' Contributions." St. Louis *Post-Dispatch,* Feb. 10, 1982, pp. 1, 8.
———. "Lawyers' Campaign Got Judges Ousted." St. Louis *Post-Dispatch,* Feb. 11, 1982, pp. 1, 9.
Lambrecht, Bill, and Robert Goodrich. "High Stakes Lawyers Joust for Maimed." St. Louis *Post-Dispatch,* Feb. 9, 1982, pp. 1, 9.
Lewin, Tamar. "Man-Made Hazards Pose More Than a Medical Problem." *New York Times,* Aug. 29, 1982, p. 4E.
Margolick, David. "Lawyers' Inner Circle Meets to Swap Secrets of the Personal Injury Trade." *New York Times,* Aug. 29, 1983, p. A12.
Mathewson, Mark. "Plaintiffs' Paradise." *Illinois Times,* Springfield, Ill., July 13–19, 1984, pp. 3–5.
Peer, Dr. Irwin N. "A New Danger for Journalists and TV Reporters." Letter to editor: *Wall Street Journal,* Oct. 31, 1983, p. 31.

Randolph, Eleanor, and Fred Barbash. "20 Years After Landmark Libel Case, Legal Costs on Media Minds." *Washington Post,* Mar. 9, 1984, p. A2.

Russell, John. "The Piasa: An Indian Tradition of Illinois." *The Evangelical Magazine and Gospel Advocate,* Utica, N.Y., July 1848, p. 18.

Stewart, James B., Jr. "Plaintiffs' County, USA." *The American Lawyer,* New York, Apr. 1983, pp. 88–93.

St. Louis Business Journal. "Ralph Ingersoll: 'We are heading for a showdown with Pulitzer.'" July 8–14, 1985, pp. 1, 15A.

Thomason, Arthur J. "Will the *Alton Telegraph* Die?" St. Louis *Globe-Democrat,* May 2–3, 1981. p. 15A.

Tybor, Joseph R. "Libel Award Puts Paper on Map." *National Law Journal,* July 14, 1980, pp. 3, 17.

———. "Burger Assails Lawyers on Ads, Percentage Fees." *Chicago Tribune,* Aug. 6, 1984, p. 4.

Wander, Barney. "The War on Gangsterism: A Study of Madison County, Illinois." *Focus Midwest* magazine, St. Louis, 1966, vol. 5, no. 34, pp. 8–10, 19–21.

Wehling, Robert J. "Rex Carr Defends 'Little People.'" St. Louis *Post-Dispatch,* Sept. 22, 1968, p. 10B.

Notes

Chapter 1. In a Plaintiff's Paradise

1. For stories of the Lock and Dam 26 funding controversy in Congress, see the *Washington Post,* Oct. 14, 1978, and the *Chicago Tribune,* Oct. 30, 1977, sec. 1, p. 1.
2. Russell, "The Piasa."
3. Chapman biographical details. Profile by Carla Baranauckas in *Edwardsville Intelligencer,* Jan. 31, 1980, p. 1.
4. Stewart, "Plaintiffs' County," p. 88.
5. Lambrecht, "Land of Multimillion-Dollar Judgments," series beginning Feb. 7, 1982, and continuing through Feb. 11, 1982. See also Mathewson, "Plaintiffs' Paradise," p. 3.
6. Stewart, "Plaintiffs' County," p. 92.
7. The account of Judge Chapman's editorial endorsement visit to the *Telegraph* is primarily as recounted by Steve Cousley. After first telling me that he would be happy to talk about the *Telegraph* case when all the related litigation had been resolved, Judge Chapman changed his mind and told me by phone that he would not meet with me to discuss that matter or any other matter. He is quoted in Stewart, "Plaintiffs' County," p. 92, as saying the *Telegraph* meeting was routine and had no bearing on the trial.

Chapter 2. Enter Jim Green the Builder

1. Eastman, *River Bend: An Area That Knows No Panics,* p. 11.
2. Phelan, *Scandals, Scamps and Scoundrels,* p. 40.
3. Norton, *Centennial History of Madison County,* p. 311.
4. Jensen, "Lucas Pfeiffenberger, Architect," p. 47.
5. Norton, *Centennial History of Madison County,* p. 306.
6. Simon, *Lovejoy,* p. 25. See also Beecher, *Narrative of Riots at Alton;* Lincoln, *Alton Trials of Winthrop S. Gilman.*

7. Robinson, *Advancement of Alton*, p. 41.
8. Kimball, *East Europeans in Southwestern Illinois*, p. 5.

Chapter 3. Roll-overs and Straw Parties

1. Wander, "War on Gangsterism," p. 21.
2. *Metro East Journal* (East St. Louis, Ill.), July 8, 1969.
3. See testimony of Clarence Bruckner in *Green v. Illini Federal et al.*, No. 74-L-228.
4. Arrest record. Bureau of Criminal Identification and Investigation, Illinois Department of Public Safety, report dated Aug. 27, 1959.
5. See "Statement of Facts," p. 1 in appellant-receiver FSLIC brief to the Illinois Supreme Court in *PSL Realty et al. v. Granite Investment et al.*, No. 52598.
6. See Kozielek's testimony with the jury absent in the trial of *Green v. Illini Federal et al.*, No. 74-L-228.
7. The most concise summaries of FSLIC/FHLBB allegations against Green are in the FSLIC's brief filed with the Illinois Supreme Court Apr. 2, 1980, in *PSL Realty et al. v. Granite Investment et al.*, No. 52598; and the counterclaim filed Sept. 6, 1977, in *Granite Investment v. PSL Realty et al.*, No. 73-L-1677.

Chapter 4. Blue Pencils at the *Telegraph*

1. Fairbanks, "History of Newspaper Journalism in Alton, Ill.," p. 92.
2. *Alton Evening Telegraph*, "Ye Editorial Staff Takes Its Stand."
3. Ibid.
4. Barrett, *Joseph Pulitzer and his World*, p. 24.
5. Markham, *Bovard of the "Post-Dispatch,"* p. 140.
6. Phelan, *Scandals, Scamps and Scoundrels*, p. 40.
7. *Kefauver Committee Report on Organized Crime*, pp. 24, 143–44, 166.
8. Wander, "War on Gangsterism," p. 8.
9. Ibid., p. 20.
10. Phelan, *Scandals, Scamps and Scoundrels*, p. 44.
11. Fairbanks, "History of Newspaper Journalism in Alton, Ill.," p. 187.

Chapter 5. A True Newspaper in Alton

1. Harrison and Stein, *Muckraking: Past, Present and Future*, p. 148.
2. *Editor & Publisher*, June 25, 1983, p. 13.

3. Because the Telegraph Co. filed for reorganization under the federal bankruptcy laws (No. 81-BK50082), the newspaper financial data are part of the court record.
4. See Bogart, *Press and Public*.

Chapter 6. The Memorandum

1. Behrens, *Typewriter Guerrillas*, p. xv.
2. See *Chicago Journalism Review*, June 1969, p. 3.
3. Feldman's *amicus* brief on behalf of the *Sun-Times* was one of several filed by news organizations but not accepted by the Fifth District Illinois Appellate Court in 1981.
4. For a discussion of reporter–law enforcement collaboration, see Goldstein, "Odd Couple: Prosecutors and the Press," p. 23. The Hersh and Mollenhoff quotes are from that article.
5. The Melosi-Lhotka memo was entered into evidence at the 1980 trial of *Green v. Alton Telegraph Printing Co. et al.*, No. 77-L-66.

Chapter 7. The Fall of Piasa

1. The 1969 correspondence from Will Wilson, assistant attorney general in charge of the criminal division of the Justice Department, to Frank Dorer at the FHLBB, and then from Dorer to Meller was introduced in evidence at the Green libel trial.
2. From DeGrand's testimony in the Green libel trial, May 1, 1980. Christie did not testify and is now deceased.
3. Discovery deposition taken Aug. 3, 1975, in *Robert L. DeGrand v. Alton Telegraph Printing Co., Joseph Melosi, and William Lhotka*, Madison County Circuit Court, No. 75-L-139.
4. *Alton Telegraph*, July 9, 1969.
5. The tax shelter implications of Gale's partnership interest were explored at the June 1979 ne exeat trial of *Green v. Illini Federal et al.* at which Gale was a witness.
6. DeGrand's reaction to the stories of his resignation is related in his undated written statement labeled "The Piasa Story."
7. Deposition in *DeGrand v. Alton Telegraph Printing Co. et al.* taken July 31, 1978.
8. See *Alton Telegraph*, Mar. 13, 14, 15, 1971, for stories of the Piasa–Illini Federal merger.
9. Preston Martin letter dated Mar. 19, 1971.
10. St. Louis *Post-Dispatch*, Apr. 25, 1971.

11. See brief of appellant-receiver FSLIC filed with Illinois Supreme Court, Apr. 2, 1980, in *PSL Realty et al.* v. *Granite Investment et al.,* No. 52598.
12. The "skimming" of the rents was testified to by both Hackmann and Green in the June 1979 ne exeat trial of *Green* v. *Illini Federal et al.*
13. The events leading up to the injunction against Green are as testified to by Hackmann in the June 1979 ne exeat trial.
14. As testified to by Green in the June 1979 ne exeat trial.
15. Layman quoted in *Alton Telegraph,* May 10, 1972, p. 1.
16. Carr's ownership interest in Green Investors was discussed in Judge Mosele's chambers during the June 1979 ne exeat trial, according to the trial transcript.

Chapter 8. Jury Selection in Metro East

1. Conference on judges and the media, University of Illinois at Urbana-Champaign, June 1, 1984.
2. Jenkins, "Betting on the Verdict," p. 95.
3. Lambrecht, "Trial Lawyers' Million-Dollar Club," p. 9A.
4. Knorr, "Rex Carr," p. B1.
5. St. Louis *Post-Dispatch,* Aug. 22, 1968.
6. For background of railroad worker injury law, see Mathewson, "Plaintiffs' Paradise."
7. Quoted in Jenkins, "Betting on the Verdict."
8. Tybor, "Burger Assails Lawyers on Ads, Percentage Fees," p. 4.
9. Fiske, "President of Harvard Brands Legal System Costly and Complex," p. 1.
10. Jenkins, "Betting on the Verdict."
11. See the trial transcript for May 24, 1979. Walch's subsequent comments are in a letter to the author dated Jan. 25, 1985.

Chapter 9. The Law of Libel

1. *Elvin (Bert) Simpson* v. *Alton Telegraph Printing Co., Joseph Melosi, and William Lhotka,* Mar. 9, 1978, Madison County Circuit Court, No. 78-L-224.
2. Hanson, *Libel and Related Torts,* vol. 1, p. 1.
3. In an address to the Illinois First Amendment Congress, Springfield, Mar. 12, 1983.

4. For the description of libel law, the author borrowed from Hanson, *Libel and Related Torts;* Ernst and Lindey, *Hold Your Tongue;* Gavin, *Foul, False and Infamous;* Stevens, *Shaping the First Amendment.*

5. The Illinois innocent construction rule was established in *John* v. *Tribune Co.,* 24 Ill. 2d 437, 1962, an Illinois Supreme Court case.

6. Luke DeGrand interview.

Chapter 10. An Odyssean Journey

1. Judge Bauer's opinion cited in 630 F. 2d 515 (1980).
2. Opinion 594, File No. 78-CI-641, Apr. 4, 1978.
3. Summary of litigation is chiefly as reconstructed from Judge Bauer's opinion; the Illinois Supreme Court opinion by Justice Ryan in *PSL Realty et al.* v. *Granite Investment et al.,* No. 52598; a calendar of events submitted by Carr in his brief to the Illinois Supreme Court, and in Patterson's brief to the same court.
4. The receivership reports listed these dollar amounts of rents and expenditures for the various projects during the fifty-four months of receivership:

	Gross Income	Total Disbursements
Chateau Commercial	158,815	151,591
Chateau Apartments	795,614	812,520
Kingston Estates	232,584	274,519
MacArthur Park	1,598,205	876,836
2911 Sunset Drive	0	3,099
Arlington Heights	537,016	299,388
Gaslight Walk	529,666	357,910
Maryland Plaza	143,103	72,060
Mitchell Commercial	9,551	16,286
Hamelot Court	90,179	59,203
Lafayette Square	90,588	629,944
University Gardens	455,796	314,228
Wood River Gardens	272,542	282,250

5. The ne exeat trial details are from the transcript of that trial (No. 74-L-228 in the Madison County Circuit Court), decided June 7, 1979, and of the post-trial motion hearing, Nov. 21, 1979.

6. *Alton Telegraph,* June 7, 1979.

Chapter 11. Give Him the Money

1. Speech to Illinois Press Association convention, Decatur, Sept. 11, 1982.
2. Deposition date Aug. 3, 1975.
3. Letter dated July 19, 1974.
4. Cox's letter to FHLBB, Mar. 1, 1978; FHLBB response, Mar. 7, 1978.
5. Cox's letter to Carr, Apr. 8, 1980; Carr response, Apr. 9, 1980. Both are in the libel case files of the *Alton Telegraph*.
6. Ability of stockholder to recover damages suffered by a nonparty corporation discussed at p. 64 of appellant's brief to the Fifth District Illinois Appellate Court.
7. Pragacz interview in his home.
8. Rhodes, Wagner, Imel comments quoted in *Alton Telegraph* story, June 4, 1980.
9. *Granite City Press-Record*, June 5, 1980.
10. *National Law Journal*, July 14, 1980.
11. Post-trial party as described in Pragacz interview.
12. Details of the campaign to unseat Judges Mosele and DeLaurenti from Lambrecht, "Lawyers' Campaign Got Judges Ousted," p. 9; and Broadway and Orso, "3 Lawyers Gave Big to Judicial Campaigns," p. 9A.

Chapter 12. The Struggle to Appeal

1. Denniston, "A Punishing Verdict in Illinois," p. 52. Reprinted by permission from the *Washington Journalism Review*, Mar. 1982.
2. St. Louis *Post-Dispatch*, May 12, 1981.
3. *Granite City Press-Record*, May 7, 1981, p. 20.
4. Letter dated Mar. 17, 1981.
5. Letter to author from David P. Sanders, Feb. 14, 1986.
6. For a story on the effects of federal bankruptcy laws on other litigation, see Lewin, "Man-Made Hazards Pose More Than a Medical Problem," p. 4E.
7. Quoted in *Editor & Publisher*, Apr. 4, 1981, p. 15.
8. Safer comments in Springfield, Ill., July 30, 1982.
9. Date of this order: Jan. 22, 1982.

Chapter 13. The Settlement

1. Judge Bauer's opinion (630 F. 2d 515), case decided Sept. 12, 1980.
2. Justice Ryan's opinion (86 Ill. 2d 291), filed Sept. 30, 1981.
3. Memorandum filed with Madison County Recorder of Deeds, dated Oct. 22, 1981.
4. The projects acquired by Midwest Multi-Family Management, Inc., the management subsidiary of Security Pacific, were: University Gardens, Wood River Gardens, and Lafayette Square in Wood River; Gaslight Walk and Arlington Heights in the Granite City area; Chateau Townhouses (formerly Chateau des Fleurs) and Kingston Estates in Bethalto; and Hamelot in Hamel.
5. Peter McAdams' interview.
6. Details of the libel settlements from *Alton Telegraph*, Apr. 14, 1982, p. 1; May 6, 1982, p. 1; May 27, 1982, p. 2. I have also drawn on the 1982 Freedom of Information Report of the Illinois AP Editors Association by D. G. Schumacher, executive editor of the *Telegraph*.
7. *Editor & Publisher*, Apr. 24, 1982.
8. *Editor & Publisher*, May 15, 1982, p. 7.
9. Curley, "How Libel Suit Sapped the Crusading Spirit of a Small Newspaper," p. 1.

Chapter 14. The Chilling Effect

1. *Alton Telegraph*, "McAdams Family Sells its *Telegraph* Minority Share," p. A1.
2. Berman, "Quixotic Father's Acquisitive Son," p. 105.
3. Lester Bernstein book review, *New York Times* book section, Nov. 17, 1985, p. 35.
4. Berman, "Quixotic Father's Acquisitive Son."
5. Curley, "How Libel Suit Sapped the Crusading Spirit of a Small Newspaper."
6. Speech to Illinois First Amendment Congress, Springfield, Mar. 12, 1983.
7. Ingersoll purchase of Cousley shares. *Advertising Age*, June 27, 1985, p. 37; *Editor & Publisher*, June 1, 1985, p. 18; *Alton Telegraph*, May 21, 1985, p. 1; *St. Louis Business Journal*, July 8–14, 1985, p. 1.

8. Speech to Suburban Newspapers of America convention, New Orleans, La., June 4, 1986.
9. Ibid.
10. Speech to Illinois Press Association, Springfield, Sept. 12, 1986.
11. See *St. Louis Business Journal,* July 8–14, 1985, p. 1.

Chapter 15. The Price We Pay

1. Peer, "New Danger for Journalists."
2. Bok, "A Flawed System," p. 38.
3. Barbash, "*Alton Telegraph* Libel Judgment Sends Fearful Message to Press," p. A3.
4. Randolph and Barbash, "20 Years After Landmark Libel Case, Legal Costs on Media Minds," *Washington Post,* Mar. 9, 1984, p. A2.
5. Barth, "Plea for a 'Slightly Irresponsible Press,'" p. 16.
6. Feldman and Hanachette quotes. *Editor & Publisher,* "Is Investigative Reporting Dead?" p. 14.

Index

Ackerman, Judge J. Waldo, 103–4, 107–8, 164
Alton, Ill.: description of, 1, 3, 19; development of, 1, 12, 16, 19, 23; poverty in, 19 (*see also* Robinson, Charles Mulford); provincialism, 43; race relations, 21–22; Riverfront Park, 21; social climate, 17, 18, 20, 21
Alton Daily Times, 37
Alton Daily Republican, 4, 32
Alton Observer, 17
Alton Telegraph: Broz, under, 39–42; Cousley sale of family interest, 191; economics of, 43–45; FHLBB chairman praise, 72; founding of, 4, 29–30; Ingersoll, under, 191–93; Lovejoy, death of, 17; McAdams family sale, 187; reputation, 1
—Libel case: "chilling effect," 190; settlement, 180–81; trial, 125
—mergers: *Daily Republican,* 32; *Daily Times,* 37
American Bottoms (Metro East) industrialization, 3, 11, 12, 23
Appeal bond controversy, 161–63
Apple, Hope Cousley, 39, 170

Bankruptcy petitions: *Alton Telegraph,* 164–65, 173; Granite Investment Co., 107, 164, 177
Barr, Judge Joseph J., 76, 105
Barth, Alan, 198–99
Bauer, Judge William J., 103, 177
Beatty, Judge William, 66, 76, 95, 181
Beecher, Edward, 18

Bell, U.S. Atty. Gen. Griffin, 94
Bethalto, Ill., 25, 53, 73, 120–21
Bok, Derek C., 83, 195
Bovard, Oliver K., 34, 39, 40, 42, 51, 193, 199
Branch banking policy in Illinois, 72–73
Broz, Elmer: as city editor of the *Telegraph,* 40–42, 66, 198; death of, 95; and the Green-Piasa investigation, 48–49; and investigative journalism, 48–49
Bruckner, Clarence, 110
Burger, Chief Justice Warren E., 83
Burroughs, the Rev. Cortley: social climate of Alton, 20–21; Paulie Cousley's Zenger Award, 183–84
Button, Harry, 155

Carl, Robert L., 192
Carr, Rex: afterthoughts, 188; DeGrand, 87; First Amendment, view of, 196; Green's business, financial interest in, 77, 104–5, 179; ne exeat suit, 86; ne exeat trial, 102, 109–13; other Green litigation, 91, 106–8, 166–68, 178; personal background and characteristics, 78–84; *Post-Dispatch* editorial, response to, 154–55; *Telegraph* appeal bond, 163; *Telegraph* bankruptcy proceedings, 172–73
—Libel case against *Telegraph,* 96; post-trial hearing, 158–60; settlement, 176, 182; trial, 115, 118–21, 124–43, 147, 148, 149, 150, 151

Index

Cassling, Donald, 174
Chapman, Judge Charles W.: defeat in 1980 primary, 114; election in 1982, 161; endorsement interview, 5, 8–9; Green libel trial, 118, 119, 123, 135, 136, 143, 146, 147, 150, 151; Green libel trial post-trial hearing, 155, 159–61; judicial appointment, 7; judicial reappointment, 161; Morris Chapman firm, 82; personal background, 7
Chapman, Morris, 7, 82, 151
Chicago Tribune, 49, 99, 100
Christie, Clarence McCord, 63–64, 117, 119, 124
Commercial Union (libel insurance), 156, 189
Conboy, Brian: changes jobs, 62; Harder case, 50; Melosi contacts, 56; memo from Melosi and Lhotka, 60, 61, 117, 129, 131
Cousley, Alex (brother of Paul B.), 39
Cousley, David R. (brother of Stephen C.), 187, 192
Cousley, John A. (first of the *Telegraph* Cousleys, grandfather of Paul S. C.), 4, 30, 31, 184
Cousley, Mary Lou Williamson (wife of Stephen C.), 39
Cousley, Paul Bliss (son of John C.), 14, 32, 33, 37, 38
Cousley, Paul Sparks ("Paulie"), 4; Chapman endorsement interview, 8–9; death of, 186; DeGrand libel suit, 117; early years, 37–38; Green libel trial, 130–33; Pragacz evaluation, 133; group ownership views, 46; and "the memo," 62; Mudge, Dick, 91; Pfeiffenberger, Dr. Mather, 69–70; *Telegraph,* bankruptcy, 173; *Telegraph* and Broz, Elmer, 42; retirement, 180; Zenger Award, 183
Cousley, Richard (father of Stephen C.), 39
Cousley, Stephen A., 4; aftereffects, 187, 188, 190; Chapman endorsement visit, 8–9; early years, 39; First Presbyterian Church, 20; Granite City, 193

—Green libel case: appeal attempt, 157; appeal bond, 162; trial, 114, 123, 131, 132, 146, 147; settlement, 176, 181
—*Telegraph:* and Broz, 42; as editor, 45, 66, 67, 70, 71; and "the memo," 62; resignation, 193; sale to Ingersoll, 191
Cox, William M.: afterthoughts, 189; bankruptcy, *Telegraph,* 164; fees in 1980, 163; personal background, 115–16
—Green libel case: appeal, 156, 157; trial, 115–19, 122, 125, 126, 130, 134, 135, 137, 139, 141, 143, 147, 148, 149
Crime in Metro East, 23, 24, 34–37, 40, 60, 197

DeGrand, Alfred (father of Robert DeG.), 27
DeGrand, Nancy Hellrung (wife of Robert DeG.), 27, 101, 173, 181, 182
DeGrand, Robert L., 10; after Piasa, 87, 88, 100, 102; death, 171; family life, 27–28; FBI-IRS clearance, 117; Green association, 13, 16, 67, 72, 73; Green libel trial, 118, 124, 126–30, 133, 134, 135, 140, 141, 142, 147, 148, 149; Green ne exeat trial, 109; Mudge death, 101; "60 Minutes," 171
—Piasa: and Hazel, 25, 52; management, 14, 15, 55, 64, 65; resignation, 69, 197; Wuellner relationship, 68
DeGrand, Robert L., Jr., 28, 124
DeLaurenti, Judge John D., 151, 152, 161
Denniston, Lyle, 153
Dorer, Frank, 63
Dunlap, William H., 73
Dykeman, Martin A., 183

Easton, Rufus, 11
East St. Louis, Ill., 20, 33, 42, 72, 78, 79
Eckert, Edward A., 65, 69, 117, 124, 138, 142, 189

Edwardsville, Ill., 7, 9, 11, 42–43, 57, 91, 120
Edwardsville Intelligencer, 45

Federal Home Loan Bank Board (FHLBB), 14, 63; Carr litigation, 96; and DeGrand, 87, 88, 89; merger of Piasa and Illini Federal, 70–72, 77, 197; Piasa audits, 25, 26, 63–65, 68, 90; *Telegraph* libel case, 117–19, 124, 126, 132
Federal Savings and Loan Insurance Corp., 14; Carr litigation, 108, 109, 111; purchases Green mortgages, 107; receiver for Green properties, 102; settlement with Carr, 177, 178, 179; *Telegraph* libel case, 117–19, 124
Feldman, A. Daniel, 51, 199
Fenderson, Albion, 69; Green libel trial, 117, 124, 134–39, 141–42, 178; post-trial hearing, 160
Findley, U.S. Rep. Paul, 91, 155
First Presbyterian Church (Alton), 18, 20, 184
Focht, John, 40, 42, 192
Francis, Terryl, 75, 77
Fraundorf, Barney, 52, 54, 95
Freedom of Information Act, use of by Mudge, 94
Friendly, Fred W., 97

Gale, Mark, 68, 74, 77, 105
Gilman, Winthrop, 18, 19
Gold, Mary Alice, 145, 150
Goldenhersh, Justice Joseph P.: Chapman judicial appointments, role in, 7, 114, 161; chief justice, Illinois Supreme Court, 156; election to Illinois Appellate Court, 66–67; Matoesian judicial appointment, role in, 8
Granite City, Ill., 7, 12, 142; black population, 22; Cousley, Steve, 193; Matoesian from, 8; newspapers in, 187; suburbs of, 23; Toncoff childhood, 137
Granite Investment Co.: bankruptcy, 107, 177–78; Carr litigation, 92, 96; Green's business activities, 68, 74, 77; settlement, property, 178–79; Steele transaction, 106
Green, James C., 10, 180; afterthoughts, 189–90; Carr financial arrangements, 179; FBI-IRS probe, 92, 117; and Hazel, 25, 52; libel case, post-trial hearing, 159, 160; libel case, *Telegraph* appeal, 169; libel case trial, 117–50; "the memo," knowledge of, 95, 96; ne exeat case, 75, 76, 86, 97, 109–13; Piasa, relationship with, 13, 26, 65, 67, 197; starting in business, 12, 13, 15, 16, 24, 25; summary of libel case, 9
Green, Mrs. Shirley, 75, 92
Green libel suit trial (*Green* v. *Alton Telegraph Printing Co. et al.*), 9, 10; closing arguments, 139–43; Cousley, Paul, testimony, 130–31; Cosley, Steve, testimony, 131–32; damages, calculation of, 133; DeGrand testimony, 128–29; Fenderson testimony, 134–38; filed, 96; FSLIC participation, 117; Green testimony, 126–27; instructions to jury, 143–44; jury deliberations, 144–46; jury selection, 120–22; jury verdict, 146; Lhotka testimony, 129; Melosi testimony, 129–30; opening statements, 124–26; preliminary (*in limine*) conference, 118–19; pretrial settlement offer, 118
Green ne exeat trial (*Green* v. *Illini Federal et al.*), 108–12; closing arguments, 111; damages, calculation of, 111; denial of post-trial motions, 113; jury deliberations, 112; jury verdict, 112; post-trial motions, 112
Group ownership controversy, 42, 44, 45

Hackmann, John: afterthoughts, 195; libel trial, 139; PSL Realty management, 73, 74, 75; and settlement, 178
Halbrook, Alice, 145–46
Hanachette, John, 199

Index

Hanson, Arthur B. (Tim), 99, 115, 156
Harder, William, 50, 56, 58
Harris, Luther, 57, 59
Hazel, Donald: death, 118; Green acquaintance, 127; Green libel trial, 124, 127, 130; libel suit against *Telegraph*, 96; "the memo," mention in, 57, 58, 59, 60; Piasa relationship, 25, 52, 53, 54, 58, 71, 130
Henkhaus, Nina, 85
Hersh, Seymour, 51
Hyde Park Club (Madison County), 34

Illini Federal Savings and Loan Assn.: dealings with Green companies, 74, 75, 76, 197; merger with Piasa, 70–71; and ne exeat trial, 109; sale of mortgages to FSLIC, 107
Illinois Glass Co., 19, 32
Imel, William H., 147
Ingersoll, Ralph M., I, 187
Ingersoll, Ralph M., II, 187, 191–94
Inner Circle of Advocates, 82
Investigative reporting, 32–33, 48, 49

Jenner, Albert E., 156, 163
Jones, Justice Charles E., 103–4, 174–75
Judicial system in Madison County, Ill., 5, 6, 18, 150, 196
Jury deliberations in Green libel trial, 144–47
Jury instructions in Green libel trial, 143
Jury post-trial barbecue, 150
Jury selection in Green libel trial, 120–23
Jury selection in Madison County, 84–86

Kasserman, Judge George W., Jr., 175
Korein, Sandor, 83
Kowalski, Stanley, 57, 96, 173, 182
Kozielek, Raymond: Green association, 24, 64; "the memo," mention in, 58, 59; libel suit against *Telegraph*, 96; ne exeat trial, 111; settlement, 181; settlement in *Telegraph* reorganization proposed by Carr, 173

Labor unions in Metro East, 24, 49, 58, 59, 192
Lakin, Thomas L., 151
Lambrecht, Bill, 161
Layman, Darrell, 74–76
Lee, John E. (Doc), 66
Lee, Pinky, 81
Legal fees, 163, 179, 182
Leu, Bob, 58, 59, 60
Lhotka, William, 9; Judge Beatty story, 95; Conboy and Martin dealings, 56–57, 60, 62; family background, 49, 50; FHLBB officials meeting, 71; Green collection efforts, 166, 172; Libel trial, 117, 123–25, 129; and Demos Nicholas, 52, 54, 55
Libel law, 95–100; innocent construction rule in Illinois, 100; *Sullivan* v. *New York Times*, 98
Linder, Illinois Atty. Gen. Usher F., 17–18
Link, Ted, 34
Lock and Dam 26, 2
Lovejoy, Elijah, death of, 4, 16, 17, 18, 29, 97

McAdams, Henry, 45, 46, 70, 162, 182
McAdams, John D. (father of Henry McA.), 4, 32
McAdams, Peter C. (son of Henry McA.), 45, 180
McAdams, William (son of Henry McA.), 45
McGlynn, Joseph B., 81
McGovern, Richard, 74, 75, 109, 110
Madison, Ill., 7, 12, 24, 43, 52
Maeras, Stephen, 59
Martin, David H., 56, 62, 129
Martin, Preston, 72
Matoesian, Andreas, 8–9, 114, 151–52
Meller, Victor S., 63
Melosi, Joseph, 9, 198; afterthoughts, 188; and Broz, 41; Conboy and Martin, dealings with, 56, 57, 60, 62; DeGrand, later contacts with, 89, 90, 93, 197; story of DeGrand resignation, 69; and Fraundorf, 52, 54, 55; Justice Goldenhersh, 67;

Green collection efforts, 166; and Harder, 50; Darrell Layman quote, 76; Libel trial, 116, 117, 123, 126, 129, 130, 133, 134, 147; merger story (Piasa–Illini Federal), 71–72; personal background, 49; *Post-Dispatch* story, 73; Peter Simpson contacts, 89

"The memo" to Conboy, 57–60, 93

Mitchell, U.S. Atty. Gen. John N., 56

Mollenhoff, Clark, 51–52

Mosele, Judge Victor J.: Green ne exeat trial, 86, 105, 109, 110, 112, 113; retention election defeat, 151, 152

Mudge, Dick, 90, 91, 93, 94, 100, 101, 117

Nicholas, Demos, 52, 54, 95, 130

Norton, Rev. A. T., 18

Norton, Wilbur T., 31

O'Donnell, Judge Thomas P., 108

Parks, Lawson A., 30–31

Patterson, Eugene C., 196–97

Patterson, Robert W.: ethics complaint against Carr, 104–5, 179; property control settlement, 178; *Telegraph* libel trial, 124, 134, 136, 137

Pearman, Judge Ralph S., 175

Percy, U.S. Sen. Charles H., judicial appointments, 158

Peterson, Ronald, 181

Pfeiffenberger, James Mather (son of Lucas P.), 14

Pfeiffenberger, Lucas: as architect, 19, 184; John Cousley friendship, 31; Democratic party leader, 13; personal background, 13, 14

Pfeiffenberger, Dr. Mather (grandson of Lucas P.): afterthoughts, 183–85; and Broz, 41; and the Cousleys, 55, 69–70; DeGrand libel suit, 91; as "establishment" symbol, 193, 198; Green libel suit, 124, 130; First Presbyterian Church, 20, 184; and the *Telegraph*, 41, 42

Pfeiffenberger, Mrs. Mather (Marthaine), 184

Phelan, James, 34, 36, 37

Piasa First Federal Savings and Loan Assn. (Alton), 10, 185; federal audits, 64, 65; federal chartering, 14; founding of, 13; growth policy, 15; Green association, 24, 25, 26, 53, 64, 65, 169, 197; Hazel loans, 52; insurance agency, 128; merger with Illini Federal, 70, 71, 72, 73, 102; *Telegraph* libel trial, 125, 126, 138, 140

Postmaster patronage in Alton, 31, 37

Pragacz, Jerome, 121, 122, 123, 137, 138, 144, 145, 146, 148, 149, 152–53, 183

Pratt, Paul L., 151

Price, U.S. Rep. Melvin, 117

PSL Realty Co., 67, 68, 73, 76, 109, 110

Pulitzer, Joseph, 33, 40, 42

Rarick, Judge Phillip, 101

Reporter-police cooperation, 51–52

Reuben, Donald, 156, 170

Rhodes, Harold, 147

Riley, Paul E., 157

Robinson, Charles Mulford, 19–20, 32. See also Alton, Ill., poverty in

Rumsfeld, Donald, 91

Ryan, Justice Howard, 177

St. Louis *Post-Dispatch:* editorial comment, 154; Ingersoll competition, 192–193; judiciary, 6, 161; Lhotka employed, 89, 124; Metro East, attitude towards, 34; Piasa demise stories, 72, 95

Sanders, David, 162, 164, 168, 173, 174

Safer, Morley, 170–71. See also "60 Minutes"

Sasyk, Mike, 27, 64, 121

Schnuck Markets (St. Louis), 193–94

Schumacher, D. G., 192

Security Pacific Corp., 178–79

Sharp, Walt, 146

Simpson, Elvin (Bert): libel suit filed, 96; "the memo," mentioned in, 59; settlement, 181; settlement in *Tele-*

Simpson Elvin (Bert) (*continued*)
graph reorganization proposed by Carr, 173
Simpson, Peter: Alton, characterization of, 43; work for DeGrand, 88–89
"60 Minutes" (CBS television), 170–71
Smith, U.S. Sen. Ralph T., 91
Sobol, John: aftereffects, 190; Green association, 24, 64; libel suit filed, 96; settlement, 181; settlement in *Telegraph* reorganization proposed by Carr, 173
Steele, Howard, 106, 121
Stevenson, U.S. Sen. Adlai E., 88–89, 117

Thweatt, Terry, 57, 58, 59, 126
Toncoff, Helen, 122, 123, 137, 138, 145–46, 149, 150, 152
Tone, Philip W.: afterthoughts, 188; libel appeal, 157–60, 162–63, 166, 168
Trabue, Judge James D.: Granite Investment Co. bankruptcy petition, 108, 177–78; *Telegraph* bankruptcy petition, 165–67, 172–73, 182
Treadway, Richard M., 30
Trone, Robert, 54, 130

Venice, Ill., 7, 12, 43, 66

Walch, W. Stanley, 86, 105, 110–13, 114
Wander, Barney, 23. *See also* Crime in Metro East
Wershba, Joseph, 170. *See also* "60 Minutes"
Williamson, Charles: fees in 1980, 163; libel case appeal, 157; libel trial, 116, 118, 122, 126, 135, 137, 140–41, 143
Wood River, Ill., 22, 35, 49, 120, 147, 196
Wortman, Frank (Buster), 35, 58, 126. *See also* Crime in Metro East
Wuellner, Henry: death, 95; libel trial testimony about, 126, 127, 140; Piasa, deteriorating relationship with DeGrand, 65, 68–69; Hazel problem, 53; as president of Piasa, 13, 14, 15, 55

Zimbrakos, Dorothy B., 168
Zurich-American Co. (libel insurance), 156–57, 189

Thomas B. Littlewood, Professor of Journalism at the University of Illinois in Urbana-Champaign, was a *Chicago Sun-Times* correspondent in Springfield, Illinois (1955–64), and Washington, D.C. (1965–77). He was a Fellow of the John F. Kennedy Institute of Politics at Harvard University in 1975. His other books include *Bipartisan Coalition in Illinois* (1959), *Horner of Illinois* (1969), and *The Politics of Population Control* (1977).